T0030831

WILD
WITCHCRAFT

WILD WITCHCRAFT

*Folk Herbalism, Garden Magic,
and Foraging for Spells,
Rituals, and Remedies*

REBECCA
BEYER

SIMON ELEMENT

New York   London   Toronto   Sydney   New Delhi

SIMON
ELEMENT

An Imprint of Simon & Schuster, Inc.
1230 Avenue of the Americas
New York, NY 10020

Copyright © 2022 by Rebecca Beyer

This publication contains the opinions and ideas of its author. It is intended to provide helpful and informative material on the subjects addressed in the publication. It is sold with the understanding that the author and publisher are not engaged in rendering medical, health, or any other kind of personal professional services in the book. The reader should consult his or her medical, health, or other competent professional before adopting any of the suggestions in this book or drawing inferences from it.

The author and publisher specifically disclaim all responsibility for any liability, loss or risk, personal or otherwise, which is incurred as a consequence, directly or indirectly, of the use and application of any of the contents of this book.

All rights reserved, including the right to reproduce this book or portions thereof
in any form whatsoever. For information, address Simon Element Subsidiary Rights
Department, 1230 Avenue of the Americas, New York, NY 10020.

First Simon Element hardcover edition May 2022

SIMON ELEMENT is a trademark of Simon & Schuster, Inc.

For information about special discounts for bulk purchases, please contact
Simon & Schuster Special Sales at 1-866-506-1949 or business@simonandschuster.com.

The Simon & Schuster Speakers Bureau can bring authors to your live event.
For more information or to book an event, contact the Simon & Schuster Speakers
Bureau at 1-866-248-3049 or visit our website at www.simonspeakers.com.

Interior design by Laura Levatino

Manufactured in the United States of America

10 9 8 7 6 5 4 3

Library of Congress Cataloging-in-Publication Data

Names: Beyer, Rebecca (Witch), author.
Title: Wild witchcraft : folk herbalism, garden magic, and foraging for spells,
rituals, and remedies / by Rebecca Beyer
Other titles: Folk herbalism, garden magic, and foraging for spells, rituals, and remedies
Description: New York, NY : Simon Element, 2022. | Includes bibliographical references and index. |
Identifiers: LCCN 2021053266 (print) | LCCN 2021053267 (ebook) |
ISBN 9781982185626 (hardcover) | ISBN 9781982185633 (ebook)
Subjects: LCSH: Herbs—Therapeutic use. | Gardening. | Witchcraft. | Forage plants. |
Handbooks and manuals.
Classification: LCC BF1572.P43 B47 2022 (print) | LCC BF1572.P43 (ebook) |
DDC 615.3/21–dc23/eng/20211104
LC record available at https://lccn.loc.gov/2021053266
LC ebook record available at https://lccn.loc.gov/2021053267

ISBN 978-1-9821-8562-6
ISBN 978-1-9821-8563-3 (ebook)

This book is dedicated to all the people whose herbal knowledge has led to my own. Namely the Indigenous, Black, and working-class peoples of Appalachia today and of yesteryear, whose legacies have enabled me to have the relationship I do with the plants that I love.

Contents

Introduction

My name is Rebecca, and I'm a professional forager-witch. I wish I could say I came up with that moniker on my own, but I was dubbed that during an interview a few years ago, and it delighted me so dearly I adopted it as the most succinct and accurate descriptor of myself.

What makes me a professional? Well, I teach wild plant and mushroom foraging, folk herbalism, and witchcraft and Appalachian folk practice classes for a living. These aren't the only words that define me, but they are the quickest way to communicate my wacky profession (and obsessions) to new people, and despite the occasional frown, it's delightful to watch smiles break over people's faces as they take that descriptor in.

If you had asked me as a child what I wanted to be when I grew up, I would have said a farmer. At four years old, it was the only word I knew that represented a human who spent most of their time outside and could eke a living from the soil with nothing but their bare hands. It wasn't until I was 12 that I knew what I really wanted to be: a witch.

As a child, I constantly moved from place to place until I was 18. I was born in Pittsburgh, Pennsylvania, in 1987, but we only stayed there a few months. Afterward, my family moved to California, then all over the misunderstood state of New Jersey. It was here, in this seemingly wild-less land, where I first made the acquaintance of a real-life witch.

INTRODUCTION

I was raised a Unitarian Universalist, like my mother and grandmother, and we attended the Unitarian Church in a wooded area of Princeton, New Jersey. It was here that I first got a taste of paganism and witchcraft. Many UU churches have chapters within them specifically for pagans, and lucky for me, this church did too.

My Sunday-school teacher was a Wiccan. I felt like I was meeting a celebrity that first day she told us she was in fact a living, breathing witch. She conveniently looked the part as far as popular media would have it: waist-length black hair streaked with gray, full-figured, and beautiful with dark eyes. Our seventh-grade year in the Church focused on exploring other faiths, and it was through that medium she shared her own with us.

I once saw her in the parking lot dropping bread dough onto the ground. I had the feeling that she was doing something very important (and also something very strange), so I asked her why she was walking in a circle, dropping dough. She told me it was an offering to the elementals, the spirits of nature that were aligned with each of the four directions. I watched, fascinated. I think it was then that I knew *this* was what I wanted.

I expressed a great interest in what my teacher was doing, and I told her I wanted to learn more. She scribbled down book titles for me on a little piece of yellow paper, and I took it home, as if I'd won some secret prize. When we are young, we want to feel chosen, to feel special. I'd never felt more special than when I closed my fingers around that little slip of yellow paper.

At 12 I was a big reader, and my mom had one rule: I could read any book so long as she could look at it first. I asked her for the books my teacher had written down on the little yellow piece of paper I kept like some forbidden treasure in my journal, as if the paper itself held some sort of magic. My mother balked at first and asked me to show her in the dictionary what pagan meant. I found two things: a follower of a polytheistic religion (as in ancient Rome) and, unfortunately, one who has little or no religion and who delights in sensual pleasures and material goods; an irreligious or hedonistic person.

I furrowed my brow in disappointment; the dictionary had failed me. Instead, I asked her to look up Wicca on the newly born World Wide Web. There she read about nature worship and deemed my interest innocuous enough to grant me my first three books on Wicca and witchcraft. The age of 12 is when I say my real practice began.

INTRODUCTION

At the time, we lived on a little farm in Hopewell, New Jersey, which is still one of the most precious parts of my childhood. Even though I was bullied relentlessly at school for carrying around books on witchcraft (and let's be honest, for being very strange), I spent most of my time outside riding horses or talking loudly (or singing poorly) to our three goats and ragtag crew of ducks and chickens. I relished the time in the little patch of woods that surrounded our house. It was there a feeling of longing that was almost existential began to grow in me, a feeling that something or someone was waiting for me, and I for them.

As I delved into the books my Sunday-school teacher recommended, I felt that strange longing crystallize. I furiously took notes on everything witchcraft-related I could get my hands on. Luckily, I was blessed with relatively open-minded parents who relented to my book habits and allowed me to continue to teach myself when we moved to northern New Jersey when I was 14.

This move devastated me. Settling near the outskirts of New York City was a real shock to my system. I tried to find magic wherever I could. I made due. I went for long walks with our Doberman, Rocky, and explored parks and wooded areas around our home, hoping to feel that sparkle I had felt in the woods around our farm. It was different. But at least it was green.

When I left for college deep in the woods of Upstate New York, I really got to sink my teeth into what living as a witch year-round while following the seasonal celebrations could be like. It was here I joined a college club called the Circle. It was a group for alternative religions composed of kind and nerdy upperclassmen who folded us baby witches into their patient and silly embrace, hosting workshops on everything from energy work to the history of witchcraft. I was among peers, finally!

I majored in medieval history and consumed everything I could on witchcraft and herbalism from historical sources. This was where I left the comfort of my first love, Wicca, to lie with the love of my life: Traditional Witchcraft. I found in the pages of witch trials and anthropology books the direct links to historic practices I imagined my own Irish, German, and English ancestors performing. Through reading of the hardships and horrors they faced, I saw an ancestral line, and I grabbed on to it. They were not good, they were not perfect, but they were mine. By the end of my freshman year, I knew I wanted to live as closely to the Earth as possible, in tune with the seasons. I wanted to know how to cure with herbs and grow my own pumpkins. I wanted to know the history of this land I inhabited. It felt impossible, like a fantasy.

Learning about intentional communities through a friend in college was what first set the keys to my current reality in my curious hands. I visited a local cohousing unit on a very small acreage, and I was once again standing in that same feeling I'd felt in the church parking lot. I'm an extrovert, and I love being around other people. I thrive within a community. I wanted to live with a group of others who also wanted to dance the Wheel of the Year and grow food. The second half of my sophomore year of college, I suffered a mysterious illness. I was exhausted all the time; I could barely stay awake while driving. I felt a brain fog that frightened me. Trying to explain it to doctors and nurses left me with incredulous looks and a diagnosis of panic disorder. I felt the most despondent and depressed I'd ever felt in my life. Strangely enough, it was in the 1890s where I would find the beginning of my healing and my life path.

I've always been drawn to and had a deep love of old-timey practices and old ways of doing them. I didn't have the closest ties to my extended family, so I longed for some kind of ancestral connection. I wanted to know what and how the people I'd come from made their way in the world before they lost the Old Ways.

It started with my admiration for the Amish as a child, until my mom told me what being an Amish woman entailed. But the summer after my sophomore year of college, at the ripe old age of 19, I got an internship in sustainable agriculture by working on a living history farm that interpreted the 1890s called Howell Living History Farm in Lambertville, New Jersey. I drove draft horses, wore long cotton dresses, and harvested large golden bundles of wheat with sickles. Everything was right in my world. I was home. I foraged my first wineberries, the red, crystalline cousin of raspberries minus the fuzz. I milked goats and made cheese. I grew my first vegetables. This peaceful, idealized version of the 1890s seemed very rich indeed to me.

Once again, as fate would have it, I found myself surrounded by other pagans. The two women I shared our intern house with happened to also be witches. We spent our evenings without the internet knitting and listening to *The Good Life* by Helen and Scott Nearing on cassette tapes by candlelight. I killed my first chicken here, and it was here, in that little house in central New Jersey, that I started the paperwork to transfer to an organic agriculture degree at the

University of Vermont. I was going to farm, cultivate plants, raise animals, and live this life every day.

Let's fast-forward to 20. I'm still sick, but I'm used to it now. I live in Burlington, Vermont, and I'm thriving in an eco-anarchist enclave. Despite the wonderful time I'm having, I developed a dry hacking cough that would not leave. I still had the brain fog and constant tiredness, but the human body is incredibly resilient. Somehow, I got used to dealing with it. I wondered if I had chronic fatigue. I went to my college nurse one day when it was especially bad, and she asked me if I had been tested for mono. I looked at her astounded. No one had ever taken my symptoms seriously. She gave me a blood test and, lo and behold, I had a very bad case of mono, and I had had it for a long time. She palpated my liver, looking down at me anxiously as I lay prone on the exam table. It was inflamed, a sign of prolonged mono infection. Normally, mono comes and goes like any other illness, but for some reason my body could not rid itself of the persistent virus. She told me there wasn't much to do for it but rest.

I was not ready to accept there was nothing to be done for my constant unwellness. I asked around among the barefoot and black-clad comrades I had and wondered, what could I do? A friend of mine suggested I ride my bike down to the local herb shop. I will never forget it. It was called Purple Shutter Herbs and it was run by a woman named Laura Brown. I rolled in, sweaty and out of breath, and she gave me just three herbs after patiently and sternly listening to my symptoms. The best part was that I got to go into the backroom and fill my own order. An herbarium out of a storybook, hundreds of jars of every size labeled with tidy, beautiful script adorned four walls covered in shelves. I was desperately delighted as I weighed out my thyme, boneset, and goldenseal on her scales, poured them into little bags, and labeled them with the pens provided. The very act of fetching my medicine felt healing.

I made it home and simmered the herbs as she had instructed. I didn't know what to expect. I wanted to believe that herbs worked, but I needed to see something to believe it. In three days, my cough stopped. Two weeks later, I woke up feeling slightly clearheaded for the first time in about a year. I cried. I had to learn this art. I needed to. If the plants could help me, they could help others.

As I finished my time at UVM, my best friend Saro called me. She told me she was settling into her new home in Asheville, North Carolina. Saro, a

Tennessee native, told me, "You'll love it here." A quick Google search revealed two things. There was a community of primitive-skills practitioners living in bark huts, wearing buckskins, and foraging off the land near there. It was called Wildroots. The deer hide–clad people I saw on this website holding armfuls of cattails and featuring baskets laden with wild greens beckoned to me. There were also three herbalism schools in the area. I was sold. I packed my truck with nowhere to live and no job and arrived on Saro's porch 12 hours later.

I became an apprentice. Those sun-worn people I saw smiling on the internet were real; I met them. I felt starstruck when I met Natalie Bogwalker. I apprenticed with her in 2011, and it was here I was first able to confidently name the trees, shrubs, and plants that grew wildly out of every corner of my new Appalachian home. She taught me fire making, basketry, log cabin building, hide tanning, wild food cooking, and plant identification, and how to be a good listener. She is still a dear friend of mine and a lifelong mentor. She gave me a leg up the first rung of the ladder I needed to climb to become a plant person.

From there I was off. I started attending Earth skills gatherings, like large family reunions with wild people where you can attend workshops on every skill you'd ever need (and well, some you never thought you did) to live simply on the Earth. I learned spoon carving, weaving, and basketmaking and took every plant identification class I could. I learned the names, uses, and history of some of the 2,000+ species of plants and trees that grew around me. I collected a large library of books on herbalism and Appalachian folkways. Finally, I attended Appalachian State University and got an MA in Appalachian studies, focusing on Appalachian ethnobotany (or the history of how people have used plants).

So, this is how I got here. These days, I still read constantly and take classes and workshops from other plant people I admire. I've come to specialize in the folkloric history of plants, their magical uses, as well as their edible and medicinal uses. The stories of plants are what bring me to life. I'm excited to share them with you.

I

THE LEGACY

A History of Witchcraft

In an age of epic consumption and ecological destruction, it's difficult to imagine a lifeway more connected with the land we live on. It's also sometimes difficult to imagine we have the capacity and the power to heal ourselves and others. Don't get me wrong, I'm not a purist. I use Western medicine alongside herbalism because I've seen they aren't mutually exclusive. They often complement and aid each other. It's important to note the history of our medicine in the West led us to both practices.

Ancient Medicine:
A Brief History of Western Herbalism

In my opinion, understanding the history of Western herbalism is imperative before you try to practice it. In North America, so much of our body of knowledge comes from peoples who have been historically killed, enslaved, and have had their history rewritten to dampen the deep and lasting wounds inflicted upon them. It's not only important to understand and acknowledge that history, but as in all things in the history of North America, it's important to question who has written that history, to what ends, and why. Acknowledging where we get herb uses and folklore from is a vital part of battling cultural appropriation and other harmful beliefs that exclude and erase Black, brown, and Indigenous contributions to a very large body of knowledge.

Herbalism begins in prehistory. Our paleolithic ancestors ingested and interacted with many plant species, including many medicinal ones like yarrow, willow, and more. When humans began to write things down, no longer did we have to wonder how and why they used plants. The first recorded mention of herbal remedies that we know of is from over 5,000 years ago. Clay tablets found in ancient Mesopotamia described a dozen herbal recipes calling for the use of over an astonishing 250 plant species by the Sumerians.[1]

Egypt, India, and China all collected, wrote, and disseminated texts on medicine and herbs as far back as 400 BCE. They birthed some of the longest and most well-studied plant medicine traditions, namely Ayurveda and traditional Chinese medicine. These systems directly influenced and inspired where this story often begins: ancient Greece and Rome. Hippocrates, often called the father of modern medicine, was one of the first to write about the separation of illness from spiritual causes around 400 BCE. At the time it was a controversial view to dismiss that angry spirits and gods could cause illness as it seemed to tempt the Fates themselves into dealing untimely blows.

The history of Western herbalism is often mistakenly told as a European story, yet nearly every continent's people have influenced it in different and complex ways, from Asia to North America and from Africa to India.

The first and arguably most important medical school in Europe was in Salerno, Italy, in the 10th century CE. It was through a rich history of Islamic medical texts and their translations from Arabic to Latin that North African medicine made its way into the very foundations of this practice. Greek medical texts from Hippocrates and Galen were also translated at this school and integrated into this institution. This school was unique in many aspects, particularly because it supported practitioners of all genders in a time where women were not encouraged to pursue professions. One of the most famous women was Trota of Solerno, who wrote some of the most influential texts on women's medicine in the Middle Ages.[2]

Monasteries also contributed to the recording and dissemination of plant knowledge through libraries and translations. It was not until the 15th century that printing presses made the painstaking labor of hand copying herbals a thing of the past. Though literacy was still a privilege of the clergy and upper classes, more books recording the uses of plants could now circulate and begin the slow process of crossing class lines. Translating works to common languages instead of Greek and Latin also allowed for plant medicine to make its way into the hands of more diverse classes of people in Europe.

One of the most well-known and cited English-speaking herbalists of the Western herbal tradition is Nicholas Culpeper. He wrote about the 17th-century countryside, recording and printing his own English-language texts on herbal remedies and astrological medicine. He treated people for low or even no cost and sold his works for affordable prices, believing this type of healing should not be relegated to the upper class. This earned him two accusations of witchcraft as well as a close call with a prohibition from practicing medicine due to the stranglehold that the College of Physicians kept over medical knowledge.

Culpeper is important not only for his anarchic heart but also for the way his work influenced herbalism in America. *The English Physician* (now known most often as *Culpeper's Complete Herbal*) was printed in Boston in 1708. It was the first medical text and the first book on herbalism printed in North America. The ethnobotany of First Nations people in North America blended with the knowledge system European colonists brought with them and that of enslaved African peoples into the Western herbal and American folk herbal traditions we know today. Some of this information was mingled by choice, but much of it was brought together by force.

This is a very abbreviated history, but it can be helpful to think of herbalism in America as a stool with three legs: one Indigenous, one African, and one European. As time went on, many more cultures came together in North America. Today we see the fingerprints of Latinx medicinal practices, as well as many more influences from the diverse cultures that now reside here. Honor where medicine comes from, acknowledge the culture, people, and nation, and pronounce it correctly. If you make a mistake, it's okay, apologize authentically, and try again. It's always okay to ask and say, "I'm still learning." I know I am.

The Birth of the "Witch"

As a self-identified forager-witch, I am often asked where forager ends and witch begins. To me, it's nearly impossible to tease them apart. As I said before, I found my way to Traditional Witchcraft through Wicca. Many people believe they're one and the same, and while some Wiccans are witches, not all witches are Wiccans. Wicca is a modern religion born in England in the 1950s that is inspired by an eclectic blend of occult practices both Eastern and Western. Wicca shares many things with Traditional Witchcraft, but the two have important distinctions. Just as the history of Western herbalism is necessary to the practice, so too is the history of witchcraft necessary to the witch. It's good to know who died for our folkways, who suffered for our magic, and conversely, who thrived from its practice. Let's look at a brief history of witchcraft as it was practiced in history (and is still today) in the Western world.

Traditional Witchcraft is an umbrella term under which many traditions lie. Generally speaking, it means a modern witchcraft tradition based on practices and beliefs of witchcraft from Europe and America from the 1500s to the 1800s. It is unique folk magic traditions and witchcraft beliefs of the land one lives on. These practices and beliefs are generally seen to have survived Christianity in recorded folklore, songs, and superstitions.

Traditional Witchcraft isn't just what witchcraft *may* have been like centuries to millennia ago, but what it *was* like. We know this through surviving documentation, oral lore, and folk practices that exist today in different cultures. What sets Traditional Witchcraft apart is that the practitioners base their practices in the old lores—chants, incantations, ballads, superstitions, oral lore, and documented witchcraft practices and rituals.

Some Traditional Witchcraft traditions are culture-based, such as Cornish or Balkan witchcraft, while other traditions are based on the writings of specific people, such as Robert Cochrane or the Andersons, who founded the Feri tradition. There are many subtle differences between different traditions, mostly revolving around the personalities behind the belief sets.

Modern Traditional Witchcraft largely did not exist as a term before the early 2000s. It was inspired by a group of witches writing in the 1950s–1970s, namely Robert Cochrane, Paul Huson, Joe Wilson, Robert Graves, and Victor Anderson. People like E. J. Jones, Michael Howard, Nigel Jackson, Nigel Pennick, Andrew Chumbley, and Daniel Schulke have, since 1980, gone on to help create what we know today to be Traditional Witchcraft.[3] Although many of these traditions are based on ancient practices, we're still forging what it means to practice Traditional Witchcraft in a modern world.[4] When I sunk into studying this lore, the ways in which I melded my foraging and gardening practices into these traditions felt like a perfect fit. Much of Traditional Witchcraft and our sabbaths and holidays revolve around the agricultural year. So, what better way to celebrate the Old Ways than to live them?

When was witchcraft as well known as it is today? What informed the legacy modern-day witches continue? It begins before the written word, when our ancient ancestors worshipped the animistic world that pulsed with life around them through prayer, offering, dance, song, and ritual. In the written word, it begins in 1750 BCE with the Code of Hammurabi. This was one of the first written law codes containing sections dealing with magic and legal charges of sorcery and witchcraft.

Time Line of the History of Witchcraft

(Based on Michael Bailey's A Dictionary of Witchcraft)[5]

The word *magia* first began to appear in Latin in the first century BCE. The first use of the truly general concept of "magic" in Roman usage was found late in the century (23–79 BCE) by the poet Virgil. Below is a brief historical list of what follows.

From here Wicca and other witchcraft traditions jump to America and take off in the 1970s. Many new sects of Wicca were born in the US alongside Traditional Witchcraft traditions. Yet of course, the continuation of the long history of American folk magic practices, like Hexerei in Pennsylvania, Appalachian folk magic, and African influenced traditions like Hoodoo and Voodoo continue and flourish. This time line gets us to the present day, but how did the *folklore* of the witch arise? What *makes* a witch?

What Is a Witch?

As we can see, the understanding of witchcraft as a crime or set of heretical beliefs against the Catholic Church began in earnest in the 13th century in Europe. Actions and practices once seen as a part of someone living on the fringes of society soon became a crime punishable by death. More often than not, many were accused of being witches for being single women, mentally ill, disabled, or being different from the norm. Sometimes people were accused of being witches for owning land desired by others or because of petty interpersonal disputes. In the 15th century, when demonologists began to argue that witchcraft was heresy rather than delusion, ideas of the witches' Sabbath and the Devil took a hold of the minds of Europeans, and witchcraft confessions became the new written record of witch lore.

Much of what witchcraft was assumed to be was simply the opposite of the God-given order of the world. This means that witches brought death

400 BCE	Plato condemns *magoi*, or magic practicing priestly caste members, and they're given a negative reputation.
1022 CE	First known burning of heretics at Orleans.
1233	Pope Gregory XI issues the *Vox in Rama*, in which he describes heretics gathering to worship a demon in the form of a toad or a pallid man, then engaging in orgies much like the later descriptions of the Witches' Sabbath.
1400	One of the earliest known witch hunts in Western Europe, in the Alps, Simme Valley.
1427-1436	Major witch hunts in Europe: Savoy, Dauphine, and Valais.
1458	Nicholas Jacquier writes *Flagellum haereticorum* (Scourge of Heretical Witches), one of the first major treatises on witchcraft and witch hunting.
1486	*Malleus Maleficarum* (Hammer of the Witches) is written, outlining how to identify and hunt witches.
1575-1675	Witch hunts reach their peak in Europe.
1584	Reginald Scott, the skeptical thinker, publishes *The Discoverie of Witchcraft*.
1675-1750	Most of Europe sees reductions in witch hunts.
1692-1693	Salem witch trials in Massachusetts.
1736	Witchcraft Act is repealed in London.
1828	Karl Ernst-Jarcke argues that historical witchcraft is actually a pre-Christian religion.
1888	The Hermetic Order of the Golden Dawn, an elite secret society devoted to ritual magic, is founded in England.
1899	Amateur folkorist Charles Leland publishes *Aradia, or the Gospel of the Witches*.
1921	Margaret Murray's *The Witch-Cult in Western Europe* is published: first of three works arguing that historical witchcraft was actually a form of ancient pagan fertility worship.
1951	Witchcraft Act of 1736 is repealed.
1954	Gerald Gardner publishes *Witchcraft Today*, laying the foundations for Wicca.

and destruction, whereas God brought life and salvation. It was espoused that witches worshipped the Devil in the form of a goat, cat, or toad. They had sexual orgies with demons and one another. They raised storms to destroy crops and injure people. These were the things Church officials warned of and what most of Europe believed.

Some of these ideas were gathered from Jewish stereotypes and other Christian/Catholic heresies. These stories were affirmed by forced confessions. Many of these beliefs may also stem from the belief in the Wild Hunt, or a spectral hunting party, led by different regional Western European pagan gods and goddesses who caused thunder and lightning while gathering the wandering souls of the dead.

The shift in belief within the Church became that witchcraft and sorcery went from being delusions to dangerous crimes. Shifts in judicial proceedings in the 12th century, due to an interest in Roman law, took an inquisitorial stance rather than an accusatory one. Additionally, new interests in magical texts from ancient Roman, Arabic, and Hebrew writings gave a framework of a world inhabited by powerful demons who needed to be dealt with swiftly and severely.[6]

All of these factors (plus many more complex changes in economics), led to the development of the belief in the 15th century that there was a diabolical witch cult set on demonic worship and the destruction of the Christian world. This belief allowed for the birth of the witch hunts that would devastate parts of Europe, the echoes of which are still felt today.

Even as a modern witch, it's not uncommon for me to get hate mail or concerned messages begging me to stop doing the Devil's work from wayward Christian people. I've been accused of sacrificing animals (I raise my own meat chickens) and other strange and fantastical things due to the deep and presiding fear some people hold for what they imagine witchcraft to be. I won't say being a witch is easy or always safe—sadly, in our world, few identities and religious beliefs are completely free from danger. That won't stop me, but it does inform how I act in public places and how I share my practice with the world around me. Even being an herbalist comes with a certain set of prejudices one has to face.

A Short History of
Folk Healers in America

The history of folk healers in America begins with us deciding on a definition. Folk medicine can be defined as "represent[ing] a body of belief and practice isolated in various ways from the social and cultural 'mainstream' and intriguingly unaffected by 'modern' knowledge, with which it is frequently compared on the apparent presumption that 'folk' and 'modern' are mutually exclusive classifications."[7] American folk medicine begins as a story of Indigenous medicine. It starts in the 1500s with the arrival of the Spanish and the enslaved Africans they brought with them. The Spanish used Roman humoral medicine combined with Christian ideologies and eventually melded them with Indigenous beliefs. This was further influenced by largely West African enslaved people who brought their own healing traditions and worldviews with them. When British colonists arrived in North America, they left a medical system that relied upon class stratification and specialization. Apothecaries and surgeons were seen as lower class in comparison to the illustrious university-educated physician. However, enforcing these class differences in a wildly new country was not possible.

The lines between medical professions blurred as people met their needs however they could medically, for in America, there were no universities to train physicians or guilds for apothecaries and surgeons. It was not until the 19th century that medical schools and licensure were enforced, thus allowing for folk medical and magical practitioners to take up caring for and curing their neighbors.[8] British colonists had heard tales of the strong, tall, and healthy indigenous people populating the land they were about to arrive upon as uninvited guests. Indigenous medicine was often believed to be superior to the medicine they knew at home.

This is due to a variety of factors, namely exotification. The idea that the medicine of indigenous people was inherently more powerful than that of whites would vacillate over the next few centuries as the systematic theft of Indigenous land occurred. The fact that they were seen as both the "noble savage" and wild people who stood in the way of landholdings depended on the desires of the colonists. Indigenous peoples did not have immunity to many of the diseases that colonists carried, and in the coming years, smallpox, typhus, and many other diseases would utterly decimate their populations, paving the way for the creation of the America we know today.

Despite the racial tensions, the land was the great equalizer; it did not invite the various colonists and Indigenous inhabitants to meld their cultures. The land almost forced it. Without the knowledge the First Nations people provided to settlers, many if not most would have perished through harsh winters in a new terrain full of strange animals and plants. European beliefs also had an effect on Native Americans. For example, they went from believing that the neglect of ritual during hunting could cause illness to believing that the hunter, by inhaling bad odors, could get sick.[9] The miasma theory of disease holds that inhaling bad airs or foul smells was the root of many diseases, kind of like a proto-germ theory, and is the legacy of Hippocrates, a fourth-century Greek physician.[10]

Migrating to radically new areas requires parts of a culture that don't transfer well to be let go of, and new, more effective cultural practices—here most likely from the Native people of the area—to be adopted. The First Nations people have lived here for thousands of years and knew how things had to be done to ensure a good life in this specific bioregion. No amount of racial prejudice could totally discount their knowledge and experience. Native Americans also had a unique blend of certain African beliefs in their systems of healing, and by 1620, they'd been mingling as runaway enslaved people fled deep into the mountains away from their oppressors. Enslaved peoples often had unique medical systems distinct from white enslavers', for some permitted victims of enslavement to heal themselves in the ways they knew how. Yet, this was certainly not always the case for those who saw their practices as witchcraft and would rather they die than allow them to be treated with their native medicine.

We can see the West African worldview's fingerprint on American folk medicine in many places. Looking at specific practices is a great way to begin following the threads of diverse folk cultures back to their countries of origin. One such belief set evident in the American South is the belief that spirits could cause illness as well as their varied and complex folkways surrounding conjuration and magic. In many cultures there is a folk healing concept that living in a "right relationship," or in a mutually kind, reciprocal, and thoughtful way with other people and one's environment is not only the right thing to do but also pivotal to maintaining good health. This is a simplified way of looking at one type of shared belief between many West African cultures and Indigenous tribes who thought interpersonal and human-land relationships could affect one's health. These shared worldviews and beliefs allowed for cultural blending more readily. Conversely, due to differing worldviews, many Africans did not find much of value in the medicine of whites.[11]

Healing information was eventually shared more often between poor whites and free Black, brown, and Indigenous peoples while the lines between what beliefs came from where became more and more blurred. One could argue the foundational stones of American folk medicine were set in the antebellum South after many white people lost their wealth in the Civil War, and class lines softened to make folk healing methods cross not only race but class lines.[12] There were also certain books, like William Buchan's *Every Man His Own Doctor* from 1794, Dr. John C. Gunn's *Gunn's Domestic Medicine or Poor Man's Friend*, and English translations of a German charm book, John George Hohman's *The Long Hidden Friend*, which circulated widely throughout the earliest states of America. Their remedies, prayers, and rituals can be seen in many folk healing traditions born on this continent.

American folk healers came, and still come, in all races, ages, and genders. Specialization in one's healing realm was a common occurrence, whether it be in the form of prayers (as in a minister physician of English colonists) or the herbs used by an Appalachian yarb (herb) doctor of any lineage. Some folk healers shared information freely among themselves, like midwives and herb diggers, while others, like folk magical practitioners, operated in secrecy due to the ways mystery lent itself to their cures.[13]

Some of the most magical and fascinating parts of the diverse American folk healing traditions are the ways people are believed to become healers. As mentioned previously, many learn from another practitioner. In the cases of granny women or midwives, younger women are taught by elders. However, some are born into healing. Accidents of birth are often believed to impart magical or innate healing abilities, such as having never seen one's father or being born with a caul, or fetal membrane, still covering one's face. In Appalachia and the Ozarks, being the seventh son of a seventh son is a sure way to be a born healer. Among Spanish Americans, the fifth or sixth consecutive son or daughter would be born *saludadores*, a healer or "health giver."[14]

Many of us today were not born into unbroken lines of these old ways of herbs and charms, but it's never too late to heed the call. In all my traveling and teaching, one of the most wonderful things I've learned is that old folk healing ways are not dead, just hidden in plain sight. Many people have come to me with a story of a grandpa who could whisper the pain out of a fresh wound, or an aunt who could stop bleeding from miles away with a prayer said to the setting sun. These are classic folk healing stories, yet I've met nearly thirty people who know a folk healer personally. It makes me want to cry with relief. Just when I think magic has been cut down and paved over entirely, there—a dandelion has pushed its way out of the cracks of cement.

Herbalism Today: Why Form Relationships with Herbs?

Understanding the context and history of working with plants as medicine on this continent is imperative to finding an ethical practice, but this also leads us to the question *why*? Why bother with herbs? Why take the time in this modern world to breathe, slow down, and sink into these relationships with plants when we have modern medicine? There's not just one answer, but I'll tell you why I think it's a valuable and worthwhile practice.

The study of plant craft is relevant today, despite its antiquated associations, especially in a plant species–rich area like Appalachia where I live. There are so many opportunities to grow and gather abundant, non-endangered plant medicines and foods due to the amazing amount of species diversity. There are many opportunities to access simple medicine and nourishing foods as well as materials for our craft.

While many ecologically minded folks rally to the cry of saving the Earth for its own sake, I have to be honest and also consider the current mindset and cultural reality that most people face: many people do not ascribe an intrinsic value to nature. Many see themselves as separate, alien from the place where they dwell. This is not anyone's fault. It's been a slow and deliberate divorce brought about by centuries of economic, spiritual, and physical oppression wrought by the forces of colonization, industrialism, and capitalism against our universal animistic ancestors of all nations. Seeing a "use" in a plant can be a doorway into recognizing the true, unique life force and real being of that plant after forming a relationship with it. We don't all arrive at the party at the same time or in the same vehicle.

When a plant is seen as useful to humans, it's much more difficult to categorize it as an other or to ignore it completely when engaging in any practice. Inspiring people to see value in plants and ecosystems can help to preserve them, for we now live in an anthropocentric world, and our sustainability in the long term depends upon the choices we make now.[15] By inspiring or reinspiring perceived value in the ecosystems of our world, we can not only combat species loss and habitat destruction but also combat the loss of traditional practices and regional folkways by making this knowledge accessible. We can combat the total divorce of humans from their fellow animal, vegetable, and mineral kin.

Having a relationship with plants through gardening and foraging supports and can even help increase biological and cultural diversity. First Nations people in North America have gathered and used almost 1,800 different plants, algae, lichens, and fungi throughout their cultural life ties.[16] In contrast, only twelve plant species make up over 75 percent of America's entire food supply today, and only fifteen mammal and bird species make up more than 90 percent of global domestic livestock production. This reliance upon just a few species for global food security and medicinal compounds is dangerous due to the threats of disease and epidemics within closely related plant and animal communities.[17] Not only is biodiversity threatened but our cultural diversity is too. Seeking direct relationships with the greenwood around us is one of many diverse tactics used to address these challenges by finding meaning and value in plants and preserving their habitats and their traditional uses in different cultural contexts.

Another reason to pursue herbal studies is rooted in history. Modern medicine as we know it today is just that: modern. What it lacks in age it makes up for in innovation, but there's a very long time line in which plants, minerals, and animals provided the bulk of our healing. That time line is one of the powers of herbalism. Centuries of trying different doses, preparations, and recording outcomes in both the folk and more professional medical practioners' workings yields us a long and detailed register of which remedies are safest and most reliable. This combined with modern herbal research (which still occurs despite lack of funds) has shown us the places where herbalism dwells most readily.

Today, there are few of us who aren't affected by minor injuries and illnesses that do not necessitate a visit to the doctor but render us in need of a remedy. Herbalism provides safe and affordable—or even free—answers to these small but annoying questions. The practice can add to our overall comfort and ease in a country that's left many with little to no affordable health care. That being said, herbs aren't just for the small things. They also offer safe alternatives and supportive allies in dealing with autoimmune diseases and chronic illnesses. Where conventional Western medicine shines in acute care, herbs often steal the spotlight for long-term management of conditions. Herbalism can help fill the gaps in conventional Western medicine and can also work alongside it as we strive for a more holistic and ethical medical system.

Why Grow and Harvest Your Own Herbs?
Why Work with the Plants Around You?

Why grow and harvest your own herbs when a short online search will bring you whatever you desire for the right price? I feel there are a few reasons: intimacy, deep knowledge, and sustainability. I want to answer this from the lens I view plants through: bioregionally. Noted bioregionalist scholar Kirkpatrick Sale defines a bioregion as a "life-territory, a place defined by its life-forms, its topography, and its biota rather than by human dictates."[18] I focus my use and learning on the plants I can directly work with around where I live. This helps me address some of the biggest concerns in herbal medicine today.

There are many questions about the sustainability of wildcrafting or harvesting plants from the wild for medicine making. Some people respond to this question by suggesting that they never wildcraft, while others operate in a devil-may-care attitude of overconsumption. I believe the answer lies in nuance. In some bioregions, like in Colorado where rainfall is limited and fragile desert ecosystems don't respond well to stress, asking whether the land can handle wildcrafting is extremely important. In Appalachia where I live, the abundant rainfall and species richness renders the questions differently. We forget, since we can talk to people all over the world with the click of a button, that we're bioregionally grounded beings, just as our ancestors were.

Considering the unique location and environmental, biological, and cultural geography of the region is a great step towards moving in the direction of location-based land management ethics. This means that what works in Colorado will definitely *not* work here. Any one-size-fits-all rules about foraging—or really anything to do with the land—must be tailored to the unique place you're addressing. This fact is very hard for folks who've never lived a place-based lifestyle to grasp, and it can bring a lot of pushback, and that's okay. It's hard to begin rewilding our minds and consciously make our world a little smaller by focusing on our dwelling place. ReWild University, an educational center focused on ancestral skills like foraging and shelter building, defines rewilding: "Rewilding isn't about trying to go back to living as hunter-gatherers. Rather, it is about examining our cultural paradigms, seeing how they affect our physical, mental, and emotional health, and reclaiming our birthright as human beings."[19] The Eat Local movement is a great example of a bioregionally grounded tactic that also keeps rewilding in mind. Eating whole foods that are fresh and from where we live helps to provide us with vital nutrients while also giving us an invitation to learn more about what grows well in our climate and what is sustainable in different seasons, and allows us to walk more cyclically from what some would say is the center of our being: our gut.

Ancestral foodways have become very important for both cultural and health-based movements in Indigenous communities countrywide. Eating wild and locally grown foods can have spiritual significance, which helps foster value, pride, and sacredness in the ways food is made, eaten, and shared. Finding our own ways to connect to ancestral diets is a beautiful way to not only connect with our ancestors spiritually but also physically, even if we'll never eat with them at our tables. If we don't know who our ancestors are (as in the case of adoption), sinking into the food traditions of the place that one calls home can be a beautiful way to share in this practice.

The French coined the term *terroir* when discussing the unique character ascribed to the tastes and magic of foods from specific biogeographical places. It could be the unique combination of that locality's air, water, and soil or something undefinable that makes it special. Here in Appalachia, we have many edible plant species, wild game, and forageable mushrooms. We're blessed with abundance in this way. A unique temperate rain forest–like precipitation combined with the moderate growing season makes it possible to grow many fruits, nuts, and vegetables that would be quite difficult to obtain if we were farther north or south.

As a forager, I believe heartily in the nuances of the terroir of a place, the unique flavors and nutrients of the wild and cultivated foods fostered wherever you call home. The wonder of foraging is that we can all be foodies. We can skip the farmers market, keep our hard-earned dollars in our pockets, and graze on the abundance of food from our yards to the deep woods. The most challenging thing is finding ways to relearn that lost knowledge.

I was not raised a witch, a farmer, or a forager, but I learned it all in my young adulthood by doing an apprenticeship with Natalie Bogwalker at Wild Abundance in western North Carolina and from many, many others. I learned from books, YouTube videos, and friends. I was privileged to stumble upon the community I have in western North Carolina, and I have to say, I have finally found my home.

I was eating some kraut my friends and I made once and was thinking about the strange and unique flavors. If there is a terroir of food and plants and animals, I imagine there is too for magic. I want to advocate for a terroir of folk magic. A magic of place. A unique and special magic that only flows through the French Broad River and the Pisgah National Forest. A Western Carolinian Appalachian magic terroir. This is just an example from my home. You have a terroir in your bioregion as well. What is it like?

I think bioregional animism, or the magic of a specific place, really comes to life for me when I'm foraging. I see the unique array of plants, fungi, and animals that these mountains have fostered and marvel at the ancient rivers and springs that feed these dark and secret hollers. I love that my body is built from the unique soil I walk upon and the water I drink and swim in. I love that there's nowhere else on Earth quite like this.

Rediscovering local flavors is definitely still a hot topic as restaurants and grocery stores showcase locally grown and now even foraged fare. Rewilders and "normal" people alike can get behind eating from a bioregion since it just makes sense, and someday, it may be the only thing on the menu. Just as much as I want to support people in growing, foraging, and sharing foodways together, I want to support and defend bioregional magical practices. In defense of folk magic, I say there's no better way to honor the places where we live and the beings that dwell there than to remember and discover the ways that came before. Not just the baskets that were woven or the way songs were sung, but the way the spirits want to be seen, the way to implore the yarrow to heal our wounds or to leave offerings that will please our *genius loci*, or the spirit of a place.

I love that term. The spirit of a place. It's the terroir of the spirit world. I learned it from Marcus McCoy, one of the founders of Viridis Genii Symposium, a wonderful plant magic conference, about eight years ago from an article he wrote. I see the term more and more since he popularized it, which warms my bioregional heart. The unique flavor of beings and creatures that crawl and fly and swim in our home places. No matter where we live we can directly interact with these beings.

It's also important for us to remember, as we seek to form a relationship with the land, that we are living on stolen land. To become entrenched in the ways of the land is not an invitation to appropriate cultural or religious practices of the indigenous peoples who came before us and who still dwell here. This call is an invitation to seek out and meet the spirits, not claim them or command them. It's an invitation to listen and look, to hear and to smell, to taste the land, and to feed it. Bioregional witchcraft to me means living a practice that's informed by the beings you live among, both human and nonhuman. It's a practice that lives and grows.

I tell my students—whether we're studying medieval herbalism or Appalachian folk charms against ghosts—that some things are not meant for us. I was born in Appalachia but raised all over this country, and that means that those things to which I'm privy are different than those things that are privy to someone who was born and raised here in these mountains I now call home. I do not mourn that, for what good would that do me? It's a reality to live in the sometimes-discomfort of realizing we all have access to different things and have different work to do. Living in shame or envy is not the answer. Just as many face the privileges afforded to them by whiteness, class, or ability, we must closely and lovingly examine the traditions we engage in for spiritual gain as well.

We all have a pagan, animist past. I see a tendency to idealize old things and shun creating new things in our witchcraft practices when, in fact, what we're practicing is the piecing together of different, fragmented ancient ways. We can create, reimagine, and rebirth vibrant bioregional witchcraft practices from the broken pieces that others tried to stamp out. We can do this by forming relationships with the land around us and by weaving it together with the practices our ancestors left us. We can live something ancient by making it new and vital.

We don't have to have perfect unbroken witch-lineages, and we don't have to speak spells that were written in the year 100 CE. We can find a new way for the many of us who do not have access to unbroken traditions to live on this land and observe the seasonal changes in ways that feel authentic. We can do it without appropriative spiritual picking-and-choosing that causes harm to indigenous folks and BIPOC (Black, Indigenous, People of Color) communities. We can find a new way to forage, to farm, and to listen. It's both old and new. And this, I think, is a fine thing.

Choosing to live in a smaller world, attempting to source sustenance and resources from the places around me where sustainable, doesn't leave me with a sense of lacking. I don't see this as a loss of detail or knowledge but, in fact, as an invitation of intimacy with the animals, plants, minerals, and history that only comes with deep knowing of a particular place. This is one of the great gifts of bioregionalism to witches. What better bedrock to build a house of magic upon than one of deep knowing?

Direct Relationship with Nature for the Nature Worshipper

As I travel to and visit different conferences and talks around the country, one thing I often walk away with is a sadness that so many herbalists and witches don't truly know the plants they work with in the wild. They may know of a few here and there, but the real commitment to learning to identify, harvest, and make medicine and magic with them is often missing.

This is for many complex reasons, largely due to the inaccessibility of learning, but I believe it's also due in part to a deep-seated belief that we really are separated from nature. Perhaps this is the greatest unlearning we have to undergo to fully allow ourselves to reestablish good relations with other than the human world. Choosing to dedicate oneself to working alongside plants by deeply knowing them is in itself an act of magic. It's an initiation and a constant reestablishment of commitment to one's path.

All of our collective ancestors were animists, which was the first way in which humans interacted spiritually with the world. Animists believe "that the world is full of persons, some of whom are human."[20] Older definitions of animism mostly focused on belief in spirits, but in the more modern definition coined by Graham Harvey, professor of religious studies at Open University in the UK, a focus on how people relate to these other beings is also paramount. Most witches are also animists. We see life in all things. We see "personhood" in all things. This does not mean we personify them, but we recognize rivers, plants, insects, animals, mountains, and the diversity of beings we share this world with as having unique "selfness" worthy of respect, value, and honor.[21]

Working with plants as a witch allows for every moment to be a prayer and for every smell, taste, sound, and feeling to be an offering. By choosing to deeply know, protect, propagate, and work with plants, we can find not only more ways to see the personhood of each plant we meet but also get to let them see ours as well. We're allowed an invitation to step a foot back onto the well-worn path we all used to walk together towards living a cyclical life with the growing of food, the births of people and nonhuman creatures, and the deaths of those beloved beings as well. We get to find more ways—in a profoundly disconnected culture where feelings of unworthiness and loneliness reign—to be embraced.

Living in Sync with the Seasons

Connecting with ourselves and the other-than-human world around us is just one special way that living more seasonally can manifest connection and meaning. I know it seems strange to intentionally perform specific actions and lifestyle shifts to create meaning for ourselves, but many of us are divested from strong familial and cultural ties. I believe this is one of many reasons modern humans face so much apathy, depression, and aimlessness. Observing the changing of the seasons, whether in Michigan or South Florida, grounds us in the subtle changes, both energetically and physically, of the land and its inhabitants around us. So if we cannot see meaning that makes sense to us or is healthy for us in the lives we live, we can often make small shifts to start to make our own.

Witchcraft as a spiritual practice is essentially the worship of nature, and it's in the observations of seasonal changes that we find our most sacred celebrations. Historically, peoples of every culture chose specific agricultural and even astrological days to feast, pray, dance, and celebrate the gifts of life and the rich world around them. In witchcraft, we call these the sabbats. In some branches of Traditional Witchcraft and other modern neopagan traditions, we celebrate eight sabbats based upon ancient Irish and English pre-Christian festivals as well as the two equinoxes and solstices. I personally find that taking the time to celebrate the milestones marked out by these special days rooted in my ancestral past has filled my life with more rich symbolism and meaning than I had ever thought possible. I have also always loved the name given to this cycle of eight holidays: the Wheel of the Year.

One of the glories of being a witch is that you don't have to celebrate holidays you have no ancestral ties to, worship gods or goddesses, or really do anything you don't want to do. One of the things I love in my personal practice is tailoring my sabbat celebrations to feature foods and plants I can forage or grow here in Appalachia. For example: A traditional dish eaten on the winter holiday called Imbolc is hot cross buns. I make these with dock seeds (*Rumex crispus*) we forage and make them gluten free because I can't eat wheat no matter how much my ancestors liked it. We eat deer meat we've hunted rather than eating lamb we buy at the store, and we eat lots of wild greens we've dried, like nettles (*Urtica dioica*) and violet leaves (*Viola sororia*).

This is far from what many kitchen witch books will recommend as traditional Imbolc fare, but for us, eating these sacred foods from the land we live on *is* the way we make tradition. The beautiful thing about tradition is that it had to start somewhere. This is the space I most delight in occupying. The space between tradition and the reality of my lived experience. What ways would eating and living seasonally change your witchcraft practice?

I don't just eat seasonally, but I also harvest plants for my craft and for regular old crafts like basketmaking and weaving. When mullein (*Verbascum thapsus*) grows its stalk proud and tall in early October here in North Carolina's mountains, I know it's almost time for Samhain. I gather mullein every year to dip into beeswax and make candles for our dark moon rites and for my most favorite of all the holidays. These are called hag's tapers; they make incredible bioregional candles, especially if you buy local beeswax or even raise bees yourself. These are just a few examples of the myriad ways to sink into aligning your craft with the Wheel of the Year as it turns. In this book, I'll include rituals, spells, and herbal remedies focused on the Wheel of the Year for you to celebrate and explore as you expand your own witchcraft practice.

II

THE
RELATIONSHIP

Gardening Your Own
Magical and Healing Herbs

The land has special energy and magic. There's an intrinsic link between herbs and witchcraft as the two are natural companions. For anyone who wants to get their hands dirty and truly become a garden witch, this part of the book will introduce you to the tools and information you need to dive in.

Maintaining a Magical Garden: Organic Growing 101

Land. We're all from somewhere, but 64 percent of Americans are landless, meaning we don't own land ourselves. This doesn't mean we can't grow our own plants though. There are many ways to have access to soil to work and play in. If you do not have a space with at least six (preferably more) hours of direct sunlight on your property each day, or you don't have access to any gardenable land, here are a few options:

Community garden: Work together! Some places have affordable plot rentals and shared tools and resources for group growing (plus it's a great way to meet your green community!). See if you can start one if there isn't one near you.

Yard sharing: Some people with lots of property are happy to share. Post ads on community bulletin boards that you are looking for a little bit of ground to grow in.

Container gardening: You can grow a surprising amount and diversity of plants in pots way up high in an apartment; all you need is light and some space in your home. We'll cover this more a bit later.

In this section, I'll break down the fundamentals of what you need to know in order to start growing and maintaining your own magical garden.

Identify Your Zone

Plants respond to the changing seasons: it's why spring and summer are fruitful and winter tends to make many plants go dormant. If you live in a climate that has particularly harsh winters and frost concerns, you'll need to pay special attention to which plants can survive in your area. If you live in a place like California, you might not have to worry so much. When temperatures get too cold, that's when plants react. Annuals die and perennials will go dormant for the winter season. You can be prepared by understanding what to expect and by understanding your **climate zone**.

Climate zones are based on expected high and low temperatures of the area. You can use a map of these zones to serve as guides to help identify which plants will grow and thrive in your area. The USDA (US Department of Agriculture) has a plant hardiness map online where you can look up your region by zip code to learn about your zone (zone labeling is based on average annual minimum temperature).

Soil

Growing plants for magical uses has to start somewhere: the soil. Whether you're growing in containers on your porch or planting directly in the ground, the way we care for and even create soil is paramount to growing and sustaining healthy plants. Soil is essentially a four-part substance: mineral solids, air, water, and organic matter. There's a lot to each of those four parts, but I'll keep it very simple. The mineral solids are clay, silt, and sand. The air creates spaces, called pores, that serve as the roadways for gases like oxygen to move through the soil. Water moves the dissolved nutrients through the soil. They're all important, but the heart of organic garden soil is the organic matter. I like the way a former professor at my alma mater, the University of Vermont, and author of the amazing book *Building Soils for Better Crops*, Fred Magdoff, explains organic matter and soil science:

Soil organic matter is a mix of three different kinds of material:

The living: This part is made up of soil organisms and plant roots. They're essentially the underground livestock herd. Soil organisms carry out a diverse array of useful functions ranging from capturing solar energy and decomposing organic residues to suppressing pests.

The dead: Recently dead organic material such as crop residues, yard wastes, and animal manure. This part is generally high in nutrients and easy to decompose, so it acts as feed for the "underground herd."

The very dead: Soil humus, or the final product of all that eating and decomposing by the living. Humus is physically and chemically active, stores nutrients and water, stabilizes soil structure, degrades toxins, and promotes plant growth. Humus can be thought of as "the farm" for the underground herd—this makes up the majority of organic matter. Humus is important because of its small particle sizes. Well-decomposed organic matter has a large surface area to volume ratio, meaning the humus is in considerable contact with much of the soil. This allows for many reactions to occur in these close quarters, like the release of nutrients into the water in the soil.[1]

You don't have to be a soil scientist to have healthy soils and recognize their attributes. Just like with identifying plants, basic pattern recognition is a great way to judge a few characteristics of the soil you're working with.

Darker soils: More organic matter, good air spaces, high water-holding capacity.

Red/brownish: Good aeration and some waterlogging—the red usually indicates a high amount of clay in the soil.

Gray/olive: Much waterlogging in the soil. (Soil is regarded as waterlogged when it's saturated with water most of the time, so much so that its air spaces are restricted.)

Mottled subsoil: Fluctuating groundwater table. Flood zone perhaps.

So now that we know how important organic matter is in soil building, how do we get it in the soil we want to plant in? We can add compost! Animal manure, crop residues (like chopped straw or leaf compost), and other plant material can make up compost. We can also grow cover crop (plants grown primarily for the benefit of the soil) and either let the plant matter rot and cover it to speed up that process or gently turn it in with a shovel or garden spade and practice good mulching to keep the sun from "scorching" the nitrogen and other minerals and nutrients out of the soil.

Soil Nutrients

Plants need access to 18 chemical elements for their growth: NPK, carbon, hydrogen, oxygen, calcium, magnesium, sulfur, boron, copper, iron, chlorine, manganese, molybdenum, zinc, nickel, and cobalt. How these nutrients move through the soil and become available to our plant friends is directly related to how much organic matter we help foster in our soils.[2]

NPK are all primary nutrients, meaning they're used in large quantities for various plant growth processes and are usually the first to be depleted.

—*Nitrogen (N)*: Even though our air is composed of 78-percent nitrogen, it's incredibly volatile, which makes it hard to keep in the soil. Nitrate is the form of nitrogen that plants love, and sadly it's also very prone to runoff! That's why soils rich in organic matter with good tilth and structure can help hold onto it. It's like a sponge—soils that aren't compacted and also have good air spaces hold onto their nutrients best. Nitrogen is needed in plants for many processes, including growth and reproduction. After water, it's the second most important nutrient for plant growth. Sometimes, yellowing on foliage is an indicator you need more nitrogen. How do we get nitrogen? From compost, manure, cover crops that are legumes (like peas or fava beans), and blood, bone, or fish meal. Regular soil testing (once in spring and once in fall) is also always helpful. You can buy a home test or send one out to your local university that offers soil testing. Lastly, you can buy nitrogen-rich fertilizer. (By the way, blood meal is the name of a commercially available natural fertilizer. It's a by-product of the slaughterhouse industry that would otherwise go to waste.)

—*Phosphorus (P)*: Like nitrogen, phosphorus is an essential part of the process of photosynthesis as well as rapid growth. It encourages blooming and root growth. Phosphorus deficiency usually shows up after a few years of growing in the same spot. Sometimes purplish-red spotting on the undersides of leaves can indicate low phosphorus. By adding enough organic matter and encouraging a healthy underground food web (especially the fungal members of the web in the soil) more phosphorus can become available. Unfortunately, it often becomes bound up through chemical bonds in the soil, rendering it unavailable to plants. If we keep feeding the underground herd and adding organic matter, phosphorus can become more available. Buckwheat is a useful phosphorus accumulator and can be used as a green manure or cover crop. If you want to add a store-bought product, remember, bone meal is ideal because rock phosphate is a finite, mined product, and its production is damaging to the Earth. Many garden stores carry bone meal, as it's a common organic amendment.

—*Potassium (K)*: Potassium is absorbed by plants in large amounts, more than any other mineral element except nitrogen and calcium. It's highly leachable and usually highly removed from the soil system at harvest time. It helps in the building of protein, photosynthesis, and the reduction of plant diseases. Potassium comes from soil minerals and organic material. If you note slow growth and stunted plants when plants are little seedlings, you may have a deficiency. Bright orange spots can appear on leaves as well as yellow leaf margins. Bronzing of the leaf tissue can occur before finally browning and dying. Usually potassium can be provided by compost, cover crops, and plant residues. Manures are usually great sources of potassium except for that of poultry (don't worry, manures available for purchase usually come from cows). Greens and granite dust are other good slow-release sources. Wood ashes are high in potassium as well, but the liming effect, about two-thirds that of limestone, can raise pH too high if they aren't regulated.[3] The pH of the soil is very important for nutrient availability, and that's why soil testing can be so vital. If soil is too acidic or basic, different plants may struggle to thrive!

Secondary nutrients are calcium (Ca), magnesium (Mg), and sulfur (S). These often exist in the soil in sufficient amounts naturally, so you may not need to add them. Also, large amounts of calcium and magnesium are added when lime is applied to acidic soils. Sulfur is usually adequate in soil organic matter as a by-product of decomposition. Don't throw away your grass clippings and leaves since these can help provide all your plants' needs!

Calcium: Necessary to produce cell walls and grow leaves. This nutrient is needed in different amounts depending on what plant you're growing.

Magnesium: Magnesium is part of the chlorophyll in all green plants and essential for photosynthesis. It also helps activate many plant enzymes needed for growth. Soil minerals, organic material, fertilizers, and dolomitic limestone are sources of magnesium. I use Cal-Mag lime in my garden.

Sulfur: Essential plant food for production of protein. It promotes activity and development of enzymes and vitamins, among many other functions. Sulfur is available in rainwater and gypsum. It's also available in organic matter, of course!

Micronutrients are essential elements for plant growth needed in only very small quantities. These elements are sometimes called minor or trace elements. The micronutrients are boron (B), copper (Cu), iron (Fe), chlorine (Cl), manganese (Mn), molybdenum (Mo), and zinc (Zn). Recycling organic matter such as grass clippings and tree leaves is an excellent way of providing micronutrients (as well as macronutrients) to growing plants.[4]

Lastly, you can always buy potting soil from your local nursery.

Seeds

We love to have choices, especially when it comes to food and medicine. Humans have been choosing what food plants they want in the form of seeds for about 12,000 years. Grain agriculture as a practice was not widespread until about 9500 BCE, when it's thought the eight "founder crops" of civilization were staking their claims as cornerstones of ever-more sedentary cultures around the world. These were emmer and einkorn wheat, chickpea, flax, bitter vetch, barley, peas, and lentils.[5] It was only in the 1880s that seed companies really began to hold sway over the ways in which we save, access, and choose which plants are worth keeping and which are okay to forget.[6] Most people before this saved, traded, and sold seed to one another on a community scale. While the advent of the seed company allowed for a wider variety of species options at first, eventually, with the scientific and industrial revolutions happening in the 1920s, less and less variety became available, and production-oriented seed saving and selling reigned.

This in combination with the changes in the sciences surrounding medical healing meant that more and more people were moving away from home remedies for sickness and homegrown foods to physicians and monocrop corn products. This is a very simplified telling of these big shifts, but as people who work with seeds, it's great to know a little about how ancient an art we're practicing by starting seeds ourselves, and how it is somewhat a radical act. Choosing to start from seed herbs and flowers that were once valued by our diverse ancestors here and abroad is a special way to reconnect and ground our practice of working with plants in a lineage.

The American Heritage Dictionary defines heirloom as "a valued possession passed down through successive generations." Heirloom gardening is the preservation of old and valued plant varieties. Many varieties that were once staples of 17th- and 18th-century gardens and homesteads have been lost due to the aforementioned changes in agribusiness. However, as with the recurrent interest in primitive skills and heritage arts, so too has there been a resurgence of interest in heirloom seeds.[7] I love growing herbs and vegetables with a story.

Growing Herbs from Seed

Plants are amazing. Most have both male and female reproductive parts, with the male portion being the stamen with its filaments and pollen-filled anthers at the filament tips. These anthers will gradually ripen and then split open, exposing the pollen when they're ready to reproduce. The female portion is the pistil and consists of a stigma and style with an ovary that contains one or more ovules. The stigma is the portion that receives pollen.

When a fertile grain of pollen connects with the style, it forms a pollen tube and eventually reaches and fertilizes the ovules in the ovary. The ovary will develop into a seedpod or fruit, while the fertilized ovules become the future seeds.

Germinating seeds can be both incredibly easy *and* incredibly hard! Essentially what has to happen is the seed coat (or the outside of the seed) needs to be weakened enough for the plant to begin growing towards the light source. Some plant seeds also need temperature changes or fluctuations that imitate winter freezes or thawing springs to let them know it's time to wake up.

Stratification is that process. Certain plant and tree species' seeds need dark, moist, chilling temperatures. These changes soften the seed coat, allowing them to germinate. Seeds fall from plants and are covered by soil and leaves in nature where they remain cool and wet until spring. You can imitate this natural process by placing a seed in layers of moistened sand or sand and peat moss mix. If seeds are small, you can place them in between muslin cloth or paper towels. You can do it in the fridge or freezer if you have the space! To determine if a seed needs this, read the seed packet or familiarize yourself with the unique needs of each plant you're growing. Not all seeds need stratification, mostly just seeds with very hard coats. Lavender is an example of a plant that germinates much better after stratification.

Scarifying, or physically damaging the seed coat intentionally, is another way to weaken the seed coat and allow moisture inside to signal it's time to germinate. You can use nail files quite easily for this. I buff a little hole into *Ipomoea alba* or moonflower seeds (which are quite hard) before soaking and planting to help speed up the germination process. The act of soaking seeds in warm water before planting them is also helpful in promoting good germination. I even like to do this to my garden peas to give them a head start before tucking them into the cold, hard earth.

I like to plant heirloom or open-pollinated varieties of seeds. This means I can save seed from those plants and share them with my community. Hybrid seeds are crosses made between two different plants for some type of benefit or feature, like disease resistance, color, or other desirable characteristic.[8] These seeds will never grow true, meaning if I save them, they will revert back to their different parent plants. I cannot save seeds from hybrid plants. Lastly, you can also always purchase plants as starts from your local nursery if you'd like to skip the seeding process.

Plant Propagation

Plants can reproduce themselves in a few different ways. Sexually (through germinating seeds), is one way we've just learned about. There are many other ways to asexually, or clonally, propagate your herbs and create clones of the plants you love. There's a great and complex world of plant propagation to explore, but we'll just graze the surface of this ancient art by looking at the easiest, most affordable methods that make sense for magical herb growers.

Division

Division is any method of asexual production that involves separating a plant part from a parent (plantlets, bulbs, offshoots, suckers, scales, or tubers). The process of division is useful for a variety of reasons, one being that you can encourage more plants to grow and spread. It helps keep plants healthy by providing them more room for root growth and nutrient exploration, as well as for more airflow around plants as they become less crowded (airflow is important to prevent fungal diseases). Not every type of asexual propagation works on every type of plant, however, most herbaceous perennial herbs can be propagated this way. Herbs like lemon balm, thyme, oregano, all types of mint, lovage, bee balm, and marjoram can be divided. Simply dig up the roots of the herbs in spring before their vigorous growth begins and divide their roots. I use a hori hori for this, but a sharp trowel works great as well. Divide the plant by the root ball in half or quarters depending on how big it is, and replant and water the "new" plants right away to prevent them from drying out and dying.

Cuttings

You can propagate many herbaceous perennial plants (herbs that live longer than two years) by cutting off certain plant parts and growing a whole new plant with that part. Unlike seed growing, this isn't a whole new genetically diverse plant but a clone, or genetic copy of the parent plant. The piece of the plant you cut off is called a **cutting**. Not every part of a plant can be reproduced in this manner, but specific pieces of roots, branches, or leaves from a parent plant can be cut and replanted in soil to asexually propagate a new plant. If you're unsure if your plant can be cut, or if you're unsure which section to cut from, do a bit of research to confirm or ask your local nursery.

Plants that are hard to grow from seed or slow to grow, like rosemary, are great candidates for this propagation method. Every plant has a certain type of cutting that can be taken from it. For example, you can propagate roses by taking a cutting of the stem from that year's blooms. This can then be planted after being dipped in rooting hormones, which you can buy or even make yourself! This hormone, called auxin, tells the plant to start producing roots. While plants don't need this extra treatment, it can help increase the chances of a successful rooting. You can also get some plant cuttings to root in water. My favorite easy plant to propagate by cuttings is elderberry—simply take a cutting of the soft, new growth on a branch that's just beginning to harden and turn to a woody brown.

One of the great things about elderberry is that you can get many new plants from one branch. Just make sure to pinch off all the leaves from the lower two-thirds of the cutting but leave at least one set of leaves at the top so they can still photosynthesize. I root mine in a glass of water, placing the root cut-side down and ensuring the stick is covered halfway by the water. Just place the jar in a sunny spot and occasionally mist the cutting with a spray bottle and change the water in the glass. Roots should start to poke out by week eight! I pot them up in a potting mix soon after this and wait until they appear robust before planting them outdoors.

You can buy premixed soil for planting your divisions and cuttings, but you can also mix your own if you like. Historically, many people used river sand to propagate plants. You can use clean sand, or you can use the following recipe to make your own potting soil. Premade potting soil mixes are very convenient but are often made from finite materials, like peat moss, or vermiculite and perlite, which are mined materials. Part of grounding ourselves in Earth-based spirituality is asking questions about least harm. How can our plant magic practices also be grounded in causing least harm to the most beings? To me, making a homemade potting soil mix is wonderful because not only will I save money by not buying bagged peat moss and perlite but also I can rest assured that I sourced my soil mix from the land around me, without supporting mined materials.

This recipe for homemade potting soil is adapted from Barbara Pleasant of the iconic *Mother Earth News*:[9]

- 2 parts very well-rotted compost
  (see more on composting on the next page!)
- 1 part good soil
- 1 part rotted (untreated) sawdust or rice hulls

You can also use well-rotted leaf mold to fluff up the soil a bit more in place of rotted sawdust if you like, and if you need very well-drained potting soil, you can add clean sand one handful at a time to a quart of soil mix.

These don't have to be exact recipes, and you can get creative and make your own! The main thing to take away if you're mixing your own is not to use too much biologically active, wet compost and to try and focus on using very well-aged and almost-dry compost. There are a lot of warnings about using soil and compost in potting soil mixes, and for large-scale growers it's a real concern. The bacteria and fungi that exist naturally in these substrates can sometimes cause disease in susceptible plant starts. That said, to me, the benefits of a plant started in the soil it will eventually grow in outweigh the small chance that some of my starts will get fungal infections. I find that by making sure I don't overwater my plants and by letting the soil they're in dry out a bit between waterings, I can avoid a lot of fungal issues in my plants. Do what works for your region though! I live in a hot, wet, humid climate, so fungal diseases like bacterial wilt are common.

Transplants

Transplanting is simply the act of taking a plant you started indoors or in a greenhouse and planting it outside. I love transplanting because I can place my plants exactly where I want them and it gives them a head start regardless of the weather! Some seeds are too tender to leave all on their lonesome when starting out in the soil. If you live in a temperate climate and experience freezing temperatures, this is especially necessary. Once the dangers of frost have passed in the spring, it's time to transplant all the lovely plants you've started from seed.

Each plant has a time to sow and a time to transplant, which is available on many planting calendars and depends on the climate you live in. Check your local extension agency for a calendar that works for your special bioregion.[10]

Composting

Compost is the material left over from when plant matter decomposes **aerobically**, which means through the action of microorganisms that live in the presence of air. This process can take up to six months to produce a mature, useful batch of compost.[11]

You can speed up your composting process by shredding any woody materials you are trying to compost so they decompose faster. Most compost needs a curing time that lasts up to 30 days even after their original contents are no longer recognizable. The final product should be dark brown in color. It should not smell bad but be more neutral and soil-like in texture. I think the perfect compost looks like chocolate cake mix.

What can I compost? This is a hotly debated topic. Many people say not to use meat and dairy, as it attracts pests, but others compost whole animal carcasses from home slaughter. I have seen fine results from both, and as long as a compost is good and hot for long enough, it can reduce bone to fine soil. Generally food scraps (green plant material like grass clippings and animal manure) are considered "green," or nitrogen-providing, while dead plant material like straw, cardboard, paper, and sticks are considered "brown," or carbon-providing. The ratio between these greens and browns will determine if we have a good compost or not.

What makes up a good compost: Oxygen, water, and a carbon-to-nitrogen ratio as simple as ⅓ green to ⅔ brown with the right temperatures.

Temperature: 120 to 140 degrees Fahrenheit is ideal for making useful, nutrient-rich compost. You can think of the compost creation process as "cooking." If properly started (see following), the compost begins to heat up right away and begins to "cook." Adding water and oxygen by wetting and turning compost will readily speed up a cooling, slowly decomposing pile and yield well-decomposed, useful compost more quickly. You can add oxygen by turning the compost. I can tell my compost is slow to decompose if I see the pile is not shrinking and it stinks!

How to Build a Compost Pile

1. Start your compost pile on bare earth. This allows worms, bacteria, and other beneficial organisms to aerate the compost by climbing up in there. It also allows water to move through it into the ground after rain to prevent waterlogging and keep pore spaces open.

2. Lay twigs, leaves, straw, or other dry plant material on the bare earth. Layer it a few inches deep. This aids drainage and helps aerate the pile.

3. Alternate your compost materials in layers, moist and dry. Moist ingredients are food scraps, tea bags, seaweed, et cetera. Dry materials are straw, leaves, sawdust, and wood ashes. If you have wood ashes, sprinkle in thin layers, or they will clump together and be slow to break down. Remember that they can affect your soil's pH as well, so be mindful not to add too much. Moist and dry is another way to think of greens and browns to ensure you have the right ratios for a good compost.

4. Add actual manure or a green manure (clover, buckwheat, wheatgrass, grass clippings) or any nitrogen source. This activates the compost pile and speeds the process along by essentially inoculating it.

5. Keep compost moist. Water it occasionally, or let rain do the job. Remember to check with the moisture squeeze test if you're worried you have too much moisture.

6. Cover your compost with a tarp or build a little roof to shelter it. If you live in a rainy climate this is especially important. The cover can also help heat up the pile in cooler months.

7. You don't *have* to turn your compost. I know it's blasphemy, but my favorite cheat for this is to add sticks and brush in-between larger layers of food or green compost to help keep more air spaces and ensure it doesn't get waterlogged. I don't mind waiting a little longer for my compost to finish if I can save my back.

Moisture: How much moisture does a healthy compost pile need? You can quickly tell a pile is too wet if you squeeze a handful of compost and water comes out. If you feel no moisture at all, it's too dry.

Making leaf compost: You can compost leaves by incorporating them into your compost piles or compost them on their own. I like to compost them solo for a few reasons. They make a low-nitrogen, fluffy compost you can use as a mulch soil conditioner (an organic matter to help it support more fluffy and water-holding soil), or to grow plants that like a lower amount of nitrogen. Every plant, like every person, prefers different things.

You can make a simple leaf compost or leaf mold pile by stacking leaves and dirt. Make it 4 feet wide and 3 feet high with a layer of dirt between every foot of leaves. The pile should be damper than the ideal compost, and if you grab a bit of leaves from the center and squeeze, a few drops of water should be present. Leaves also compost quickly by themselves in about four to six months. I love when they're nearly composted and can be added as "sheets" because they stick together between my herbs to help smother weeds and hold in moisture in the soil.

Tea: You can take a burlap bag and fill it with leaves (not walnut though!) and let those sit in a bucket of water for three to five days. This is like a vitamin for your plants, but it's not a good source of nitrogen.

Manures: If you happen to have livestock, you can age any manure six months (except for rabbit and alpaca/llama manure, which can be directly applied like little slow-release fertilizer pellets!). I find it's best to mix in some wood chips, straw, or other bedding as this speeds decomposition and keeps odors down. You can also make manure tea, like leaf or compost tea, by soaking bags of manure in tubs of water. This is a nutrient-rich liquid full of microbial life and nitrogen. It's another way to use manure as a fertilizer, whether it's poured on the leaves of plants (called foliar feed) or into the soil. It also acts as a mild natural fungicide since the beneficial organisms present can help keep the balance of fungi healthy.

These are other ways we can feed our soils and build organic matter:

Mulch: Spreading leaves, lawn clippings, straw, or manure directly over the soil. Let it rot in place. This is also a great option if you have some time before you want to dig your beds. Of course, you can also purchase mulch.

Trench method: One of the oldest and simplest ways to add organic matter is simply by digging a trench or one hole at a time and burying plant matter. The trench can even be dug between plants or rows during the growing season. The organic matter is typically kitchen waste, such as food scraps or coffee grounds, but any organic matter can be added in this way.[12] Some people call this composting in place. I often bury my old kale, mustard greens, or spent lemon balm in trenches in the autumn where I want to start new beds so the decomposing plant matter will feed next year's plants.

Container Gardening

Container gardening is fun and beautiful whether you have a garden or not. I like to grow certain herbs in containers just for the beauty of it or because the plant is sensitive to cold and I can bring it inside in the winter. It makes more plants available to us even if they can't tolerate the climate we live in! Choosing what to grow in is largely up to your imagination. I've even used old sinks and bathtubs (which I love because they have drainage), and the old drain allows rainwater to flow through, preventing waterlogging. Also it's a neat way to recycle what would otherwise be in a landfill! I like to keep gardening as affordable or free as possible, and checking Craigslist or other community bulletin boards for free barrels and planters is a constant fun thrifting project.

You can also use plastic pots but try and get ones from nurseries that are getting rid of them since plastic is such a toxic industry. Plastic pots are light and portable, which is nice, but they do contribute to waste when they inevitably break. Ceramic and terra-cotta make really sustainable options for containers, but they're very heavy. They also can crack or break. The only worry with ceramic is that it dries quickly, so make sure if you're in a dry climate that you water them enough to prevent your plants from drying out.

Wooden containers are another option whether you make them or purchase barrel or box-style planters to use. I like to use the offcuts and slabs from local sawmills because they aren't perfectly square and make for unique-looking "troll pots." You can make whimsical cottage-style planters of any size this way. Just make sure they can drain water with a hole in the base! Also keep in mind that different types of wood last for different amounts of time—pine of all types decomposes quickly, and hardwoods like oak and black locust last a long time. Other long-lasting woods are cedar and cypress. I've called around to different sawmills and asked about any spare slab wood that I could have (these are the rounded outermost cuts when a tree is milled, and they are often thrown in a big pile and forgotten about). These slabs also make great garden edging. It will have to be replaced every once in a while, however, for it all eventually degrades.

Moisture regulation makes container gardening a great option if you live in a dry climate. Just remember the bigger your container, the most readily you can manage the moisture.[13] You can also help hold moisture more readily by adding a fluffy medium, like coir or leaf mold, to your potting mix. Make sure to not set your precious plant friends in furious full sun all day long if there is a partial shade spot they might enjoy more. Waterlogged soil promotes root rot and fungal diseases, which you can help prevent by allowing dry-out time between waterings, adding sticks or straw to the bottom of your containers before adding soil, and elevating the container to allow airflow under it. I elevate mine on rocks or bricks I have lying around or make sure they're set somewhere that doesn't gather water. I check the seed packets of herbs I'm growing to see if they prefer moist or dry conditions when deciding what container to place them in and how often to water them.

Easy Medicinal and Magical Herbs to Grow

There's so much to learn about all the special history and uses of these plants. This section serves as an introduction to these special beings and is by no means a complete history or herbal or *materia magica*. Feel invited to go deeper with the plants you love and read and learn more about their uses and cultivation.

Hardiness Zones: As mentioned previously, not all these plants can be grown in every climate in the US. To determine what zone you are in and if a plant can be grown outdoors in your location, start by checking your agricultural zone. Just look up your zip code and your growing zone, or plant hardiness zone, on the USDA website. I live in zone 6b, meaning I have about six months of frost-free growing months. In North America, as you move north, you get towards 3a (which is the coldest in the continental US), and south moves us to zone 11b (the warmest, not including Hawaii).

Spacing: Seeding and transplanting spacings are not an exact science. Follow the spacing given on your seed packets, or plant slightly closer. In general, the closer your plants, the more watering and fertilizing they may need. Also, remember to never ingest a plant without 100-percent certainancy of identification, and be aware of allergic reactions; it is very important to look up herbal contraindication information for all medications, especially if one is pregnant or nursing.

Calendula, Marigold (*Calendula officinalis*)

Growing Information: Easy to start from seed. Plant directly in the garden after the last frost or, for extra early flowers, plant inside six weeks before the last frost and transplant outside after it warms up. Make sure it has full sun and moderately drained soil. This plant is very hardy and can tolerate some frost; it may bloom up until the first killing frost of fall. It's a self-seeding annual, so it'll drop seed and come back year after year if you keep grasses from taking them over.

Region: Zones 3 to 10.

Parts Used: Flower petals.

Harvest Time: Bloom time, summer to early fall.

Folklore and Magic: This plant is said to be named for the Virgin Mary, Mary's gold, or "marigold." It is one of the sacred herbs of Midsummer, like the fiery sun. Many pest species dislike calendula, so it is often planted in the garden alongside vegetables as a pest deterrent. This plant has been used since 1100 CE for medicine, especially against melancholy,[14] and has had a special place in love magics and potions for a long time. In Slavic countries, men and boys would carry calendula roots wrapped in purple silk cloth to be seen as more attractive to women. A British folk belief says that the flowers should be picked while the moon is in Virgo and Jupiter in the ascendant, and by saying three Paternosters and three Ave Marias, the plant will yield a flower useful in revealing robbers.[15]

Food and Medicine: There are 20 species in the calendula family. They're originally from the Canary Islands and all throughout the Mediterranean area to Iran. Calendula is best known as a medicine for the skin and as an antifungal, though historically, it has been used for stomach ailments, jaundice, and in many other applications. I love it best as a salve for wounds and fungal issues, as well as for tea. A tea of the petals, cooled, is a wonderful wash for irritated mucous membranes or for general vaginal itching. Calendula flowers can be eaten raw and added to salads, cookies, and cakes. I love to add them to my Midsummer and Lughnasadh cakes and confections to call upon the fiery energy of the sun they reveal.

Catnip (*Nepeta cataria*)

Growing Information: This mint family plant grows readily and can become aggressive and weedy in some damp places, therefore, it makes a great container plant. You can pinch off the flowers to prevent them from spreading by seed. Start from seeds in the garden or propagate by stem cuttings or root division. *Nepeta cataria* prefers well-drained, poor soil and full sun. It is certainly not fussy.

Region: Zones 3 to 9.

Parts Used: Leaves and flowering tops.

Harvest Time: Anytime.

Folklore and Magic: Catnip was used as a rat repellent plant for both cats' fondness for it and for rats' hatred of it. It was also believed that chewing the plant created quarrelsomeness despite its medicinal usefulness as a soother of the nerves.[16] Pillows stuffed with it help with sleeplessness. There's also a legend that the hangman can never do his duty until he's chewed the root of catnip.[17]

Food and Medicine: This sweet, gently fuzzy plant was first mentioned in the 11th century herbal *De viribus herbarum* for its ability to calm occasional nervousness and promote restful sleep. In Appalachian folk medicine, it's given as a tea to babies and children for colic and restless sleep. The leaves and young shoots are also used as a condiment and were added to sauces and stews as an herb for flavor in France. Ancient Anglo-Saxons used it for lung disease when combined with raspberry leaves and a "reed spear," ground ivy, bishop's wort (*Stachys officinalis*), pellitory (most likely *Achillea ptarmica*), and catnip as a decoction.

In Southern folk medicine it's given for teething, colicky babies, and fussy children to help keep them calm and help them rest.[18] It was also given as a tea for pneumonia and is still used for chronic bronchitis.[19] Catmint (*Nepeta x faassenii*) with blue flowers has been used very similarly, and it's very easy to grow. I brew the aerial parts of this plant into a tea for anxiety and colds. I also like it a lot personally for stomach pressure from indigestion and gas.

Chamomile (*Matricaria recutita*)

Growing Information: This sweet one is cold tolerant, but you can still transplant it out after the last frost for early blooms. Directly seed in the garden after the last frost in full sun to partial shade. It appreciates well-composted soil. It will drop seeds and come back year after year.

Region: Zones 5 to 9.

Parts Used: Flowers and leaves.

Harvest Time: Summer.

Folklore and Magic: Once native to eastern and southern Europe and the Near East, this humble herb is one of the nine sacred Anglo-Saxon herbs from the Nine Herbs Charm. In the Middle Ages, it was used as a strewing herb. You can still sprinkle it around the house to keep out negative magic. Associated with divination and dreamwork, this herb blooms at full strength on Midsummer. It's sunny, yellow centers mark it as an herb of the sun, much like calendula, yet its calming, sleep inducing properties also align it with the moon. Mix with other herbs like passionflower, bay leaves, cinquefoil, yarrow, calendula, and mugwort in dream pillows or as a bath to encourage dreamwork. You can also use this tea as a wash for divinatory tools like scrying mirrors or stone pendulums. Place it in your wallet to attract money. It also symbolizes energy in adversity, for the more they're trodden the more they grow and spread.[20]

Food and Medicine: You can also use chamomile culinarily. I love to add it to vinegars for salad dressings or just add it to meals for beauty and the almost apple-like flavor. Chamomile is a very popular old medicine and is used much like catnip as a tea of the flowers for indigestion and heartburn, as well as for its calming, nervine effect. This plant is safe for children.

Chamomile is a traditional hair rinse for fair hair: simply brew a tea of the leaves and flowers and pour over freshly washed hair as a final rinse for shine. It is an ancient medicinal plant and was used by the Egyptians and Romans as a near panacea. It was used as a laxative, to address digestive upset, and to heal snakebites. It was also used to treat insomnia, neuralgia, women in labor, and externally for ulcers and wounds as a wash; the dew shaken from the flowers was used for tuberculosis in Wales.[21] In Ireland, the root was used to cure toothaches. The tea was even given to troublemaking children to stop their mischief in English folk medicine.[22]

Comfrey (*Symphytum officinale*)

Growing Information: Hardy perennial. Grows in full sun to partial shade. Dividing from roots is the easiest way to propagate this vigorous growing plant. Very aggressive and almost impossible to get rid of the deep taproots once established, so be specific about where you plant it. Sow seeds in fall in well-composted soil.

Region: Zones 3 to 9.

Parts Used: Roots, leaves, and flowers.

Harvest Time:

- **Roots:** After flowering in fall.
- **Leaves:** Anytime.
- **Flowers:** In summer. Remove the thick, juicy stems from the leaves when drying as they have too much moisture to air dry without molding in most climates.

Folklore and Magic: Comfrey is native to much of Europe. Its name is a corruption of *con firma*, an allusion to the uniting of bones it was thought to effect, and the botanical name *Symphytum* is derived from the Greek *symphyo* (to unite).[23] Wreathes of comfrey were worn to show maidenhood—a decoction of the tea was thought to restore the hymen. The Latin name means "to grow together," which speaks to this plant's long-standing history as a bone healer. To heal a broken bone, the gelatinous root matter was boiled down and applied to dry as a hard plaster and was spoken three times over with this charm in Exmoor:

> Our Lord rade,
> The foal slade,
> Sinew to sinew and bone to bone,
> In the name of the Father, Son and the Holy Spirit.[24]

The Pennsylvania Dutch perform a magical cure by placing the uprooted comfrey plant in a hernia and warming it there, then planting it. If it grows, the hernia will be cured.[25]

Food and Medicine: This plant was once eaten as a food (it was treated much like spinach). The leaves were cooked, and the flowers were added to cakes. However, due to the presence of pyrrolizidine alkaloids, which are toxic, *I do not recommend ingesting this plant*. The leaves and root were also a long-standing traditional cough remedy. In Anglo-Saxon medicine, the prescription for a dry cough was raw honey with comfrey and elecampane. Its other long-standing use was as a wound herb. The leaves were carried into battle by the Crusaders, and it was used all over the British Isles for the same purposes. Boiled roots were also applied to boils, skin eruptions, and burns.[26]

I like to add these leaves to my bath water for fungal issues or as an overall skin toner. Place fresh leaves in a cloth bag in the bath, almost as if making your bathtub into a giant cup of tea. I use this in my wound salves as well, for it is rich in an alkaloid called allantoin which is wonderful at speeding skin healing.

Elecampane, Elfdock (*Inula helenium*)

Growing Information: Easy to grow from seed or root division. Plant outside after the danger of frost or start six weeks inside before the last frost and transplant out after it grows its first two sets of leaves. This plant doesn't do great in hot or humid climates, and keep in mind it may not flower the first year. Elecampane prefers full sun and well-drained soil; the soil doesn't have to be particularly rich, but it shouldn't be very wet or waterlogged. Because this plant is perennial, its appreciates an application of compost each spring.

Region: Zones 3 to 7.

Parts Used: Roots.

Harvest Time: Fall of second or third year of growth for roots.

Folklore and Magic: Native to Europe and Asia, this plant has now naturalized in some parts of North America from Nova Scotia to North Carolina. The Latin name shows an association with Helen of Troy, as it's said she clutched a branch of elecampane when she was carried off by Paris. Other legends say it was born from the tears she shed.[27] It was used as a love charm in Guernsey, England, where it must be gathered on St. John's Eve, or Midsummer, dried, powdered, and mixed with ambergris. Then, it must be worn near the heart for nine days, after which the person whose love one wished to obtain had to swallow some of it (remember, folks, this is for entertainment purposes only and obtaining love by force is not only gross but why would you want that!?).

In Welsh folklore, this plant is lucky. Worn on a hat, it is said to have frightened off robbers and thieves. If you placed it in the hat of a deceiver, they would get red in the face, giving away their ill intent. In the Balkans, it's sewn in children's clothes to ward off witchcraft. The herb has been used for centuries as a valued medicine and was mentioned by Dioscorides and Pliny. An old Latin distich celebrates its virtues: *Enula campana reddit praecordia sana* (Elecampane will the spirits sustain).[28] One of the folk names, elf dock, speaks to the folklore of its faerie associations.

Food and Medicine: The leaves were once cooked as a potherb, much like comfrey. The young roots were also cooked as food. Ancient Romans used the boiled roots as appetizers to stimulate the appetite.[29] They were also candied and eaten as a treat. I like to candy them in honey. It was also used in absinthe in France and Switzerland.

This plant has a long-standing history as a medicine, so much so it was featured as the reviver of the dead in medieval "mumming" plays. The roots are the most medicinally potent part of the plant and have long been used as cough medicine for both humans and animals. This plant is my favorite remedy for persistent, wet coughs. I use a tincture and tea made from the root. You can also use an elecampane-infused honey mixed into warm water with lemon for a stubborn cough. This plant is also high in inulin, like dandelion, which acts as a probiotic and feeds our gut flora.

Fennel (*Foeniculum vulgare*)

Growing Information: Prefers dry and sunny locations like its native home in the Mediterranean. Plant in spring after the last frost in fertile, well-drained soil. You can grow in a container; just don't allow it to get too wet.

Region: Zones 6 to 10.

Parts Used: Leaves, stalks, bulb, and seeds.

Harvest Time:
- **Leaves and stalks:** Anytime.
- **Bulb:** Fall.
- **Seeds:** Early fall.

Folklore and Magic: Native to the Mediterranean, the Latin name means "little hay." This lovely culinary herb was used in the late Middle Ages for magical purposes, especially in conjunction with St. John's wort. Fennel is one of the herbs bearing the magical power of the sun at Midsummer. It was hung over doorways on Midsummer Eve to ward off sorcery, witchcraft, dwarves, demons, and fire. Fennel is also included in the famous Nine Herbs Charm and was sacred to the Anglo-Saxons. The plant is an amulet against evil spirits in Italian folklore.[30]

Food and Medicine: Fennel is a celebrated food plant. I love it roasted in a cast-iron Dutch oven with trout and good butter. Make a compound butter by finely chopping the feathery leaves and mixing into room-temperature butter. Roll it up with some salt and a piece of wax paper and you have a beautiful herbal butter to add to various savory dishes or to spread on toast. The seeds are an excellent digestive and are wonderful as a cordial to help with gas and bloating following a rich meal. Take a clean quart mason jar and fill it a quarter of the way with crushed fennel seeds. Fill the jar three-quarters full of brandy and the last quarter to the jar rim with honey. Steep two weeks, shaking occasionally, and strain. Take two tablespoons in a small favorite glass over an ice cube and topped with sparkling water as an aperitif or after a meal when one may have overdone it.

Feverfew (*Tanacetum parthenium*)

Growing Information: Wonderful container herb. Easy to grow from seed. Sprinkle the very seeds on the surface of the soil and do not cover them; they prefer well-drained soils. Cut down in fall and this short-lived perennial will appear again in spring.

Region: Zones 5 to 9.

Parts Used: Flowers and leaves.

Harvest Time: Midsummer when flowering.

Folklore and Magic: Feverfew is a small-flowered, daisy-like plant in the aster family whose sunny, yellow center opens around Midsummer every year. This has earned it one of its many folk names, Midsummer daisy, due to its June bloom time and, well, looking like a daisy. Other names it's earned historically are featherfoil, featherfowl, and parthenium. Avicenna, in his *Canon of*

Medicine, one of the most influential medical books in history, assigns feverfew to the natures of heating and drying. In late Anglo-Saxon lore, feverfew was a remedy for "elfshot,"[31] or what some in Appalachia call "witch balls," a mysterious pain in the body with no apparent cause. It was believed to come from an arrow shot by an elf, a hag, or a witch.

According to 16th-century herbalist and botanist John Gerard, the method of picking must be done just so to ensure the magic of the herb remains intact: it must be harvested with the left hand specifically, while also reciting aloud the name of the sufferer, and at no time looking behind oneself.[32] The plant was also used to magically soothe unruly horses by the renowned horsemen of East Anglia in England who were known to have certain secrets in the world of horsemanship. This little flower was thought to aid those suffering from melancholy when one can barely speak from sadness. It was even used to help counteract the effects of an overindulgence of opium.[33]

The Latin name, *Tanacetum*, comes from the name Thanatos, the Greek god of death.[34] This also yielded this plant's lesser known folk name, devil's daisy. This may be due to its strange odor, which I've found to be very polarizing. I enjoy the mugwort-like scent, but occasionally certain people smell it and abhor it strongly, comparing it to a bodily smell. Romans and Greeks associated this plant with the underworld, relating the scent to corpses, for this fragrant plant, for better or worse, was used to mask the scent of the dead in funerary rites. So, as is often the case, this summer flower stands as an emblem of the life-giving sun and as an accompaniment to death.[35] This association has given feverfew a powerful magical influence as a plant of protection, Midsummer power, and finally, the liminal spaces between life and death.

Food and Medicine: Feverfew continued to be used as a pain-relieving herb in history through the Romani community and was also used in place of chamomile, most likely due to their similar appearance. It was likewise used as a sedative tea, just as chamomile is. Today, feverfew is known best as a reliever of migraine headaches. Eating a fresh leaf of feverfew on a piece of bread to avoid an upset stomach is a traditional way to help prevent migraines. You can also use a tea of the leaves and flowers for headaches, but it is best not to do so for an extended period of time as too much can cause mouth ulcers.

Hyssop (*Hyssopus officinalis*)

Growing Information: This easy-to-grow plant can thrive in poor soil and is drought tolerant. Easy to grow from seed, cuttings, and root division. Bees love this plant.

    Region: Zones 4 to 9.

    Parts Used: Aerial parts.

    Harvest Time: For medicine, right before it goes to seed. For magic, anytime.

    Folklore and Magic: Hyssop is one of the herbs infused with the power of the Midsummer sun and is sacred to this day. There's a plant called hyssop mentioned in the Bible imbued with many powers and used in the ancient Jewish rites of purification. However, the identity of that plant is still unknown so it would be irresponsible to assert they are indeed the same. Hyssop was used in Bulgaria by bundling it with wormwood and lovage to protect people from female spirits of the crossroads, who could raise whirlwinds and lure people to their doom by their singing.[36] Hyssop is a traditional herb of cleansing and purification, and newlyweds hang it in their homes to bring luck. It can also be hung after the house has been thoroughly cleaned to spiritually cleanse it. It's said to be hated by evil spirits.[37]

    Food and Medicine: Native to southern and eastern Europe, hyssop has long been used as a respiratory medicine and is an antiviral like many of its mint family relatives. It has naturalized in some parts of the US and can be found in wayside places. This plant is wonderful for congested lungs and wet coughs. It's also been a long-standing remedy against asthma. A cup of hyssop tea, sweetened with honey, is an excellent idea at the first signs of a cold or flu when a low fever is present. This makes an excellent oxymel with fresh herb in flower and can be given for bronchitis, coughs, colds, and the flu (one teaspoon every hour with warm water). Avoid prolonged use and do not use during pregnancy or lactation. If you have a medical condition or take pharmaceutical drugs please consult your doctor prior to use as it may interfere with certain types of medications, such as those used to treat epilepsy.

Lemon Balm (*Melissa officinalis*)

Growing Information: This woody perennial is easy to grow but spreads aggressively, so be sure you want it where you end up planting it. Easy to start from seed, cuttings, or root division, you should start seeds indoors six weeks before the last frost and transplant it out after the danger of frost passes. This is also a great plant to grow in a container. Mulch the plant in winter in colder climates to prevent winter killing. This plant prefers moist, composted soil in a partially shaded spot. Harvest to help control them or divide roots and share plants with friends to prevent them from taking over the whole herb garden.

Region: Zones 3 to 7.

Parts Used: Leaves and flowers.

Harvest Time: Anytime.

Folklore and Magic: Lemon balm is another protective hanging herb to keep away harmful magics. It was included in Midsummer bundles above the door to keep away evil on that night. In Germany, sprigs of lemon balm were tucked into babies' diapers to keep away evil spirits and flatulence.[98] Wearing lemon balm helps to attract a lover into one's life and is also said to be sacred to the Greek goddess Diana.

Food and Medicine: As a spice, lemon balm is overlooked. Use anywhere lemon goes nicely. Chopped fresh, dried, and crumbled as a dry rub, lemon balm can go many places in sweet and savory dishes. Medicinally, lemon balm is a powerful antiviral and nervine. I love taking infusions of lemon balm every day for a week to help calm my anxiety during hard life transitions. Lemon balm helps calm the occurrence of cold sores, as a tincture or tea taken at the first tingle of a pesky sore.

Mint (*Mentha* spp.)

There are many species of mint due to the ready cross-pollination and hybridization of different varieties. Some of the most popular are water mint (*Mentha aquatica*), apple mint (*Mentha suaveolens*), peppermint (*Mentha × piperita*), and spearmint (*Mentha spicata* var. *spicata*).

Growing Information: Mints love loose, damp, humus-rich soil. They're often found along waterways and creeksides. I dug some of my mints from friend's gardens and wild places where they were abundant and transplanted them into the damp, lower corners of my garden. Mint spreads by growing roots from stems that touch the soil. It must be harvested frequently to prevent it taking over a garden. Plant in large containers to help contain their amazing growth.

Region: Zones 3 to 8.

Parts Used: Leaves and flowers.

Harvest Time: On a sunny day, just after the dew has dried, or at any time of year when the plants look lush.

Folklore and Magic: This plant is native to the Mediterranean but was brought to England by the Romans. Now peppermint can be found almost worldwide! Mints of all types have long been used in garlanding and as stewing herbs to help spiritually cleanse spaces and rid them of pests and disease. John Gerard, a famous 16th-century herbalist, spoke to the gladness the wonderful fragrance of mint inspires when he said, "The savor or smell . . . recoyceth the heart of man, for which cause they use to strew it in chambers." Watermint is sacred to Aphrodite and is still included in bridal garlands in Greece.[39] Mints have long been thought to be stimulating in a variety of ways, especially in provoking lust, according to ancient herbalist Dioscurides and his many successors in the Western herbal tradition. Mint was also associated with the dead in Greece and burned in funerary rites and planted on graves. All mints were seen as protective plants against witches and worms and helped to cure diseases caused by bewitchment.[40]

Food and Medicine: Mints are excellent food and medicine. They're a part of many traditional cuisines of the world, like tzatziki sauces and raita from Greece and India. I like to add diced mint leaves to salads, crushed leaves into herbal iced teas or water, and frozen leaves into ice cubes for extra-special summer beverages. I love peppermint tea for stomach complaints of all types. The strong volatile oils of the mint family, which make themselves known to us through their amazing fragrances, are antimicrobial. I like a teaspoon of dried mint and one of chamomile steeped for 10 minutes in boiling water for gas and bloating. Combine dried mint leaves with elderflowers and yarrow flowers and leaves for colds and flus. This combination is one of my favorites for these common respiratory grievances. Peppermint tea is also a gentle nervine, and a hot cup of mint tea has been used to ease anxiety in folk medicine around the world. Cool tea dipped in a clean cloth and applied to feverish foreheads and headaches is also a lovely soother of pain and inflammation.

Rose (*Rosa* spp.)

Like the mints, there are many species of roses. Some have little scent, yet for magic and medicine I prefer the fragrant and medicinal: *Rosa rugosa*, *Rosa canina*, and *Rosa damascena*.

Growing Information: Most roses prefer well-drained soil, some so much so that they prefer sandy, coastal soils. Other species of roses are hedge plants and prefer damper, richer woodland soils. You can grow roses in full sun to partial shade, and they are always best grown as cuttings or divisions. Roses can be tricky and prone to disease so I like to stick to the hardier species like the rugosa rose (*Rosa rugosa*). Disease resistance and best flowers are produced in full sun.

Region: Roses can grow in a wide variety of climates. Check which rose species does best in your zone. Rugosa rose can grow in almost any temperate climate with winter protection.

Parts Used: Flowers and fruits (rose hips).

Harvest Time: Spring to early summer when the fragrant flowers have just opened, early fall when the hips are red and ripe.

Folklore and Magic: Roses most likely originated in ancient northern Persia. Roses have enough lore to fill a book unto themselves, and are associated with love, death, and much more. To find true love in Appalachian folk magic, you gather a rose at midnight on Midsummer Eve without speaking a word and wrap it up in clean paper. Don't look at it, and leave it to dry until midwinter. Wear it on your bosom on the winter solstice, and whoever plucks it off shall be your true love.[41] Roses, though beautiful, bear nasty thorns. Thorns have extensive uses in folk magic of all cultures and can be used in protective witch bottles when buried outside the house. To dream of roses means success in love is coming.[42] Throwing rose leaves on a fire will bring good luck.[43] I like to save and dry the leaves at the end of the season for this purpose. Try burning rose petals as an incense in your love workings and wear a rose pinned to your favorite shirt to draw love near.

Food and Medicine: Roses have been used as food and medicine throughout history. The hip, or fruit of the rose plant, is rich in vitamin C and beneficial flavonoids. Both of these nutrients help to support a healthful immune response and give roses some of their healing magic. You can make rose hip jam just as you would any other fruit preserve and enjoy on buttered toast. The hips also dry nicely and make a lovely tea for cold and flu season to help boost vitamin C in the body. Be careful not to overheat the tea, however, or boil the hips, as high temperatures damage vitamin C.

The seeds have hairs that can be irritating, so typically just the fruit surrounding them is used. Rose-petal tea is astringent, meaning it tightens inflamed tissues, and is great as a wash for sore eyes or inflamed mucus membranes or as a drink for a sore mouth. Make a soothing warm wash by mixing equal parts calendula and yarrow for irritated urogenital tissues. Rose also makes a beautiful hydrosol or perfume and has been used as such for ages. Make a rose petal tea and use as a toner to soothe irritated or reddened skin. I love preserving wilted rose petals in honey for aphrodisiac evenings, drizzled on apple slices or stirred into warm brews.

Rosemary (*Rosmarinus officinalis*)

Growing Information: As rosemary is very slow to sprout from seed and has a low germination rate, I prefer to grow rosemary from cuttings or buy plants from a nursery. Rosemary grows best in full sun in well-drained, sandy soil. Rosemary goes great in a terra-cotta planter as it prefers it on the dry side. I love bringing ours indoors in the winter and enjoying the scent.

Thoroughly water it when the soil feels dry, but allow it to dry out between waterings. If you live in zone 6, plant near a brick wall or south-facing side of a house to get the ambient heat of the day in the winter to protect your rosemary from too much freezing. You can take a branch of a mature rosemary plant and propagate by air layering, or burying the branch, waiting for roots to form where the branch is beneath the soil, and then cutting the now-rooted branch from the original plant and replanting. Rosemary can live many years with proper care and occasional fertilization.

Region: Zone 6 with occasional winter protection, zones 7 to 10.

Parts Used: Sprigs and leaves.

Harvest Time: Anytime. Avoid taking more than one-third of the plant at a harvest. The leaves dry very easily when hung in bunches.

Folklore and Magic: *Rosmarinus* means "mist of the sea." Rosemary originated in the Mediterranean and thrives in sunny, drier climes. Rosemary is an herb of remembrance, so it is ideal for the ancestor worshipping time of Samhain. It was often carried at funerals in England. It was also believed to make old folks young again. In Derbyshire, young women customarily placed a sprig of rosemary or a crooked sixpence under their pillow on Halloween in order to dream of their future husbands.

The Romans said that its odor helped to preserve the dead. This most likely aided its use as an emblem of eternity. It was also known to mean remembrance and was included in bouquets and wreaths for friendship, fidelity, bridal wreaths, and funerals. Though it is debated, rosemary may have been one of the plants that opened to hide Mary from Herod's soldiers. Its periwinkle flowers have taken on the color of Mary's mantle in memory of rosemary's service to the Holy Mother.[44] However, it has more sinister associations in Sicily and Portugal, where it was considered a heathen plant that fairies nestled beneath disguised as snakes. This makes sense as it was once burned as an incense to the Olympian gods. Despite this it was also worn as an amulet against the evil eye. In England, a sprig worn in the buttonhole ensures the wearer of success in all their tasks.[45]

Like other evergreens, the boughs of rosemary were also brought indoors to provide scent and brighten dark Roman and medieval halls. It decked winter solstice or Christmas feasting halls and the wassail bowl. During the Middle Ages, rosemary was spread on the floor at midnight on Christmas Eve so as people walked on it the fragrance would fill the air; this in the belief that those who smelled rosemary on Christmas Eve would have a year of health and happiness. This started the long tradition of rosemary in Christmas wreaths and other holiday decorations.[46] An old French name for rosemary was "incensier." It was an old practice to burn rosemary in hospitals, and it was often paired with juniper berries to prevent infection and purify the air in sick chambers.[47] I like to save my rosemary twigs for incense and fumitory bundles to cleanse spaces and prepare my witches' tools for workings.

Food and Medicine: Rosemary is a common and popular culinary plant and is used around the world as a spice (in Italian cuisine especially). Rosemary is thought to alleviate sadness and grief in Italian folk magic.[48] Rosemary goes fantastically with potatoes and chicken and almost all other savory dishes. I like to use it in healing broths and soups for both the warming flavor and antibacterial properties. Rosemary is a powerful antioxidant and is useful for the scavenging of free radicals from the body. Rosemary is rich in volatile oils that are antiseptic and help support heart health through stimulating good circulation. Add rosemary springs to a hot bath to clear the mind, revive the sinuses, and sooth sore muscles and joints. I also use rosemary tea for sore throats and to clear congestion.

Sage (*Salvia officinalis*)

Growing Information: Sage can be grown in the same manner as rosemary: cuttings or layering. Sage loves to grow with rosemary as a companion, and funnily enough, cabbages do well when planted near sage. It is considered unlucky to grow sage from seed in old gardener's wisdom.[49] As sage does not like wet soil, make sure to plant it somewhere well-draining.

Region: Zones 5 to 8.

Parts Used: Leaves, woody stems for incense.

Harvest Time: Pinch off leaves here and there anytime but be sure to not pick them too bare. Flowers in summer.

Folklore and Magic: A southern European native to the mint family, *Salvia* means "to be saved," which speaks to the diverse medicinal and magical powers of this plant genus. In ancient Rome it was taboo to harvest this plant with any tool containing iron. Sage was even said to be used by burglars in aiding them to magically pick locks. Sage has long been used in historical women's medicine, as an abortifacient and as a way to dry up milk in lactating persons. Sage is also associated with serpents and toads, in some beliefs repelling them and in others attracting them.[50]

Food and Medicine: Sage tea is good for colds, and we commonly use it in Appalachian folk medicine for all types of respiratory infections. Sage is strongly antibacterial and antifungal due to a compound it contains called thujone. This means it should not be taken in pregnancy or during breastfeeding! Sage is also commonly used in flavoring pork sausage and other fatty meat dishes. You can grow and dry your own sage for cooking meat, mushrooms, and much more.

St. John's Wort (*Hypericum perforatum*)

There are over 350 species in this genus, but this is a very common one used worldwide in medicine.

Growing Information: Soak the seeds in warm water for a few hours or overnight before planting in a good potting mix. Plant out in early spring after the danger of frost has passed, and make sure to transplant when seedlings are around two inches tall into composted, well-drained soil. Many species can tolerate mild flooding and drought, but even watering will help support the best blooms; they love to grow in a place with nice bright morning sun and afternoon shade. This plant can also spread wildly and is considered invasive in some locations, so container gardening is a great option. Don't overwater.

Region: Zones 5 to 10.

Parts Used: Flowers.

Harvest Time: Midsummer.

Folklore and Magic: This plant is native to temperate Eurasia but is now considered an invasive weed in many places around the world (including North America). St. John's wort is one of the most storied magical plants in European witchcraft traditions. English country folks hung St. John's wort over the doors of their houses, barns, stables, and cowsheds to protect themselves from meddling spirits and faeries on Midsummer Eve. Another yellow, sunny flower, it often blooms around this time of year. Traditionally, the flowers of St. John's wort are collected on Midsummer Day to be made into remedies and charms along with other seasonal herbs.

It is said to be best to harvest the flowers while naked, of course! Since the herb is very protective, use it in charms to protect against heartbreak and to develop a courageous heart. It is also useful in love magic—combine with rose petals and other herbs aligned for workings of love to open a cold heart. In Scandinavian mythology this plant is sacred to Baldur.[51] In Irish folklore it is one of the seven herbs—including speedwell, vervain, eyebright, mallow, yarrow, and self-heal—nothing supernatural could injure.[52] In Germany, a love divination may be made with St. John's wort by rubbing the plant between two fingers while saying:

> If our love is right,
> Then the blood is red;
> If our love is dead,
> Then the water's white.[53]

This charm relies upon the pigment from the species *Hypericum perforatum*, which is my favorite species to use for medicine and grows abundantly where I live. Some species do not yield this red color when their leaves are rubbed, thus leaving a disappointed charmer.

St. John's wort has volumes of lore associated with it. I love the sunny yellow flowers, used for so long to drive away melancholy, and standing tall for harvest at Midsummer. They remind us that in the depths of winter, at the winter solstice, they will hold all the power of the warmth of the summer sun to brighten our dreary days.

Food and Medicine: St. John's wort has long been used for a wide variety of medical ailments from lumbago to insanity. It was originally believed to cure diseases caused by witchcraft and demons.[54] The plant's red pigment, evident in its oil and alcohol extracts, was seen as the "blood" of the plant and through the old medical belief in the doctrine of signatures, this means that the plant was ideal for healing wounds and burns.[55] This plant has also long been used to treat melancholy, or depressed emotional states. St. John's wort is good for digestive issues and mild depression internally and wounds, burns, and nerve pain externally. I like to make an oil extraction of the fresh, wilted flowers with a good olive oil to apply to painful joints and nerve pains. *Be aware some people are very sensitive to this plant, and it can cause photodermatitis in full sun if worn on the skin. It can also interact with birth control pills and other medications so please check for contraindications before consuming.*

Thyme (*Thymus* spp.)

There are 300 species of thyme. Some grow prostrate and creep along the ground making beautiful ground cover, while others stand more upright. My favorites are common thyme (*T. vulgaris*) and lemon thyme (*T. × citriodorus*).

Growing Information: Thyme hates wet feet and does great in a well-draining container in full sun. Plant out in the garden after the danger of frost has passed. Like rosemary, thyme is very hard to grow from seed; I like to get a division or cutting from a friend or buy a plant from a nursery I love. They aren't very picky and do not need a ton of fertilization, but amending their space in the garden with compost is always a great idea.

Region: Zones 2 to 10 with those zones below 5 using winter mulches and protection from frost damage.

Parts Used: Leaves.

Harvest Time: Anytime.

Folklore and Magic: Thyme has been an important folk medicine and magic herb from Greece, Iran, North America, and almost everywhere in between. Thyme was one of the first plants I used to heal myself of a prolonged, hacking cough after a long bout of mono and I adore this humble garden herb. Thyme is a mint family plant native to southern Europe and the Mediterranean but has spread throughout the world, becoming an important part of many nations' folk medicine and folkloric plant practices.

To the Greeks, thyme was a symbol of courage, a belief that spread in the Middle Ages into other parts of Europe. Thyme is also a plant of the bees, and it is customary to rub it on hives for their well-being. In the Middle Ages, even embroidering a bee and a bit of thyme on a cloth was enough to confer courage to the knight it was gifted to. Wild thyme has been burned since antiquity in Greece, Mongolia, and Siberia as an incense plant. Before frankincense resin was used, thyme was the most important incense plant in Greece—it was burned to fend off disease-bringing demons, for it keeps away many evil and devilish things.[56]

The sometimes reliable but never boring Madame Grieve writes,

The name Thyme, in its Greek form, was first given to the plant as a derivative of a word which meant "to fumigate," either because they used it as incense, for its balsamic odour, or because it was taken as a type of all sweet-smelling herbs.[57]

It was included in the mix of special herbs strewn on the birthing bed in Germany alongside common bedstraw (*Galium aparine*). Not only was it a birth herb to be used in this manner but it was also used as a tea to bring on menses, the birth itself, and later, the passing of the afterbirth. The fae are said to especially love thyme, and despite its use in the birthing bed, it was, in some places, spoken of as an unlucky plant to bring indoors.[58]

Its use as a funerary herb may shed some light on this curious custom. The Order of the Oddfellows carried sprigs of thyme at the funerals of their brothers, while in certain areas of England, it was customary to drop a sprig of thyme onto the coffin before burial. It is interestingly also associated with murder, and the scent, perhaps due to its use at funerals, is said to be the smell of a murdered man's ghost.[59] This is curious because that means that my chicken soup is not complete without essence of murder.

Pennsylvania Germans have a particular practice around the planting of thyme. It is said it cannot grow and flourish if you do not sit on it after planting. If you've ever transplanted large carpets of thyme, this is actually a very helpful practice and is also uniquely enjoyable.

In Scotland and England, there is a love divination that can be performed with thyme on St. Agnes' Night, January 20. Take a sprig of rosemary and one of thyme and sprinkle water on them three times each. Upon going to bed, put one in each shoe and place a shoe on each side of the bed. You must then invoke St. Agnes:

> St. Agnes that's to lovers kind,
> Come ease the troubles of my mind.

And the future will be revealed in a dream once you drift to sleep, revealing the identity of your true love.[60]

Food and Medicine: In the British Isles, it was used for coughs and respiratory ailments, and even for quite serious ones such as tuberculosis and whooping cough. In England, many would drink thyme tea to calm the nerves, and today, it is still used as a gentle nervine. It was drunk almost universally in remote parts of Scotland, and aside from being a nervine, it was used to prevent bad dreams. In Suffolk, it was specific for headaches. In Ireland, its use was less common, but it was still used for respiratory trouble and headache when sniffed, rather than when drunk as a tea. For tuberculosis, or consumption as it was known historically, an infusion was mixed with the antiviral plant honeysuckle and wild sage.[61]

In Southern folk medicine, thyme was used to treat typhoid in conjunction with other diaphoretic plants like sassafras root bark, pine needles, mustard seeds, boneset leaves, and pennyroyal as an infusion. It was also used for promoting birth to "women in Travail" and moving the afterbirth, as well as topically as a hot ointment for swellings and warts.[62] In African American folk healing, thyme was used for respiratory illnesses, as a gargle for sore throat, and as a hot fresh leaf poultice for cuts and wounds to prevent infection.[63] I like to use it for coughs and respiratory illnesses of all types. It has been indicated for both dry, raspy coughs and productive coughs depending on the herbal tradition, but I have personally benefited from thyme in both cases.

You can make a lovely, simple **cough syrup** from it by combining it with horehound (*Marrubium vulgare*). I mix two parts horehound dry leaf and one part thyme dry leaf. Steep in freshly boiled water for 15 minutes. You can leave it longer to make a stronger infusion, but honestly it can get a bit bitter if that is off-putting. If I end up with two cups of liquid after squeezing out the herbs, I add one cup of honey for a 2:1 ratio of water to honey. I warm the tea in a pot gently to dissolve the honey and then pour into a very clean jar and label. This will keep in cold storage in a fridge for about two months. I take 1 teaspoon up to four times a day for coughs. I also just use the tea, simply infusing one teaspoon of dried thyme leaf in about one cup of water and drinking that three times a day for digestive issues. For urinary tract issues like a UTI (urinary tract infection), I like to combine it with goldenrod, another favorite friend, as a tea.

Thyme is also lovely as a spice and has been used for ages as a culinary herb for roasts, stews, and soups. I love it on chicken or fish as well as sautéed for a minute or two in butter before I cook the mushrooms we forage. When food and medicine meet, there I fall in love with the complex interlacings of folklore, magic, and tradition that we are all writing together as we relearn and rediscover these folk practices.

Wormwood (*Artemisia absinthium*)

Growing Information: Wormwood is a very resilient and wonderful container plant. They don't love wet soil and prefer warm, dry conditions; they like dry, rocky, and even salty soils and make a wonderful rock garden plant. They are tenacious growers and can spread, so containers are lovely to hold them. Wormwood is drought tolerant, but will need well-drained soil and appreciates some compost when being planted out. They grow readily from seed or root divisions and cuttings. Sow the seed directly in the garden after the danger of frost has passed in spring and water adequately in a composted, well-drained place in the garden with full sun.

Region: Zones 4 to 9.

Parts Used: Leaves and flowers.

Harvest Time: Best to let this perennial grow two years before harvesting large amounts.

Folklore and Magic: Wormwood is native to Europe, Crimea, and Siberia, with its Latin name coming from the ancient Greek name of the goddess Artemis, who was known as Diana to the Greeks. She is the goddess of the moon, wild animals, and hunting. It is another of the plants sacred to Mid-summer. The others are rosemary, vervain, hyssop, fern, mullein, basil, lav-ender, thyme, and fennel, and the flowers rose, daisy, marigold, cornflower, and calendula. Wormwood has long been used strewn about the house to repel pests of various types, like fleas and flies. The power of its medicine was so esteemed that a mixture of wormwood and vinegar was carried as a remedy for the Black Death in Europe. Wormwood has even been used as a symbol of health.[64] Sixteenth-century herbalist John Gerard says that, mixed with vin-egar, wormwood is a good antidote to the poison of mushrooms or toadstools, and when taken with wine, counteracts the poisonous effects of hemlock and the bites of the shrew mouse and sea dragon.

Wormwood was often used as protection against harmful magics at im-portant life ceremonies like weddings and burials. In many places in Europe, wormwood is worn by lovers to prevent the envy of witches. Some say if worm-wood grows tall in fall then heavy snows will come in winter.[65] Dreams con-nected with wormwood are considered of good augury, implying happiness and domestic enjoyment. Wormwood, like its relative mugwort, was also used as a charm against weariness by travelers by laying a sprig in the shoe or on one's person.[66] Wormwood is a favorite protective plant of mine. It has been used almost everywhere it grows to hang as a protective bundle, repelling not only flies but evil spirits and the envy of others. I also use dried wormwood as an incense, including the leaves, flowers, and dried twigs, as well as to stuff sachets to hide as protective talismans anywhere they are needed.

Food and Medicine: Wormwood's bitter taste and pungent, beautiful scent has given it many uses worldwide. Wormwood has been used as an an-tiparasitic against worms, for digestion, and for many other illnesses. It was also the ingredient in absinthe, the infamous drink that was claimed to have driven so many artistic souls to madness in the 19th century. This controversial beverage born in Switzerland in the 18th century began as a tonic beverage made with other strong herbs like fennel and anise. Some believe the toxicity or hallucinogenic nature of this beverage has been greatly overstated, for the chemical that wormwood contains that has come under fire, thujone, is only present in trace amounts in old recipes for absinthe.[67]

That said, wormwood is still a valuable digestive remedy; a cup of weak wormwood tea for gas, bloating, or weak digestion is very effective. However, pregnant or nursing people should never take wormwood, for it is also a powerful emmenagogue, or menstrual stimulant, and was used as an abortifacient in the past. Wormwood is a medicine to use in small doses for short periods of time, for even if the effects of absinthe were overhyped, thujone is still toxic to the liver over long periods of time. I add a teaspoon of dried herb to a cup of hot water and steep for 10 minutes for occasional safeguarding against intestinal parasites. Some people make a homemade herbal wine by steeping a loose cup of chopped wormwood leaves in a good red wine and drinking a cup occasionally as a digestive.

THE
POISON
GARDEN

None of the information supplied in this section is for anything other than entertainment and historical inquiry. DO NOT attempt to ingest, apply, smoke, or even handle these plants without extreme caution or a wish for certain death, or a fate worse than being trapped in the mouth of madness.

Veneficium concerns the intersection of magic and poison, originating in remotest antiquity and reaching into the present day. Beyond their functions as agents of bodily harm, poisons have also served as gateways of religious ecstasy, occult knowledge, and sensorial aberration, as well as the basis of cures.

Daniel Schulke, from the publisher's remarks in *Veneficium*[68]

What can cure can also kill. This old saying reminds us that even though humankind likes to categorize things as safe and unsafe, good and evil, things are rarely that simple. The plant world presents us with this conundrum especially, for many plants, even the sweet apple or peach, can kill when the dose is too high. This space that exists between cure and poison is where some witches walk. They use the power of the liminal space between to commune with the spirits of powerful plants who can kill or teach, punish or reward.

The Poison Path is a newer term when referring to specific Traditional Witchcraft practices and was coined by Dale Pendell, a fantastic author and human who writes on entheogens, philosophy, and much more. It refers to that peculiar branch of witchcraft that concerns wortcunning and the ancient plant arts. The Poison Path is a veer-off into the dark woods on the moonlit path of Traditional Craft, a branch of wortcunning that is alluring and damning, just as it probably was to our ancestors. The witch was often accused of poisoning people, animals, and crops, while she was also looked to for healing. The art of poisoning has always been associated with the witch. For what better tool than poison for those who are oppressed? These dichotomies are the playground of those who practice our art.

Poison is power. Poison is a great transmuter. It can corrode flesh, change DNA, cure cancer, and kill flowers. Poison is magic, for isn't magic simply change facilitated by intent? This path requires humbleness and constant checking of one's ego. It requires facing that there is always more we do not know than that which we do. Why practice this path? Why do something so difficult if you do not have to? I believe that by working with the poison plants, we can tap into their immense innate power that exists here chemically and elsewhere magically and use them for our workings, learn from them and their harsh whispers, and seat understanding where fear once lounged.

The way the poisons move you changes you; this is the way one can walk the Poison Path. Of course, there are always many ways to traverse a path. This does not always mean ingesting poisons. Wearing an amulet of hemlock root can bring the practitioner in close contact with the spirit of this being to mingle, rather than risk life and limb to ingest this deadly being. Because these plants draw their energy and life force from deep beneath the earth, they are a direct link to the underworld and its denizens. The Poison Path often involves holding court with such beings.

There are many ways to commune and work with these energies and powers, and in all of the different methods, there needs to be constant vigilance as to our intentions, ego, and desires. The word *veneficium* in Latin can refer to magic, poison, or drugs. This definition is as multifaceted as the witch herself who shall never be defined as wholly good or evil. Meet the iconic plants that have been associated with witches for centuries, and if you choose to grow them and know them, be humble, be patient, and be ever blessed by their strange beauty.

Belladonna (*Atropa belladonna*)

The Latin name of this plant should alone strike fear, or at least respect, into the heart of humans. *Atropos*, meaning the terrible and merciless, is one of the Three Fates who determine life and death. It is indicative of her deadly powers, as it is Atropos who makes the final cut to the thread of life. Like her brethren mandrake, belladonna was also added to beers and wines, namely in the East, and was known as an aphrodisiac. It is interesting to see how many deadly or poisonous plants moonlight as sexual stimulants. "The little death" is given new meaning. Long associated with witches, pagan rituals, and flying ointments, this plant has gaps in its recorded historical uses but is infamous nonetheless.

Its powerful poisons have rendered belladona a unique place in the poison pantheon, for it can produce deadly results more readily than henbane or mandrake. It is indigenous to central and southern Europe and Asia Minor. Though it has since spread throughout Western Europe and into northern Africa. Belladonna has even been used as a chemical weapon in war in the Far North. It was added to the dark beers of the Scots. The Danes greedily guzzled it, rendering them helpless and delirious afterwards, and all too easy to eliminate in the 11th century. Christian mystic, herbalist, and visionary Hildegard von Bingen lets us know about the demonization of this powerful plant as Christianity swept through Europe:

> The deadly nightshade has coldness in it, and yet holds disgust and paralysis in this coldness, and in the earth at the place where it grows, the devilish prompting has a certain part and a role in its arts. And it is dangerous for a man to eat and to drink, for it destroys his spirit, as if he were dead.[69]

It is known as belladonna, or "beautiful woman" in Italian, and it was the herbalist Matthiolus who said that Italian women would drip the juice of the plant into their eyes to dilate the pupils to make themselves appear more comely. Today, atropine is still used in ophthalmology.

As recently as 1930 people were still prescribed belladonna-leaf cigarettes that had been dipped in opium tincture; they were smoked for pain and gastrointestinal issues. As little as 3 to 4 berries are regarded as psychoactive aphrodisiacs, while 10 to 20 berries are an adult lethal dose. For children it can be as little as two. It appears that using the smoke is the safest way to interact with this plant, for even the smallest doses can cause unpredictable effects in people and even death. While the berries were added to wines and beers in the past, it is highly recommended to *never* ingest this plant or its berries. Why risk it? Herbalist John Gerard advises us:

> If you will follow my counsel, deal not with the same in any case, and banish it from your gardens, and the use of it also, being a plant so furious and deadly, for it bringeth such as have eaten thereof into a dead sleep, wherein many have died.[70]

It has been used, sometimes interchangeably, like mandrake since antiquity. There are myths surrounding its harvest, much like the dog lore of mandrake. In Hungary, belladonna is to be dug up on the night of St. George while naked and a bread offering is made, "as if to an elfish monster."[71] In Germany, one of its folk names is "wolf's eye." The wolf is one of the animals of Wotan (Odin), and belladonna was associated with his daughters as well, for it has also been known as the "Valkyrie tree," leaving anyone who ate the berries at the mercy of the Valkyries. In southern Germany, hunters under the tutelage of Wotan would eat three to four belladonna berries before hunting to ensure sharpened perception. The famous natural philosopher Giovanni Battista della Porta mentioned that by using a formula that was chiefly made from belladonna, one could transform themselves into a bird, fish, or goose (all winter solstice animals perfect for sacrifice to Wotan historically).

Though demonized by the Church, belladonna has been a healer of depression, psychosis, and spiritual diseases. It was used as a remedy for the "traveling diseases," or conditions caused by demonic possession. The powerful hallucinations brought about by belladonna are described as profoundly dark and frightening, even diabolical. In Bohemia, the devil himself is said to watch over this plant but can be persuaded to leave by letting loose a black hen, which he apparently cannot resist chasing.

Constituents: Tropane alkaloids, mostly hyoscyamine, which following harvesting and drying transforms to atropine. The chemicals can even transfer into the tissues of animals. Rabbits can eat the plant without ill effect, but if a person eats that rabbit's meat, hallucinations can occur.

Effects: From the urge to laugh, great euphoria, strong desire to move, frenzy, rage, madness, to death. There is sometimes a feeling of timelessness. Many who have used it for psychoactive experiences state terror and no desire to try it again.

Growing Belladonna: *If you have children or very curious pets, growing these particular plants is not advisable. Belladonna makes big, dark beautiful berries that look very tempting to eat but are deadly.*

Belladonna will self-seed from fallen berries once established, but the seeds require cold stratification if you purchase them to plant. Place them in a container of cold water in the refrigerator for two weeks, changing the water daily. To start indoors, sprinkle over the surface of the potting mix and keep evenly moist. Their germination can take weeks! Plant them outside once the danger of frost has passed in spring in the garden with a clear label. They prefer partial to full shade.

Datura, Jimsonweed, Thorn Apple (*Datura stramonium*)

This beautiful plant has debated botanical origins, but its effects on the human body have offered little to debate about. Some botanists say it may have originated in the Caspian Sea region, while others postulate it comes from Mexico. In 1676, it earned its name jimsonweed in Jamestown, Virginia. A cook mistook the leaves for a wholesome food and served it to soldiers there, who apparently acted delirious and idiotic for days afterwards. This is how it became known as Jamestown weed, and eventually through the folk vernacular, jimsonweed.[72] It was believed that the Romani brought the thorn apple to Europe, but as aforementioned, it is up for botanical debate. It was eventually claimed that many of the Romanis' miraculous healing and magical practices all stemmed from their uses of the thorn apple.

In Mexico and the surrounding regions *D. stramonium* is used similarly to *D. innoxia*. The Mixe in Oaxaca believed this plant contained a spirit in the form of an old woman and is sometimes referred to as "grandmother." The seeds were swallowed for use in ritual divination. As with other plants in this maligned family, the uses of datura in Mexico are often done in shadowy places for in local Catholic circles it was believed that the plant was created by the devil himself. It was used by many different South American and North American Indigenous peoples for many sacred rituals, divination, and education-based vision questing.

Most writers in antiquity seemed to fear the datura plant. Dosages are described by Theophrastus that will drive a man to permanent madness and death. Its reported use in the cults of Kali as driving the worshippers to legendary frenzied human sacrifice also aided in the creation of the darkness behind this plant's name. The plant came to North America with the earliest European colonists, which confused many botanists in colonized America, who assumed it was indigenous.

In Europe, the thorn apple was associated with witches and flying ointments, and the seeds were added to beers in Germany, Russia, and China to lend them narcotic properties. The seeds were also used as an incense, which was said to have come from the Romani. It was burned to chase away ghosts or conversely to invoke spirits. A type of weather divination was also performed by throwing seeds left out for a night in the fire and watching their crackle patterns. If they burned with loud cracklings, the winter would be dry but very cold. They also used the seeds by throwing them upon animal skin drums and hitting them with a mallet a certain number of times. The way the seeds fell in relation to the lines drawn on the skin drum could then be used to answer questions about whether a sick person would heal, the location of stolen objects, and other useful things.

In Germany it was used in love philters, or love potions. These uses granted it associations with love and bending people to love against their will. This, and its reported use as an ingredient in witches' ointments, also lent it another folk name, the "sorcerer's herb."

Constituents: Tropane alkaloids, hyoscyamine, scopolamine, and atropine, the content of which varies widely.

Effects: Dry mouth, difficulty swallowing, pupil dilation, confusion, and hallucinations, all of which can persist for days. Positive experiences are only rarely mentioned. Deaths can also result from the use of this plant.

Growing Datura: This plant prefers a sunny, dry spot in the garden, and will grow in poor soil. I often see datura in wayside places on the edges of pastures in full sun. Sow seeds in spring after the last frost has passed. If you start them in pots, start them in a cactus mix. Barely cover seed and tamp well, then water and allow to dry out before watering again. Don't overwater. When handling these plants I wear gloves, for their powerful chemicals can seep through the skin and cause dizziness and disorientation.

Henbane

Black Henbane (*Hyoscyamus nigra*)

Ethnobotanist Wolf-Dieter Storl has conjectured that henbane has been in use for ritual and shamanic purposes in Eurasia since Paleolithic times. Black henbane is the most widely distributed species of all. It grows from Europe to Asia, from the Iberian Peninsula to Scandinavia. It has now become naturalized in North America and Australia.

It was used as a ritual plant by the pre–Indo-European people of central

Europe. An early Bronze Age urn of henbane seeds along with bones and snail shells was unearthed in Austria. It was believed, according to Carl Ruck, professor of classical studies at Boston University, that henbane, known as *hyoskyamos*, was sacred to Deo-Demeter-Persephone due to her sacred animal being the sow; one translation of henbane's name was derived from the term "pig bean."

It was used elsewhere in Europe as well. In Celtic regions, the plant was *belinuntia* (the plant of the sun god Bel). The Gauls poisoned their javelins with a decoction of henbane while the medieval Anglo-Saxon herbals mentioned its medicinal uses. Albertus Magnus, in his *De Vegetabilibus* (ca. 1250) stated that necromancers used the smoke to invoke the souls of the dead as well as demons. Henbane takes a more erotic turn in the medieval bathhouses of the late Middle Ages, where the seeds were strewn over hot coals to incite, how do we say, titillating feelings.[73]

The associations between henbane and witchcraft as we know them today began in the Middle Ages: "The witches drank the decoction of henbane and had those dreams for which they were tortured and executed. It was used for witches' ointments and was used for making weather and conjuring spirits. If there was a great drought, then a stalk of henbane would be dipped into a spring and the sun baked sand would be sprinkled with this."[74]

It was especially associated with divination and love magic. After monkshood, it was also a favorite of poisoners. It was believed that carrying the root on one's person would render them invulnerable to the witchcraft of others. Fight poison with poison, perhaps? The smoke of the leaves was used to make one invisible, and it was smoked in a pipe to achieve this purpose. *Oleum hyoscyamin infusum* (henbane oil) was made by infusing the leaves on gentle heat in oil. This made for a fine erotic massage oil or therapeutic treatment for soreness. As we shall see, if any plants were truly used in witches' ointments, it would most likely be henbane.

Henbane was also used as an ingredient in psychoactive beer, which ended with the Bavarian Purity Laws in 1516. Even though its use in ritual was namely as an incense of the seeds, the Germans loved their henbane beers, so they planted gardens of henbane just for this purpose, which were believed to be under the protection of Woden/Odin, father of Donar. These henbane gardens have left their mark on Germany's history with place names like *Bilsensee* (Henbane Lake) and *Billendorf* (Henbane village).

The seeds were used by the Assyrians as well, combined with sulfur to protect against magic. Persian visionaries also undertook astral journeys under the influence of henbane wines and concoctions. The Celts knew black henbane as *beleno* and burned it as an offering to Belenus, the god of oracles and the sun. Druids and bards also inhaled the smoke to travel to the realms of the fae and otherworldly beings.

The Vikings placed considerable importance on henbane, which we know due to the hundreds of seeds found in graves. A woman known as the Fyrkat woman was unearthed in Denmark wearing a pouch of henbane seeds. The earliest known record that mentions Germanic uses of the plant come from the time of Bishop Burchard von Worms, who passed in 1025. It describes a confessional in great detail that illustrates a rain ritual:

> . . . they gather several girls and select from these a small maiden as a kind of leader. They disrobe her and take her out of the settlement to a place where they can find hyoscyamus, which is known as *bilse* in German. They have her pull this out with the little finger of the right hand and tie the uprooted plant to the small toe of the right foot with any kind of string. Then the girls, each of whom is holding a rod in her hands, lead the aforementioned maiden to the next river, pulling the plant behind her. The girls then use the rods to sprinkle the young maiden with river water, and in this way they hope to cause rain through their magic. They take the young maiden, as naked as she is, who puts down her feet and moves herself in the manner of a crab, by the hands and lead her from the river back to the settlement.[75]

The seeds served as fumigants for necromantic arts and to conjure the dead for Renaissance magical practitioners, as it does today. Foundational occultist Agrippa writes in 1531:

> So, they say, that if of coriander, smallage, henbane, and hemlock, be made a fume, that spirits will presently come together; hence they are called spirit's herbs. Also, it is said, that fume made of the root of the reedy herb sagapen, with the juice of hemlock and henbane, and

the herb tapsus barbatus, red sanders, and black poppy, makes spirits and strange shapes appear; and if smallage be added to them, the fume chaseth away spirits from any place and destroys their visions.[76]

The root was also used as an amulet. Alexander of Tralles (CE 550) frequently prescribed a mixture of an amulet and wise words designed to create magical protection. He was a follower of Gnosticism, a complex religious movement that flourished in the pre- and early-Christian era. One of his prescribed amulets was henbane root hung about the neck of a patient for magical pain relief. Then again for gout, some henbane, before sunset when the moon is in Aquarius or Pisces, must be dug up with the thumb and third finger of the left hand, and it must be said:

I declare, I declare holy wort, to thee; I invite thee tomorrow to the house of Fileas, to stop the rheum of the feet of M. or N. and say, I invoke thee, the great name, Jehovah, Sabaoth, the God who steadied the earth and stayed the sea, the filler of flowing rivers, who dried up Lot's wife, and made her a pillar of salt, take the breath of thy mother earth and her power, and dry the rheum of the feet or hands of N. or M. The next day, before sunrise, take a bone of some dead animal, and dig the root up with this bone, and say, I invoke thee by the holy name Iao, Sabaoth, Adonai, Eloi, and put on the root one handful of salt, saying, "As this salt will not increase, so may not the disorder of N. or M." And hang the end of this root [henbane] periapt on the sufferer.[77]

So intimately tied was this plant with thoughts of witchery, that possession of it was enough to convict one of witchcraft. There are many mentions of it in 16th- and 17th-century witch trials as proof of malevolent intent. With the advent of the Bavarian beer purity laws, henbane fell from popular usage to await rediscovery by those hungry for magic centuries later.

Constituents: The entire plant contains tropane alkaloids hyoscyamine and scopolamine, aposcopolamine, norscopolamine, littorine, tropine, cuscohygrine, tigloidine, and tigloyloxytropane.

Yellow Henbane (*Hyoscyamus alba*)

There are many types of henbane, but yellow henbane (*Hyoscyamus alba*) was the most commonly used magically and medicinally in European antiquity. It was called white henbane, as we can see in its Latin name, though today it is commonly known as yellow. It has been written about since the time of Dioscorides who claimed it was the most medicinally potent species. It interestingly also has many name associations with tobacco. Tobacco (*Nicotiana rustica*, *N. tabacum*) was originally identified as a species of henbane, and many herbs associated with the word *tobacco* meant the plant was used as a smoke. This is a good indicator of henbane's use as a ritual smoke.

This species of henbane was ingested and used by soothsayers and seers to induce a trance state. It was the "dragon plant" of Gaia, the "madness-inducing" plant of the Colchic oracle of the witch-goddess Hecate, and the intoxicant of many others in antiquity. The seeds were used on their own or combined with others as ritual incense and inhaled. The leaves were also added to wine and drunk. Grecian priests and priestesses would inhale this smoke or drink the wine and allow their god, usually Apollo, to possess them so they could deliver his messages to humankind.

Today, the seeds are still used for psychoactive incenses in Morocco. On Cyprus, crushed leaves are still used as an analgesic plaster, and the dried leaves, mixed with tobacco, are smoked for asthma. In Israel, preparations of the leaves are used for various skin ailments, open wounds, headaches, rheumatism, inflammation of the eye, and insect stings.

Constituents: The entire plant contains tropane alkaloids hyoscyamine and scopolamine, aposcopolamine, norscopolamine, littorine, tropine, cuscohygrine, tigloidine, and tigloyloxytropane in concentrations similar to those in black henbane (*Hyoscyamus nigra*).

Effects: *Overdose of henbane can lead to dryness of mouth, locomotor disturbances, farsightedness, coma, respiratory paralysis and death. The lethal dose is not known.*

In ancient times, the effects of henbane were known as a type of mania, or madness. The Greeks used this word to indicate a dramatic alteration of consciousness. Oftentimes it was a divine alteration. The effects last three to four hours, but the aftereffects can last as long as three days. Dry mouth, locomotor disturbance, and farsightedness can all occur. Beer brewed with the plant can cause delirium, confusion, and memory disturbances in doses from two to three liters.

Growing Henbane: Stratify just like belladonna. Put seeds in water and store in the fridge for two weeks and change the water daily. You can then sow in pots in a well-draining potting mix. Do not overwater these beauties because they are prone to damping off or flopping over from fungal issues. Transplant when they get two inches tall to a sunny, sandy, well-drained area. They don't mind growing close together, but if they get too hot in a container they may fall over, so keep an eye on them in the summer.

Mandrake (*Mandragora officinarum*)

This root is so shrouded in mystery and folklore it may be considered the most infamous of the witch's plants. Though not the most toxic of the *Solanaceae*, it certainly could be said to have been regarded as one of the most powerful and frightening of them all. Originally hailing from the eastern Mediterranean, the Egyptians were familiar with the plant and used the roots and berries for various medicinal purposes but mainly as an aphrodisiac. Pieces of the roots were found in burial chambers, and the plant is mentioned in the famous Ebers Papyrus from between 1700 to 1600 BCE. It is also mentioned in the Bible twice: once when Rachel barters with them for Leah to become fertile and again in reference to lovemaking between the young Shulammite and her beloved. Clearly, this root fascinated many, and it comes as no surprise that it should be so titillating and tempting when associated with all sorts of sordid and forbidden acts.

The oldest written mention of the mandrake occurs in the cuneiform tablets of the Assyrians and the Old Testament. It may have been referring to mandrake wine, which was often mentioned in later tablets. The Greek doctor Theophrastus discussed its uses as a soporific and aphrodisiac, but more interestingly, he described curious rituals that were performed before the harvest of the alluring root. It required three circles to be drawn with a knife in the earth around the plant, after which the top of the plant was cut off while facing west. Before the best of the root is dug and cut, one must dance about it while saying as much as one can about the mysteries of love, or essentially, repeating as many indecent things as possible. If one acts lewdly enough, it is possible to frighten demons away, freeing the root from interference with lingering spirits of ill intent. It seems clear that mandrake maintained a firm grip on the vivid images of love and lovemaking throughout history in different cultures.

This love association enabled the mandrake to become associated with salacious acts in the Middle Ages. To the ancient Greeks, Aphrodite was also known as Mandragoritis, "she of the mandragora." It was one of the plants sacred to her. It was also sacred to the infamous goddess of witches, Hecate. She was both the poison goddess and the goddess of birth and aphrodisiacs. It was said of her garden, as described by Orpheus, that "many mandrakes grow within."

Josephus Flavius (37–c. 100), the Jewish historian, diplomat, and general, claimed this wonderful plant emitted a glowing red light at night, and that the shy plant would withdraw if it saw someone approaching. Others claimed this ghostly glow as well, and it was shortly after this time in antiquity we see the dog come into play in the story of the mandrake. Aelian (c. 175–c. 235) instructed one to tie a starving dog to the plant and to place some meat within smelling distance. The poor beast would pull the plant up, killing itself by hearing the mandrake's ungodly cry, and be buried afterwards in the plant's place in a ceremony honoring the gift of life for its master's conquest.[78]

The shape of the mandrake is likely one of its characteristics that made it most amenable to magic. The roots often resemble a human being, like that of another famous root, ginseng, which also came to be known as a panacea, or cure-all, of the human body. It is hard to say where the mandrake went from a useful and mysterious medicinal plant to sinister homunculus. Harold Hansen postulates that it may stem from the story of Jason's "dragon men," but it is most likely from early Christianity. It was said that the mandrake was a first draft of man that God discarded after creating Adam from the red earth of Paradise, hence its eerie humanlike form.

The German name for mandrake is Alraune, which comes from Alrun, and may have meant "he who knows the runes." Germanic oracles, who were known far and wide in ancient times, would use the mandrake in concoctions to enter prophetic states. Though sadly, as Christianization overtook Europe, so too did the associations of mandrake go from seer's plant to an almost demonic entity. It was in early medieval Germany that new traditions and beliefs formed around the mysterious root and perhaps brought about some of its most sinister associations.

Its folk names now included gallow's man and dragon doll, for it was said to only grow at the base of the gallows where, in the throes of death, a hanged man's urine or semen stained the earth. This ensured the powerful mandrake was a rare and strange occurrence. Due to this, many would pay high prices for the mandrake, for it practically did it all: luck in love, healed the diseases brought about, brought in wealth, and acted with a power no woman could resist.

To convince the root to do these things for you, however, required careful ritual, for the mandrake still bore hatred for mankind for being chucked aside as a prototype on God's drafting desk. It must be bathed in wine and wrapped in red or white silk cloth, as well as a little velvet cloak. It must also be fed. What to feed it varied depending on who you asked. Some of the most powerful foods were Communion wafers saved in the mouth from Church, spittle from a fasting person, or even earth from Paradise.[79]

These roots continued to be known as *alruna* or *alraunes* in Germany and England. Even with the best care, however, sometimes the mandrake would tire of its owner and stop working. In these instances it had to be sold right away lest it turned the tides and caused misfortune for its master. Interestingly, it could only be sold for less than one had bought it for, and if the owner died, it must go to the grave with them and be prepared to be judged alongside them at Heaven's gates.

They have lived on in German and English folklore where it was said that well-kept *alraun* were dressed in silk and velvet and "fed" meals of milk and cookies. Dr. Faust of the iconic German Renaissance legend was said to have an *alraun*. In 1888, it was said such manikins could be found among the Pennsylvania Dutch. In Renaissance-era magic it was also, like henbane, used as a magical incense associated with the moon and placed under the pillow for prophetic dreams.[80]

Hildegard von Bingen was one of the first to record her criticisms of the mandrake:

> With this plant, however, also because of it's [sic] similarity to a person, there is more diabolical whispering than with other plants and it lays snares for him. For this reason, a person is driven by his desires, whether they are good or bad, as he also once did with the idols. . . .
> It is harmful through much that is corruptive of the magicians and phantoms, as many bad things were once caused by the idols.[81]

Yet she also prescribed its use, still paying homage to the powerful plant for depression of sorts, saying that a person should place a spring-washed mandrake root whole with him in his bed while he sleeps. There is even a little charm that accompanies it, though Hildegard would have never called it such: "God, who makes humans from the dirt of the earth without pain. Now I place this earth, which has never been stepped over, beside me, so that my earth will also feel that peace which you have created."[82]

Constituents: It contains the potent alkaloids scopalamine, hyoscyamine, atropine, apoatropine, and many more. The effects are little written about despite the popularity and notoriety of this root. It is poisonous but less so than our other *Solanaceae* friends.

Growing Mandrakes: One of the most difficult to grow of the witches' plants. Stratify them in the fridge like belladonna and henbane. Their germination is staggered, for in the wild if all plants come up at once, a late frost could kill them all. Staggering germination is a survival tactic. They can grow outdoors in zones 8 to 10, but we have seen them grown in our 6b area with frost protective mulch. They need loose, well-drained soil in full sun to avoid rot. Some keep them in containers, but they are sensitive to their roots hitting the bottom. Some people plant them in large garbage cans or even pipes! They grow natively in places with rocky, alkaline soil, so adding oyster shells or limestones to the bed they will ultimately rest in can help.[83]

Your Harvest: Basic Processing and Storage

After plants are grown and tended to, how do you harvest them? Every plant has different parts that are useful and different times for harvest, but once you harvest your herbs, there are a few things you can do with them to preserve and store them.

Drying the leaves, flowers, and (some) roots of plants is a great way to store them for later use in our magic rites. I dry plants in a dehydrator and follow the instructions for which plant part I'm drying. Roots have a higher moisture content and are thicker, so they take a higher temperature and a longer time to dry. Leaves and flowers are more delicate and generally less moist, meaning I won't use as high of a temperature and may even hang them to dry.

If you'd like to hang dry herbs, which have a beautiful aesthetic value all their own, I like to bundle them with twine around the stems and tie them to the rafters of my kitchen or make a special herb-drying rack. You can drive two nails into a wall that's out of direct light as too much direct sunlight can damage delicate oils in herbs. Then, simply tie a string firmly between them and hang your bundles of herbs from this string, either by tying on each bundle with their own little string or by using paper clips as little hooks. I try to make sure there's plenty of airflow by moving them occasionally and checking for any mold. When they feel dry and slightly crunchy, I take them down and crumble them with my hands into a large bowl. Using a clean mason jar, I store them in a cool, dark, *not* damp spot.

Make sure to always label your jars! I'm guilty of forgetting this vital step, and sometimes after time has passed it's difficult to remember just what herb, potion, or concoction I have! On my labels I include the following:

- Common name
- Latin name
- Date harvested
- Moon phase when harvested

You can add other astrological information that feels meaningful to your practice, like the zodiac sign, the name of the person who harvested the plant, or where it was harvested if you foraged it. Your labels can be as simple or as complex and detailed as you desire. Just be sure to keep any herbs that are not safe for children out of reach.

You can also store herbs as vinegars, salts, sugars, meads, and tinctures. Get to know the herbs you're working with and see what speaks to you! I store most of mine as dry herbs.

III

FORAGING YOUR OWN MAGICAL AND HEALING HERBS

Foraging Basics for the Wild Witch

There are so many reasons to forage for food and medicine. Some are practical, insofar as obtaining food and medicine is a way to practically meet our human needs; others are more spiritual. Knowing the flora of your home area is a way to dive deep into a relationship with the land and all the beings—human and otherwise—around you. Interesting work has been done looking at how engaging with the local environment—in this instance through foraging for plants and mushrooms—can lead to grounding place-based identities and strong relationships with the other-than-human life of a bioregion.

A 2014 study examined the ways in which foraging for plants and mushrooms informed three topics: cultural belonging and identity, belonging and place, and belonging and more-than-human agency. By interviewing informants from different cultures as well as recent immigrants who inhabited the Seattle area they were studying, the researchers noted that plant and mushroom foraging aided people in establishing connections to places.[1] Interestingly, it also reinforced differences between people who related with nature and places distinctly through their unique cultural lenses with which they viewed the world. Contrary to ideas held by its critics, bioregionalism is not a homogenizing force, but allows for distinct cultures and lifestyles to coexist within the same locale. To me, the idea of finding home in the place we live, respecting the unique perspectives we each bring to a bioregion, and honing a relationship with that land is reason enough to get out and see what's growing.

Safety and Ecology/Sustainability

But isn't it hurting nature to forage? Don't the animals need it? Why not just go to the grocery store? You destructive, bad human, you.

Wild food foraging and the harvesting of wild plants for food and medicine has come under fire since the early 1990s due to a variety of factors that are inherently damaging to the environment.[2] Unfortunately, the seeds of humankind's disconnection to nature are planted so deeply it is difficult for scientists today to see the ways in which human activity in nature, when properly managed, is not ipso facto destructive. Just as the Forest Service manages the access hikers have to the woods and how the public can interact with them, wild foraging can be, and in some places already is, regulated. By sharing and making more accessible information about the proper harvesting techniques for each plant, shrub, and tree in question in a locale, we can provide tools to avoid improper harvest and overharvest of rare or culturally significant species.

It's difficult not to see the world in all-or-nothing ideologies. I see this happen so often in the realms of herbalism, foraging, and witchcraft (which for me all make up a single place, but for many are three separate places). Some of the key things to take note of when asking about the sustainability of foraging wild plants is that it's not being promoted as an activity all people would, can, or should want to do. It does not have to sustain the whole populace to be a sustainable activity.[3]

The Nuances of Foraging

It is often painful for humans to humble ourselves. For all of us, the idea of sinking into a feeling of "sometimes I'm wrong" is very scary and hard. I understand because I feel the same way! I hate the feeling of being wrong. However, I believe that to hold any safe, respectful, and meaningful practice with foraging from the wild, you have to engage with nuanced, place-specific rules and constantly ask questions. You also have to be okay learning new things constantly and not practicing black-or-white thinking in the face of an ever-evolving and deepening practice. These are all part of the reconnecting and remembering of how to be in good relationships with the wild world.

There's a lot to consider before picking a plant, and over time, just like a new exercise, the thought process and ethical quandaries become a new normal. In that same measure, I also lament the gatekeeping I see around herbalism and foraging that keeps many people, especially BIPOC individuals, from feeling comfortable and welcome working with plants. This is something we must address as well.

Here are some good places to start when asking yourself whether you should harvest a plant, shrub, or tree:

- Always ensure a 100-percent identification before ingesting. No matter how advanced you are, this should always mean asking a real human, not Google or a book, to make sure. While we cannot always do this in real life, sending good, detailed pictures with the location and date found to a university or reputable plant group online can be a great help. As we learn to ID plants, having multiple points of identification is key. Note the season, the growth stage, the physical characteristics, the smell, and the relationships to other plants around. At the end of the day, it's up to each of us to be responsible for seeking this confirmation.

- Don't forage in places of contamination. Roadsides and residential areas can be contaminated with lead and other industrial waste. Make sure you check out the history of an area before harvesting.

- Don't forage on people's private property without permission. Also be aware of local regulations concerning foraging on public lands because if you are caught you could be fined if it's illegal.

- Focus on the abundant plants.

- Educate yourself on culturally significant plants in your region and be sensitive to the issues of First Nations access to plants sacred to them. One example would be white sage (*Salvia apiana*).

In addition, ask yourself the following questions:

- Am I prepared to be honest with myself in regard to making decisions about my impact on this stand of plants and the ecosystem in which they live?

- How much medicine do I realistically need? We often harvest more than we use. Avoid killing plants just to waste them.

- If the plant is rare, can I use a more widely available plant in its place?

- Is this stand of plants healthy? Is there observable damage to the plants?

- How large is this stand? Are there others? How large are they?

- If my harvest won't require taking the plant's life, how long will it take the harvested part(s) to grow back? If my harvest does take this plant's life, such as in the harvest of roots, how will I support its propagation in the future if needed?

- Will my impact be noticeable? Could anyone tell I've been here?

- Is there evidence of others harvesting here? How intense is that evidence?[4]

The answers to these questions require a variety of things. They require an ever-deepening knowledge of your specific location's history, current management practices, and much more. This can make harvesting on public lands—which is often illegal or heavily regulated—very hard, but if you have permission to harvest on private lands, it's more accessible if you can ask the land owner about the land use history. I find a great way to manage and add to this information is keeping a **foraging binder**. You could also use Google Drive or a phone app, but just keep a section for each new plant and tree, expanding and adding to it over time with new information about the plants and the places where you identify them and harvest them.

Region-Specific Questions:

- Know the rare and endangered plants of the area and don't harvest them.

- Know the poisonous or plants that pose dangers (like poison ivy) before harvesting in a new region.

- Pick from different stands or spots in a stand to minimize impact.

- Care for and develop a relationship with the stand. Educate yourself on those plants' propagation and help them!

- Don't harvest the oldest and largest plants in a stand as they are the most successful survivors with the strongest genes.

- Leave any area you harvest from in the same or better condition than you found it. Fill in holes after harvesting roots. Don't leave discarded leaves or other plant parts lying around where others can see them. Whenever appropriate, replant root crowns or scatter seeds. Pick up trash and help maintain the area.

- Keep notes on different wildcrafting populations. Observe the stand over time so that you can continue to refine your personal assessments of where it is safe and ethical to harvest from that spot each year.[5]

How Much Can I Take?

If you Google "foraging" online, you'll come across many different numbers, proportions, and percentages of what's appropriate to harvest from any given patch of wild plants. I've always struggled with this for a few reasons. The first reason is that they're often speaking about foraging generally, so there's a kind of one-size-fits-all approach. This is problematic for a few reasons. In certain ecosystems, like desert highlands where water is limited and plants grow more sporadically, taking any amount from a population can be devastating, yet harvesting plants here in Appalachia, especially non-natives and invasives, can actually be helpful!

We can help control invasive plants like garlic mustard and Japanese knotweed by eating them and making medicine with them. There's no rule about how much to take that does not depend completely on the location, population size, species, and climate you're foraging in. I would instead learn about each new plant in your region and how prevalent it is on a case by case basis, always asking questions and watching the populations grow and change over time.

Natives, Naturalized, and Invasives

Invasive plants are defined by US executive order as "a species that is 1) non-native (or alien) to the ecosystem under consideration and 2) whose introduction causes or is likely to cause economic or environmental harm or harm to human health."[6] They are taken very seriously and cast as almost evil entities by many speaking about environmentalism and conservation. Using invasive plants as a means to control their populations has faced much criticism, most likely due to a lack of nuanced thinking. Critics' claims vary and involve everything from fears that the product made from the plants will become culturally significant and therefore become a protected resource by the populace, to concerns over the creation of a market demand for the invader.[7] Both of these arguments are dependent upon wider markets and grander scales of production, which we're not dealing with here. When capitalism is applied to our plant practices, it can quickly warp them.

These suppositions also follow very all-or-nothing approaches to plant use that are not realistic or always applicable in small-scale situations, as in our personal foraging practices. The fears around invaders and invasives go far deeper than the ecological world and are important issues to address as an aside before delineating which plants are "good" and which plants are "bad." Things are so much more nuanced and complex than that. Invasive plants can often be found in public spaces too, which is another benefit of working with them!

If you're unclear about legal areas to forage, here again, your favorite hunter friend or relative can be a great resource for learning about public lands open for foraging and hunting, and they may even know private property owners to whom you can seek permission for access. On that note—also be aware of hunting season schedules and take proper safety measures during those times of the year.

Tools of the Trade

Foraging really requires as few tools as your hands and a basket to hold your bounty. However, having the right tools can make foraging more fun and easier on your body, and help to more sustainably remove plant portions you're after. Here are the tools in my foraging bag that I keep in my car at all times.

Baskets: It's no secret that I'm a basket hoarder. I have probably 20 different sizes and types I've thrifted, bought, or made. I love different baskets for different harvests. If I'm going to get many small daisies, I will use a small, tightly woven basket. If I'm harvesting stinging nettle to dry for winter soups and stews, I'll use a big basket with a wider weave to let any little bits of dirt that get in to fall out and keep my harvest tidy.

Pruners: These are ideal for snipping the fragrant branches of birch or pine and for taking cuttings of plants like elderberry to propagate at home. I also use them to prune back my raspberries in the fall. When foraging, I cut back any invasive species like kudzu (which I then take home and weave a basket from!) choking out my favorite harvest spots. Pruners are so useful for lots of tasks in both foraging and gardening.

Hori Hori: This Japanese tool is like a sharp trowel. Mine has one serrated side, which makes cutting through roots like dandelion and dock a breeze. I use this tool constantly in my garden for transplanting and dividing my mints and bee balm.

Cloth Bags (various sizes): Keeping my harvest clean and separated for later processing is a huge help. Keeping everything in separate bags also helps ensure I didn't sneak any plants I didn't mean to into my basket. I use little drawstring bags of various sizes to hold my harvest and separate things as I go. Moving slowly and staying tidy when bagging up your herbs is a great way to ease your processing tasks later. You won't regret it when you get home and need to bundle everything up to dry or chop it up for supper.

Small Shovel: This is most useful for large roots like burdock or sassafras. I have a little camp shovel in my car that is perfect for this purpose.

Knife: I use the knife to trim my plants up before placing them in baskets or bags. I can trim off very dirty bits or cut soft mugwort stems one at a time for later bundling. I like Morakniv-brand bushcraft knives that can take a beating and stay sharp.

Brush: I use a small, clean paintbrush just for this purpose to quickly clean any roots I harvest of loose dirt before adding them to my harvest basket.

Work Gloves: I love to wear gloves while I harvest certain plants like stinging nettle or wild roses to avoid thorns and stickers. They can also help keep my hands clean when I'm digging up daylilies or trying to transplant a sochan plant.

Wild Tending: Stewarding Wild Populations of Plants

Wild tending is a very old idea. It is the idea that rather than remove all the wild plants growing in an area and planting a garden there, you support the growth of desired plants in the places they are already growing. All of our ancestors wild tended in the diverse places where they dwelt within the bounds of their unique bioregions. Wild tending is most visible today in places with intact Indigenous land management and in places where various groups of people are intentionally returning to a traditional land management ethic using Traditional Ecological Knowledge. Traditional Ecological Knowledge, or what is known as TEK in academic circles, is defined as "a cumulative body of knowledge, practice, and belief, evolving by adaptive processes and handed down through generations by cultural transmission, about the relationship of living beings (including humans) with one another and with their environment."[8]

When these knowledge bases are interrupted or destroyed, the chaos that ensures inland management and natural resource access is remarkable, to say the least. The arrival of Europeans on North American soil is a great example of these interruptions, for without the First Nation's wisdom, both shared and stolen, European settlers would have starved.

Europeans had been divorced from a sustainable land ethic long before their arrival. It would take another few hundred years for them to see beyond the profit in their soil and monetary value of the land beneath their feet, but by then their once kind hosts would be nearly physically and culturally eradicated, much like the ecological communities and great forests Europeans had written about with awe in the 1600s.

Wild foraging, or wildcrafting as it's often called today, is a practice informed by Traditional Ecological Knowledge. Indigenous peoples have a unique insight into the location that they have historically inhabited, namely due to the powers of long-term observation and the strength of oral tradition among many other important and sacred factors. Looking to Indigenous knowledge on how and when to harvest certain plants as well as honoring and educating oneself on the issues surrounding Indigenous access to wild plants is essential in my opinion if you want to practice foraging in America.

Inspired by this concept, I have begun a personal practice of wild tending that is grounded in the spirit of long-term observation and land stewardship. I believe that by gardening and foraging I can help add to the health of the ecosystem around me through listening to Indigenous voices about how land management can look with the idea that humans are not inherently destructive or terrible, but are in fact part of the natural world and can even be beneficial when living in good relationships with the world around them. I can combine that with my use of non-native and invasive plants from my own ancestors and look to that old knowledge about how best to use, harvest, and grow those particular plants. As a witch, this idea is woven into the fabric of my beliefs, so it makes sense that it should be woven into my plant practice too.

Asking how I can use my privilege to protect and advocate for Indigenous land access, control, and management of their ancestral lands and access to the knowledge and practices that have been forcibly removed from them is also imperative. I do this by donating my time and resources to Indigenous-led food sovereignty organizations and by offering a certain number of tickets to all my foraging classes to BIPOC for free. I feel that as a person who is sustained by this land, as a teacher of plant identification and herbalism, and as a European-ancestored person, this is just the very least I can do to say thank you for the knowledge I have as well as work in solidarity with my Indigenous community to help repair that which has long been broken by colonization.

Wild tending for me looks a few different ways, but these are the two that make up the majority of my practice:

1. Observing and protecting specific plant populations that I harvest from and monitoring their health. I have gone to the same patches of elderberries to harvest for the last 10 years. It's been such a gift to see how much they grow and change every year. Elderberries are a native species here, and while not particularly endangered, they are growing ever popular among herbalists, and I want to ensure there are enough for the animals and for us. I can do this by watching how many blooms I harvest, and knowing that if I take all the flowers, I will get no berries, and neither will anyone else. Watching this patch and propagating their genetics is one way I can wild tend this patch.

2. Transplanting and propagating wild plants I love at my home so I don't need to wild forage them and can actually add to their numbers.

As we learned in the plant propagation section of this work, elderberry is very easy to propagate by cuttings! I take cuttings from these plants and will root them and grow their kin on our land. We will have elderberries from here and many other spots we come across as we carefully harvest cuttings from different places. This means that not only will we remove harvest pressure from those patches, we will start new plants in new places, which birds and rodents will ingest seeds from and spread elsewhere. It's really spectacular. Other plants I love to transplant and propagate from the wild into my half-wild garden are:

- Daylily: *Hemerocallis fulva*
- Stinging nettle: *Urtica dioica*
- Wood nettle: *Laportea canadensis*
- Blackberry: *Rubus* spp.
- Raspberry: *Rubus idaeus*

- Wineberry: *Rubus phoenicolasius*
- Sochan, green-headed coneflower: *Rudbeckia laciniata*
- Oxeye daisy: *Leucanthemum vulgare*
- Onion grass: *Allium vineale*

These are a few of my favorites. Our sochan patch started as three little plants three years ago and is now so large that I gift plants to our students regularly for their gardens!

Common Forageable Herbs

Agrimony (*Agrimonia* spp.)

There are around 15 agrimony species, at least 4 of which have strong herbal traditions: The first, *Agrimonia eupatoria*, is native to Europe, North Africa, southwest Asia, and Macaronesia and was introduced to North America.[9] The next, *Agrimonia pilosa*, is native to Asia and eastern Europe. Lastly, *Agrimonia gryposepala* and *A. parviflora* are native to North America.[10]

Habitat: Woods, edges, fields, and wayside places. Native to the temperate Northern Hemisphere and one species in Africa. *Agrimonia gryposepala* is the most widely distributed of the seven native North American species. Agrimony is found in most states except those in the Rocky Mountains and Florida. It prefers moderately to very moist habitats.

Identification: This erect perennial plant can be identified from afar by the spike that can grow one foot or more of five-petaled yellow flowers throughout the summer. Each flower develops into a ruddy-brown dry fruit, deeply furrowed and fringed with hooked bristles. Young leaves grow in a basal rosette with deeply veined pinnate leaves. The terminal leaflet is often the largest.

Parts Used: Flowering tops and leaves. Flowers from May to early fall in temperate climates.

Folklore and Magic: This astringent herb was once used to help beer keep better. Much like hops, agrimony is associated with sleep; you could make one fall asleep by placing agrimony beneath their pillow:

If it be leyd under mann's heed,

He shal sleepyn as he were deed;

He shal never drede ne wakyn

Till fro under his heed it be takyn'.[11]

In England, a divination was done with agrimony. You'd take two fronds of the plant, each with nine leaflets, and place them crossed beneath a pillow secured with two new pins (which were also crossed). This would cause one's future husband to appear in a dream. Agrimony also guards against spells, especially when combined with green broom, elder leaves, and betony.[12] Agrimony also bound with broom-straw, maidenhair, rue, and ground ivy in Tyrol allows the bearer to see witches and when hung over the doors forbids them from entering a dwelling.[13]

Food and Medicine: Agrimony makes a lovely tea and was once drank commonly for pleasure by French and English country folk.[14] Historically, this plant was used as a medicine for the liver and as a tonic. Romani people used it for coughs.[15] Agrimony was also believed to help the eyes, according to Anglo-Saxon herbals, and was used for poisonous bites from serpents. Agrimony has had a plethora of different medicinal uses around the world. The tannins in agrimony are the key to the medicinal power, which makes sense for this small member of the rose family. Many rose family plants are rich in astringent tannins.

I like to gather the leaves and flowering tops for tea. The mild, slightly astringent tea is an excellent wash for itchy skin and inflammation, as well as a pleasant drink for a cold or a sore throat. It's also a great remedy for diarrhea, which is another long-standing historical use of this sweet little plant.

Blackberry (*Rubus* spp.)

There are many species of blackberries, all with subtle differences, and all edible and medicinal. Some are invasive in certain areas.

Habitat: Disturbed areas in temperate forests. Abundant in eastern woodlands and the Pacific Northwest.

Identification: Palmately compound leaves with 5 to 7 leaflets each on their own stalk. Berries often ripen all at the same time due to uniform flowering time. The berries each hang from their own stem. This makes picking a large amount at once possible!

Parts Used: Fruits, leaves, roots, and dried stems.

Folklore and Magic: On St. Simon and St. Jude's Day (October 28), tradition says that Satan sets his foot on the bramble, after which day not a single edible blackberry can be found. In Sussex, they say that, after Old Michaelmas Day (October 10), the Devil goes around the county and spits on the blackberries. In Scotland, it is thought that, late in the autumn, the Devil throws his cloak over the blackberries and renders them unwholesome.

In antiquity, people deemed both the fruit and flowers of the bramble good medicine for the bites of serpents. Like other rose family members, the astringency accounts for much of the medicine of blackberry. It was believed that due to this intense astringency, even its young shoots, when eaten as a salad, would fasten teeth that were loose.

In Cornwall, bramble-leaves, wetted with spring water, are employed as a charm for a scald or burn. The moistened leaves are applied to the burn while the patient repeats the following formula:

> There came three angels out of the East,
> One brought fire, and two brought frost;
> Out fire and in frost;
> In the name of the Father, Son, and Holy Ghost.
> Amen.

Brambles are ruled by Mars. Dreaming of them is also a portent of things to come. To dream of passing through places covered with brambles portends troubles; if they prick you, secret enemies will do you an injury with your friends; if they draw blood, expect heavy losses in trade. To dream of passing through brambles unhurt denotes a triumph over enemies.[16]

There are taboos around when you can eat blackberries safely in England. If you eat them after Michaelmas day (September 29) in England you may die! The Devil or the pooka, a goblin, spits on them and makes them sour. This is because some say on Satan's fall from heaven, the plant broke his long fall, so he hates the blackberry.[17] Any plant hated by the Devil made a good protective charm, so wreaths of brambles were hung to protect against evil witches in England.

Burning brambles offered protection as well, and it is one of my favorite local incenses for this reason. I take the twigs carefully, with a gloved hand of course, and snip off the thorns with pruners. I cut the twigs into roughly six-inch lengths and bind one end together with red thread, and it is the untied end of this little broom-like creation that I light on fire and blow out, creating a smoking tool that one can whisk about, banishing evil energies from a space before magical workings.

Cecil Williamson, founder of the incredible Witchcraft Museum in Boscastle, England, describes it best:

> . . . made of dried out blackberry stems and with the end bound to form a handle. Here in the south west (of England) when a witch decides to make magic she first selects a spot or place where she will work, be the chosen place inside or out. The next thing to be done is that of cleansing the chosen spot of all evil forces. This is where the bundle of blackberry twigs comes in. She sets a light to the twigs and with them smouldering, burning, and making smoke, she dances and weaves her way in and around and around over and over again. So this is one might call it: "a witch's devil scarer."[18]

Food and Medicine: Blackberries are a delicious food and full of antioxidants. The fruits are easy to identify because they are segmented. You can easily tell a blackberry from a black raspberry by pulling on the fruit. The raspberries pop off like a cap while blackberries retain their center, leaving a little stem. I love the root tea made out of blackberries: one chopped teaspoon of dried root steeped in hot water 20 minutes then strained for loose bowels, but be careful not to overdo it, for it is powerfully astringent. This is a classic Appalachian folk remedy for diarrhea.

The leaves also make a lovely tea that was used historically for everything from sore throat to wound washes. It is high in vitamin C and antioxidants as well! I use it much like raspberry leaf and you can even ferment the leaves by bruising them fresh, packing them into a very clear, dry jar, and letting them ferment for two or more weeks. Dry them out after, and they will taste much like black tea. A decoction of the leaves is a great wound wash or wash for poison ivy or other itchy skin conditions. These plants are often invasive in certain places and "eating the invaders" is a great way to nourish ourselves physically, spiritually, and mentally by practicing the sacred act of foraging and making our own food and medicine while helping to control the spread of plants out of balance.

Black Walnut (*Juglans nigra*)

Habitat: From the East Coast to the Great Plains and from Texas and Georgia, north to central Minnesota, Wisconsin, Michigan, and up to Ontario, Canada.

Identification: Large tree with light gray-brown, thick, rough bark. Often has a straight, dominant trunk. Smooth, brown, thick twigs. Pinnately compound leaves with 13 to 21 leaflets with the terminal leaflet often missing. There are four species of western walnuts that can be used similarly: Arizona walnut, *J. major*; California walnut, *J. californica*; Texas walnut, *J. microcarpa*; and Hinds walnut, *J. hindsii*.[19]

Parts Used: Hulls, nuts, wood.

Folklore and Magic: *Juglans* means "nut of Jupiter" in Latin, and *nut* may in fact refer to the "glans of Jupiter." This may account for the walnut's connection with fertility and love in legends. The ancient Greeks apparently stewed walnuts and ate them to increase fertility. Carrying a walnut in the shell was also believed to increase fertility, an interesting practice in comparison with our hickory and buckeye nut lore here in Appalachia as a charm for good luck when carried on one's person. The Romans ascribed more feminine aspects to the walnut and associated it with Juno (Jupiter's wife) and the Roman goddess of women and marriage. In fact, one of the Roman wedding customs was to throw walnuts at the bride and groom to encourage fertility.[20] This seems unadvisable!

European walnuts feature prominently in folklore and fairy tales throughout the rest of the continent, especially in Italy. There, walnut shells are often seen to be containers for magical or precious objects. They also believed that walnut branches or wood could protect one from lightning strikes. It was sometimes called "roots of evil" due to its poisonous nature, as well as its links to witches in Italian folklore. After all, it was said that witches preferred to meet under the poisonous shade of the noxious walnut tree, one of the most famous coming from the legend of the witches of Benevento, which may also be the first time flying to a Sabbath was mentioned in accusations from a 1428 testimony by accused witch Matteuccia da Todi in Italy. The following was recited by many of the women accused of witchcraft at their trials:

Unguento, unguento
portami al noce di Benevento
sopra l'acqua e sopra il vento
e sopra ogni altro maltempo.

"Unguent, unguent,
Carry me to the walnut tree of Benevento,
Above the water and above the wind,
And above all other bad weather." [21]

I find myself quite at home in the shade of any walnut tree. Perhaps in conjunction with its association with malevolent practices, falling asleep beneath a walnut tree was thought to cause madness or prophetic dreams; two paths one's mind may take that often lead to one another. Aside from its medieval associations with evil, in Europe the walnut was seen as promoting fertility, strengthening the heart, and helping to dispel the evils of rheumatism. [22]

In North America, in the Ozarks, walnuts draw lightning, and to plant a walnut tree near one's house was seen as a terrible idea. I wonder if this has to do with the incessant crashing of walnuts in the fall upon the roof, rather than solely a fear that this tree, above others, draws lightning to it. Another Ozark belief held that walnut shells must not be burned or bad luck would come. Dreaming of opening or eating walnuts means money is coming soon. [23]

I love to carve wood, and black walnut is a lovely one to carve. It's very hard so a good sharp carving knife is needed. I've made many spoons and wands from this lovely, chocolate-brown wood.

Food and Medicine: The black walnut has been in North America at least since the Pleistocene era, and has a long history of use as a food and medicine source for First Nations people in North America. Because of the beautiful, rich brown color of the heartwood, black walnut has become one of the most valuable hardwoods native to North America. Its natural resistance to decay and insect damage, as well as its large size, have helped it remain on top in the rankings of useful woods. One of the most interesting things about black walnuts is their poisonous nature. The tree is allelopathic, which means it releases chemicals from its roots and decaying bark and leaves that stunt other plants' growth. Black walnuts produce juglone, which is the allelopathic chemical that is exuded by this majestic tree. It is the tree's built-in method of cutting down on competition by nearby growing plants. People made note of this potent chemical as early as 77 CE and parts of the walnut have been used as herbicides and medicines for centuries.

Black walnuts are a wonderful food, rich in healthful fats and vitamin E, which is great for brain health, interestingly enough. This nut has a long history as a cure-all of mental ills due to its closeness in appearance to a brain according to the doctrine of signatures. These can be gathered in the fall. I like to remove the hulls (with gloves, as they stain everything a dark brown) and save them for dye by air-drying them on tarps. You can boil them in a pot just for this purpose and add a dash of vinegar to dye natural materials like linen and cotton a beautiful warm brown. I like to dye my altar cloths with natural dyes, and brown is always in season.

I tincture the green hulls when they are younger around summer's end for their antifungal and antiparasitic medicine. I chop a mason jar full of young green walnuts (with gloves on) and then cover them in good vodka and label. I strain this four to six weeks later (I make sure to do this outside because of staining) and use the tincture for short-term applications with my wormwood tincture for worms and other internal parasites. One dose is 20 drops. Take three times a day for a parasite cleanse for *no longer* than two weeks at a time. *Black walnut is not to be used when pregnant or nursing.*

Burdock (*Arctium minus, A. lappa*)

Habitat: Ranges across northern portion of US and southern Canada. They are often found in disturbed ground and on edges of fields and forests.

Identification: Large biennial or perennial rosette herb with ovate leaves. Heart-shaped lobes at the base of green topped leaves with fuzzy white wool underneath. The first-year burdock is a rosette of basal leaves, which, during the second, puts up a stalk with hook-covered, burr-covered seeds with alternate branches. *A. minus*, common burdock, has hollow petiole, but *A. lappa*, great burdock, does not and has thinner stalks.

Parts Used: Roots, stalks.

Folklore and Magic: Burdock was considered a "bear" plant by the Celts and Germanic peoples, and was sacred to Thor, god of thunder. The name *Arctium* comes from the Greek term *arktos*, which means "bear." This is a reference to the

A Recipe for Midsummer
Green Walnut Liquor, Nocino

1. Take as many green Walnuts as you please, about the middle of July, try them all with a pin, if it goes easily through them they are fit for your purpose.

2. Lay them in Water for nine days, washing and shifting them Morning and Night; then boil them in water until they be a little Soft, lay them to drain.

3. Then pierce them through with a Wooden Sciver, and in the hole put a Clove, and in some a bit of Cinnamon, and in some the rind of a Citron Candi'd.

4. Then take the weight of your Nuts in Sugar, or a little more; make it into a syrup, in which boil your Nuts (scimming them) till they be tender; then put them up in Gally potts, and cover them close.

5. When you lay them to drain, wipe them with a Course cloth to take off a thin green Skin. They are Cordial and Stomachal.'

From *The Family Physician*, by Geo. Hartman, Phylo Chymist, who liv'd and Travell'd with the Honourable Sir Kenelm Digby, in several parts of Europe the space of Seven Years till he died.[24]

bristly, bear fur–like burs. The species name, *lappa*, also means "bur," or "thorn," in Latin. Burdock was gathered at midsummer and placed in homes and stables to protect against lightning and giants. There is a legend of a "midsummer coal" that dwells in the roots of burdock and can be discovered during the noon hour of the longest day of the year, the summer solstice. This is also legendarily hidden beneath mugwort as well. It is said if you brave handling the red hot "coal" you will have no bad luck or sorrows.[25] Farmers braided it into their cows' tails to protect them from evil. "Piskies" or "pixies," a race of fairies or "small people" in Cornwall, are said to have ridden colts furiously around the fields and braided their manes or tangled them with "Billy buttons," or burrs of the burdock.[26]

These beliefs survived into North America, where necklaces of dried burdock roots were worn by children against witchcraft in the Ozarks.[27] Burdock is also associated with the planet Venus, rendering it a fine option for love workings. To win a lover in Ozark folk magic, carve a burdock root into their shape and carry it with you or wear it in a bag.[28]

Food and Medicine: This Eurasian herb had naturalized and was noted growing wild in the piedmont region of North Carolina by 1764.[29] Burdock root has traditionally been used as a blood purifier, for rashes, as a diuretic, and as an aid for digestion. In American folk medicine traditions, it is considered one of the most powerful blood purifiers, and in Appalachia, it was drunk as a cold water infusion. A wash from the leaves is also useful for poison ivy if jewelweed isn't available. Many rashes are helped by it. Like dandelion, the roots are rich in inulin, which is a wonderful prebiotic and was used as a folk remedy for diabetes.[30]

Burdock root is called *gobo* in Japan and is eaten as a vegetable. You can dig up young, first-year plants in spring or fall when the energy of the plant is under the earth, and scrape the dark outer skin off the root, wash it, and cook it. I like to either sauté and season or boil until tender and then add butter and salt. You can also eat the stalks of the leaves (tender ones without too many strings) and peel the outer skin off those as well with a sharp knife. Boil or steam and serve with your favorite fat and spice blend. I like to use the root for tea as well to help heal skin troubles from the inside out. Drink the tea as a nutritive tonic to help support the liver, and in turn, the skin. Burdock can help skin on the outside too. The leaves can be cooked into a mash and applied warm, but not scalding, to skin eruptions, burns, and sores.

Chickweed (*Stellaria media*)

Habitat: Native to Europe, chickweed is now found all over the world in abundance, especially in Asia and North America.

Identification: Chickweed grows in mats, creeping across the ground with thin stems adorned with small sets of opposite tender leaves with no teeth. There is a thin mohawk of fine hairs running along the stems. This line of hair switches directions each time at the juncture of a set of leaves. The flowers have five petals that are cleft so they appear to have ten petals. Chickweed is forageable in spring and fall but can't bear the heat and dies back in summer.

Parts Used: Aerial parts.

Folklore and Magic: Chickweed helps to foretell the weather, for it shall not rain for a day when the leaves fully unfurl.[31] It was considered good luck when grown in a pot outside the home in certain parts of England, and the dew that clung to the little leaves when washed onto the face would make one beautiful.[32] Carry a bit of dried chickweed in a pouch for luck.

Food and Medicine: This annual plant is often the first forageable plant people learn. One reason is that it tastes very mild and is palatable to those who detest all bitter flavors. This ubiquitous treat bedecked in tiny white starlike flowers is a delicious spring salad staple. Chickweed contains many minerals, including calcium, iron, magnesium, manganese, selenium, silica, sodium, phosphorus, potassium, and zinc. It also contains vitamin A, vitamin B_1, vitamin B_2, niacin, and vitamin C. Think of it like this: it has six times the amount of vitamin C, twelve times more calcium, and eighty-three times more iron than spinach. Wild plants have to fight to survive, unlike our garden vegetables, and the chemical compounds they use to deter insects and face the elements are also often good for us!

Chickweed is helpful for liver, kidney, and bladder issues due to its mineral-rich nature and promotion of urine flow: it's a diuretic. It is considered a cooling medicine. In Irish folk medicine, chickweed was used to make poultices for boils.[33] In Appalachian folk medicine, chickweed is a remedy for weight loss due to its diuretic action. It was also used as a cough and cold medicine in a tea by both Romani and Appalachians alike.

As a food, I love this plant almost best of all the wild greens. I say almost, because like a child, I cannot pick a favorite. These tender greens are mild and sweet, and when finely chopped, they make an excellent salad. I love the cooling, moist medicine they provide as food. I love to mix them with violet leaves and eat chickweed in the cool seasons when it is available. I use scissors to cut the tips off and avoid eating the dirty, yellowed older bits that hug the ground. I love to make a big mason jar of the tea from the freshly harvested leaves to give my system a blast of good minerals and green goodness. I prefer to blend my chickweed tea, though, and eat it! The best way to get the minerals out of both chickweed and the other mineral powerhouse, stinging nettle, is to actually ingest the tea. I like to blend my tea and drink the whole thing, leaves and all. You can also add it to bone broth or mushroom broth. Delicious and nourishing.

Cleavers, Sticky Willie, Goosegrass (*Galium aparine*)

Habitat: Native to Europe but now widely naturalized. Found on all continents except Antarctica. It thrives in a variety of habitats, from forest to field, and can survive in a range of temperatures.

Identification: Cleavers are hard to miss. Covered in small hooklike hairs that stick to you and feel like sandpaper. Hence the English name "sticky willie." The leaves grow in whorls, meaning they come out of the stem in a radial circle of six to eight leaves. There are many species, but none are toxic in small doses.

Parts Used: Aerial parts, during flowering, before going to seed.

Folklore and Magic: Indigenous Cowlitz women would bathe in it to attract love.[34] It was also used for love divinations in England, by throwing a wad of it onto a girl's back. If it stuck without her being aware of it, she had a sweetheart. If she took it off and dropped it, it would form the initial of the sweetheart-to-be.[35] The plant was also used to strain milk in cheese making, and the roots were used for a red dye. This plant is in the bedstraw family, and many of these long-stemmed plants were used in birthing beds historically and were sacred to mothers and the process of birth.

Food and Medicine: Cleavers get things moving. A long-standing tonic for the lymphatic system, it is traditionally taken in the spring to clear out any lingering toxins in the body; it can be made into tea or juiced. The water content in this lunar herb is very high, making it less suitable for tincturing in alcohol for long-term storage. Don't take your desire for spring cleaning too far though; more than one to two ounces of the green juice a day, and it becomes a purgative.[36] Whenever the lymph nodes are swollen, especially around the head and neck, it's time to call on cleavers. You can save your juice for later too with an ice cube tray! Just freeze servings of the juice for when you need a lymphatic pick me up or to run over a fresh sunburn for both the cold and the skin-healing property of the cleavers.

I finely chop cleavers and cook them up; mixed with other wild greens, they are lovely in a stir-fry. The texture is hard to swallow raw, so I think it's best blended, juiced, or cooked. I love the plant as a poultice too for boggy, wet, and hot infections of the skin. Cleavers are wonderful on infected splinters and other small skin issues where pus is present. Just begin by crushing the plant, dunking in hot (but not boiling) water, and mashing it with clean hands, making a warm poultice. I tape it on with medical tape and change it three times a day. *The tea is also helpful with urinary tract infections, but be careful not to take cleavers if you have cystitis or other overactive bladder issues.*

Dandelion (*Taraxacum officinale*)

Habitat: One of the most common plants in the US. Native to Eurasia, it has now naturalized throughout North America, southern Africa, South America, New Zealand, Australia, and India. It occurs in all 50 states of the US and most of Canada.

Identification: Dandelion has a few look-alikes, but looking for a few key identifying factors is paramount to telling them apart, with or without flowers. Dandelion grows in a rosette with golden yellow flowers coming out of a single stem with no branches. Dandelion has a hairless stem and yields a white latex from broken leaves and stems. The leaves are deeply toothed. Dandelion means "tooth of the lion," which is how I remember this identifying feature. The leaves also end in a point. Some people confuse cat's ear (*Hypochoeris radicata*) with dandelion, but cat's ear leaves are hairy, have a rounded point, and the flowers come out of branched stems.

Parts Used: Leaves, roots, flowers.

Folklore and Magic: Dandelions can bloom throughout the year, but their initial bursting forth with sunny yellow flowers in early spring has given them an association with the Irish and Scottish springtime goddess Brigid. In Scottish Gaelic, one of the names of dandelion is Bearnon Bride, Bride being a name for Brigid. To dream of dandelions, however, is a portent of misfortune.[37] The fluffy seeds that adorn the dandelion that so many of us were delighted by as children were also used in a variety of divinations from love to weather depending on the amount of seeds left after blowing upon the seed head. The direction the seeds fly could also be the direction to seek your fortune.[38] Dandelion wine is also apparently best made on May Day, or Beltane, May 1 in England.

Medicinally, Culpepper writes that dandelion has an "opening and cleansing quality. . . . It openeth passages."[39] One could read this as a purely medicinal and physical statement or see within it a message of portals opening. Perhaps then this plant of air can also be a tool in opening passages between the worlds and giving aid to one in spirit communication.

Its magical use goes back to Greece where John Evelyn, in his *Acetaria*[40], says of dandelion: "With thie homely salley, Hecate entertained Theseus." We can see "homely salley" to mean, "humble or homely salad." Hecate is considered the goddess of witches and crossroads, and one may honor her with offerings of dandelion wine and blossoms.

In the folk tradition of German Appalachians, there was a charm to ensure the holder always made the right decision. It involved taking a skunk cabbage leaf gathered in May under the sign of Leo, then wrapping it in a laurel leaf, adding a dandelion to it, and carrying it on your person.[41] Some people prefer to use the root of dandelion to make poppets and alrauna[42] for magical workings, instead of the rare, poisonous, and faraway mandrake.

Food and Medicine: This hated lawn invader should really be celebrated for its divine nutritional content. Lowly dandelion, we are not worthy. It is very high in dietary fiber, vitamin A, vitamin C, vitamin E (alpha-tocopherol), vitamin K, thiamin, riboflavin, vitamin B_6, calcium, iron, potassium, and manganese, just to name a few.[43] The roots are also edible when young and can be diced and spiced in the stir-fry pan. They are rich in inulin, a prebiotic that aids gut health. The flowers and leaves can be eaten raw or cooked. I like to batter and fry the flowers in my favorite pancake batter to make dandelion flower fritters and dip them in honey.

Easy to find and ubiquitous, the roots are also excellent as a liver support tea and taste delicious toasted as a caffeine-free, coffee-like beverage. They were included in the traditional bitter herbs dishes during Passover, and the leaves have long been savored as a good and nourishing, if not bitter, food. Dandelion has long been used as a bitter liver tonic and diuretic for ages. I like dandelion leaf and root tea when I am focusing on my liver health. I got sober from alcohol five years ago and healing my liver is a big concern of mine.

Dandelion stimulates bile production and aids digestion. In England and other parts of Europe, dandelion was used to treat fevers, boils, eye problems, diarrhea, fluid retention, liver congestion, heartburn, and skin ailments. The white latex was used in British folk medicine to cure warts. As a powerful diuretic, it also earned the folk name "pissabeds" and was believed to cause children to wet the bed by so much as touching it. The leaves were used in Scotland and Ireland to treat stings, much like plantain and dock leaves. The leaves were also eaten in bread and butter sandwiches and believed to be an ulcer cure. It is also interesting to note that in Ireland, it was believed to be heart medicine, a uniquely Irish folk belief.

In North America, dandelion wine was used and drunk hot as a cure for colds. In Pennsylvania, a cough syrup was reputedly made from lemon, sugar, and the blossoms. In Appalachia, chickweed and dandelion leaves were cooked together, the resulting liquid mixed with vinegar and drunk as a tonic. The root can also be roasted in the oven on low heat and brewed into a fine coffee substitute. Just as with cleavers, avoid drinking lots of dandelion tea if you have bladder issues like cystitis.

Its unyielding and wild spreading has a comforting anarchy that bothers the suburbanite and delights those who watch things crumble from the shadowy hills, laughing bitterly as people attempt to destroy that which can help and heal them. It is a witch's ally through and through.

Elderberry (*Sambucus* spp.)

European black elder (*Sambucus nigra*), and American elder (*S. canadensis*) are the two most common species used for magic and medicine.

Habitat: Elder grows throughout North America, from Canada to Florida and west to Arizona and Texas. Elder can be found on the edges of fields and in the forest. I often see them on roadsides.

Identification: Elder is not so much a tree as a shrub. American elder has branching stems covered in a rough gray bark containing a large, spongy pith. The branches and leaf-stalks are very smooth, with opposite, pinnate, smooth leaves that grow in groups of five to nine. The flowers are small, white, and grow in loose cymes. They have a narrow groove that runs along the top of their leaf stem.

Parts Used: Flowers and berries.

Folklore and Magic: Few trees have as much lore surrounding them as the elder, and we could write a whole book on it alone. There are beliefs all around Europe that a spirit inhabits the tree. In Latvia, it is the Priskaitis who lived under an elder. In Denmark, it is the Hyldemoer, or elder-mother, who lives within the tree, waiting to avenge all injuries done to her.[44] Elder is a Midsummer plant and blooms in early summer, dotting the roadside with creamy, lacy blossoms. Merely stand under the tree on Midsummer to see Toly, the king of elves, and his procession. Interestingly enough, on the Isle of Man, an elder tree outside the cottage door was thought to keep witches away. It is at once food, medicine, and poison, the green parts of the plant being toxic, unripe berries included. If one was going to cut an elder, permission had to be asked. I've adapted a rhyme to ask, based on a German saying:

> Elder tree, elder tree won't you give some wood to me,
> and when I'm a tree too, I will give my wood to you.[45]

Elder was powerfully protective and hung above doors and windows to protect houses in England. Fairies were said to live in elder trees and were planted near houses to protect them as well. If a twig of elder was planted on a grave and grew, it was a sign that the dead person was happy.[46] Elder was protective, but it was a tree to be cautious of in folklore. Elder wood was never to be burned, and in some places bringing the flowers in the house was deemed unlucky, for they were believed to attract snakes.[47] In Sweden, milk was sacrificed at the base of the "house" elder, or elder planted near the home, as an offering to the household spirits dwelling there.[48]

Food and Medicine: Elderberry has been used for mead and wine making and as a preserve; the berries can also be used in pies. Elderflowers are lovely as cordials or as a tea. Paired with peppermint and yarrow, elderflowers make an excellent tea for hay fever and influenza.[49] Hot elderflower tea has been a folk remedy for colds in many traditions. Cherokees used elderberry teas and strong infusions for rheumatism, and elderflower tea as a diaphoretic.[50] Elderberries are often enjoyed as a medicinal syrup for the flu as well. There is much scientific and historical evidence of the efficacy of elderberries for influenza and as an immune stimulator.[51]

I like to use elderflower tea for colds and take elderberry syrup at the first inklings of the flu. The hot tea is diaphoretic and brings on a sweat. This also makes elderflower a great fever medicine. Elderberry does not build up the immune system so much as to provide help when illness is already underway.

Caution: Raw elderberries, leaves, twigs, branches, seeds, and roots contain cyanide-inducing glycosides, which are toxic in large doses. Do not eat raw berries or use them for medicine. Boiling or cooking destroys these compounds.

Goldenrod (*Solidago* spp.)

There are many species and all are useful! One of the most common is Canada goldenrod, *S. canadensis*, but there are 100 to 120 species.

Habitat: Goldenrod seems to be able to grow just about anywhere, which is one reason it is considered invasive in some places, even though many types are native. It grows in almost every state in the US and many parts of Canada in fields, on roadsides, and in wayward places as it can tolerate a wide variety of soil types and climates.

Identification: The lanceolate leaves are two to five inches long and have fine hairs on them. I rub them between my fingers and feel the sandpapery texture. They also have shallow teeth running along the margins, or the leaf's edge. They grow tall and erect and often droop at the weight of their many small, bright yellow flowers. I also find the leaves (when crushed) smell almost of carrots.

Parts Used: Flowering tops, leaves.

Folklore and Magic: In New Hampshire it was believed that carrying one of the galls in your pocket would prevent rheumatism. These so-called rheumaty-buds were only effective while the grub inside them was still alive. Once the grub died you would need to get another gall. (It seems kind of cruel to carry these grubs around just so they could die, but I don't think 19th-century rural folk were too concerned with the pain and suffering of insects.) I'm guessing the galls were considered effective against rheumatism because they resemble the swollen joints arthritis sometimes causes. It was once believed that if it suddenly appeared growing outside your front door, good luck would soon be coming your way. Goldenrod was also a valuable dye plant used by American colonists and home dyers in the 18th and 19th centuries. The Latin name for goldenrod is *Solidago*, which means "whole," and is thought to be a reference to its reputed healing powers. It is also known as woundwort for this reason.

Abundant goldenrod is thought to indicate the source of a hidden spring (or hidden treasure). It's also considered a sign of prosperity. In English folk belief, goldenrod will point the way towards buried gold and silver. People once used goldenrod to find water, believing that wherever it grew, a hidden spring was nearby.[52] In the US, farmer's wisdom says that when you see the first goldenrod blooms, you can expect a frost in six weeks. This flower is a symbol of wealth and good fortune. Some say that if goldenrod starts growing near your home, your family will have a run of unexpected good luck! Wear a piece of goldenrod and you will see your lover tomorrow.[53] As with elderflowers, there is also a belief that it was unlucky to take indoors.

Food and Medicine: Goldenrod is edible, medicinal, and of course, magical. Despite its many uses, it has a bad rap as an allergen, when in fact, its friend the ragweed (*Ambrosia* spp.) is the culprit. The pollen of goldenrod is too heavy and sticky to become airborne and affect us allergic humans, and it is this stickiness that causes insects to be the main purveyors of this weighty pollen. This does not mean no one is allergic to goldenrod, topically or internally, as anything can cause a reaction, but the story that goldenrod is responsible for the streaming eyes and noses of people with fall allergies is not so!

Tea from goldenrod leaves and flowers has been used for a wide variety of medicinal purposes by Indigenous people around the Americas, with large emphasis on its uses as a kidney and bladder medicine due to the yellow color of the flowers. Goldenrod is ideal for old wounds and is slow to heal sores. According to Hieronymus Bock, ancient Germanic tribes considered this plant, which they called woundwort, a most valuable wound herb. The Latin name Solidago means "whole," which most likely refers to its healing properties. Others say it comes from the phrase *in solidum ago vulnera*, or "I consolidate wounds." In Scotland it was used especially for broken bones. It was also commonly used as a tea made of the leaves and flowers in African American folk medicine for fever and chills.

I like to make goldenrod vinegar for a few reasons. It's a nice way to utilize the nutritional compounds in goldenrod, like the high vitamin A content without the harsh application of alcohol or heat. I also like to combine the powers of goldenrod and apple cider vinegar together for urinary tract infections. I use two tablespoons of this vinegar in a quart of water at the first sign of a UTI. Here is how I make it:

I chop a big head of flowering goldenrod, gathered near Lammas when it is blooming, and fill a quart jar loosely. I cover it in good organic apple cider vinegar with the mother and cover with a plastic lid. Metal lids and vinegar don't mix—it will eat right through! I let this sit about four weeks out of direct sunlight and strain. I like to mix this yellow vinegar into salad dressings and marinades for the Lammas feast table, or add two tablespoons of it to a glass of water for urinary tract infections. I will drink up to three glasses of this a day when I'm struggling with one, and it does the job great! I like to drink lots of clear water between the vinegared water to move everything through. Goldenrod leaves and flowers are also edible, and I love to make goldenrod cornbread by removing a quarter cup of flour from my favorite recipe and substituting finely chopped flowers. A good stir and bake as normal yields a harvest season treat that is almost too pretty to eat. Goldenrod always makes me smile in the way that they mark the turning of the Wheel, for when they bloom, I know autumn is soon coming.

Mugwort (*Artemisia vulgaris*)

Habitat: Mugwort is native to temperate Europe, Asia, North Africa, and Alaska, but is now naturalized worldwide and considered an invasive weed in the eastern US.

Identification: It is characterized by its tall stature despite being a shrub, and its angular, sometimes purplish-hued stems that have many smooth, dark green leaves with somewhat irregularly serrated edges, covered with fine, silvery down on the bottom. The plant is strongly scented when crushed.

Parts Used: All aboveground portions.

Folklore and Magic: Mugwort has been known by many names: mugwort, on foot, felon herb, St. John's herb, moxa, cingulum sancti Johannis, motherwort, cronewort, artimisia, witch herb, old man, old Uncle Harry, muggons, sailors' tobacco, smotherwort, maiden wort, and muggins. It has been used since the Iron Age by humans for food, medicine, and magic. Mugwort was once called the mater herbarum in early Europe, or the "mother of all herbs" in the Salernitan herbals, as well as by the infamous herbalist Culpeper. Some say it got its name from flavoring drinks, hence the word mug, and others say it in fact comes from its use in repelling moths, or the Old English moughte, as it was strewn about in clothes and used as insecticide. Mugwort is one of the most significant plants in Germanic pagan practice (especially as a ritual incense plant, and fresh bundles were stroked over the sick then burned to dispel disease-causing spirits). A plant sacred to Midsummer, it is also an herb of Saint John.

On Samhain, or Halloween, Germanic women would go out "flying" by fumigating or rubbing their bodies with mugwort. Legend has it that they would then kill a goose to honor Frau Holle and mix the goose fat and "flying herbs" together for a nocturnal, astral journey.[54] Mugwort is associated with dreaming and the moon in modern magical practices. Because of this association with the dream world and between states, it is used as a wash for divination tools, especially crystal balls and other gazing instruments. It is said that placing it sewn up in a pillow beneath the head at night will grant the sleeper remembrance of their dreams upon waking. Mugwort was not only used in European folk medicine and magic but also in Chinese medicine, in which it is known as moxa. Moxibustion is the process of burning specially processed mugwort near the skin in alignment with acupuncture for a variety of health issues.[55]

Mugwort is my favorite incense herb to wildcraft. It is both a traditional European incense herb and, as mentioned before, a long-time repellent of evil and disease. It is an excellent fumitory, or burning herb, and is a wonderful alternative to white sage as a smudge, which has issues of both cultural appropriation of Indigenous smudge practices and is damaging wild plant populations with overharvest due to increased demand. It is good to make sure as we seek connection with the land that we do so with the knowledge and understanding of who it affects and how.

Food and Medicine: Mugwort has a long history as a brewing herb and was used in beer brewing from the early Iron Age or 500 BCE onward. Mugwort remains have been found at Eberdingen-Hochdorf in Germany alongside charred barley, henbane seeds, and carrot seeds. These may have added more psychedelic, intoxicating effects to their brews. Mugwort was also added to beer in medieval times, most likely as a seed. Gruitbier was, in its time, some 500 to 1,000 years ago, clearly the most common beer style in the world. *Gruit* is old German for "herbs," which is what most medieval brewers used to flavor their beers before hops became a universal beer-flavoring agent starting around the 15th century.[56]

I like to make wild herbal sodas with mugwort for use in ritual preparation or celebrations in our witching community. The bitter, perfume-like taste is beautiful paired with local honey and dandelion flowers or roses. Mugwort has long been associated with the moon and identified as a woman's herb. Hildegard von Bingen, Paracelsus, and Culpeper, as well as many other Renaissance-era herbalists, speak of it almost exclusively as a female remedy. Today it is still considered a uterine stimulant, emmenagogue, and spasmodic among many other uses. It was often used as a poultice, or mash of leaves in hot water, on the stomach of a laboring mother in folk medicine. It was also drunk as a tea and given as a footbath to promote easy birth.[57]

This silvery, soft plant does have a bit of a bite to it just as its toothy leaves suggest. It contains thujone, a menthol-scented monoterpene. It is often blamed as the guilty constituent in wormwood, mugwort's cousin, that caused the madness associated with old absinthe recipes. However, mugwort is generally considered the gentlest of the Artemesias and contains small amounts that make it safe to take in small doses, so long as it is not for too long. It is not safe to take during pregnancy or while nursing or for long periods of time.

Mullein (*Verbascum thapsus*)

Habitat: It was brought here from Europe and Asia where it originated. Now commonly found in zones 3 to 9 worldwide.

Identification: Mullein is a biennial. The first year it grows in a beautiful reset of large, very velvety, fuzzy leaves with no serrations. The second year it sends up a tall stalk, sometimes five or more feet high, with bright yellow flowers, almost like a torch in the distance.

Parts Used: Leaves, roots, and blooms.

Folklore and Magic: Mullein is also known by some as hag's tapers, flannel leaf, and Aaron's rod. The bright yellow flowers glow with the power of the sun, and the soft leaves are an excellent remedy for many a skin and musculoskeletal condition. This is what gives it its Saturn alignment. Burn mullein along with mugwort in your Midsummer balefire for protection. In Ireland, ashes of fires with certain herbs, or from certain days, were gathered for use in charms. Gather the ashes of mullein to use in protection and healing charms throughout the year.

Mullein was a key ingredient in folk magic as well in Appalachia, just as it was in Europe. If you bent a stick of mullein towards the house of the one you fancied, you could tell if they felt the same way about you by checking in a

To Make a Mullein Leaf Candle
for Necromantic Works

Take a single mullein leaf and when it is dry but not terribly crispy, roll it gently into a long tube. Dip this into beeswax or tallow and light it. I stand them in sand in a fireproof bowl, like my cast-iron cauldron. They are smoky, but the light and flame are lovely. Use these in rites of the dark year or for spirit work.

To Make a Hag Taper

Gather entire dried stalks and dip or brush with tallow or wax. Stand these in the same manner as mentioned above, or drive into the ground (away from flammables) and watch carefully. As All Hallows approaches, imagine your harvest rites lit by grand torches. It has quite an effect, I think.

few days to see if it had grown up straight again. If it was standing tall again, your true love loved you back; if it was dead, well, you get the picture.[58] In the Ozarks it goes a little different. If the mullein bends towards a person's house, the one who tends the mullein loves them. Mullein is also a powerful protector, according to the Anglo-Saxons. In the Anglo-Saxon version of Apuleius translated by Cockayne: "If one beareth with him one twig of this wort, he will not be terrified with any awe, nor will a wild beast hurt him, or any evil coming near."[59]

In Germany the Himmelbrand (heavenly fire), or Konigskerze (king's candle) was used during the rites of harvest times. In the Middle Ages it was said that Mary herself traveled through the land this time of year blessing all the mullein. This is where another name for it, Our Lady's Candle, comes from. A saying arose from this as well· "Our beloved Lady goes through the land, she carries mullein in her hand!" It was even said sometimes she touched the sick with the wand of mullein and healed them. From the excellent book *Witchcraft Medicine* we get the ritual involved in picking the mullein and other herbs for use in the rites of this time of the year.

The herbs for the August festival (Lammas) must be picked before sunrise by women who are barefoot, speaking the charms, silently and naked, without being seen and without thinking any thought. Never cut with an iron knife or dig with an iron spade, for it would take away the herb's power. According to Frazer in *The Golden Bough*, it was passed through the Midsummer fire to make a charm to protect the cattle herd. It was also placed in butter churns in Ireland if the butter would not come.[60] Mullein is so useful it has gained a host of astrological associations. Culpepper ascribed it to the influence of Saturn, Agrippa said it was under Mercury, Junius gave it Jupiter, but today many give it to the sun for its merry yellow flowers.

Food and Medicine: Some say it traveled with the Puritans for use in the physic gardens of the New World. This garden escapee quickly naturalized throughout North America and entered the folk medicine and magical systems of peoples across this land. It was mullein's usefulness in medicine that made it so popular. This plant was used to treat many things, but overwhelmingly it was used to treat respiratory illnesses and colds. The leaves were smoked or made into a tea, often sweetened with honey. This practice can be seen in many places worldwide and in America from the Ozarks to Appalachia, and even all the way to Canada.[61] Though often considered a gentle medicine, it was used in more serious respiratory conditions like tuberculosis (or consumption, as it was called, due to the way it consumed you).

In Appalachia it was one of the most popular plants used in herbal medicine. It was chewed, smoked, and made into tea for all manner of lung ailments including TB. It was eventually incorporated into the medical practices of Indigenous peoples in the area as well as the African American folk medicine lexicon. Sometimes it was mixed with brown sugar and wild cherry bark or rabbit tobacco and horehound for coughs. Salt and mullein tea was used to bathe swollen body parts, and the leaves themselves were bound around limbs to reduce swelling in injuries. Whooping cough and malaria also called for mullein. It doesn't seem like there was much mullein couldn't soothe.[62]

I used the roots of mullein for a stubborn bladder infection with much success. The root decoction was used in Appalachia for this purpose, and I had never heard of this use before. After doing some research, I tried it on myself, and I was pleased with it all around. I chopped a ¼ cup of root, steeped it for 15 minutes in a mason jar, and drank the tea throughout the day. By the following morning my urgency to urinate, pain, and awareness of the discomfort I had been feeling had passed. I did it for one more day after to ensure it was really passed. This is one of the reasons I love folk medicine, for that week I also lost my health insurance, and I was able to provide for myself by looking into the wisdom of the people who lived here before. I harvested this mullein from the land and made it fresh. Bless this land. Bless these herbs.

Plantain (*Plantago major, P. lanceolata, P. rugelii*)

Habitat: Plantain prefers the waste places. Compacted, poor soil; roadsides; and along places where foot traffic is heavy and soil disturbance is recent. It now grows worldwide.

Identification: Broadleaf plantain (*P. major*) has broad, oval shaped leaves with parallel veins that grow in a basal rosette. They put up a remarkable seed stalk with a long narrow stem, topped by a seed head of many seeds. The thick stems, when broken, reveal strings much like celery. Blackseed plantain (*P. rugelii*) looks much like a taller version of broadleaf plantain but with purple stems where the stem meets the leaf. Ribwort plantain (*P. lanceolata*), or narrowleaf plantain, also has parallel veins but is much narrower, and the leaves end in a point.

Parts Used: Leaves and seeds.

Folklore and Magic: Plantain is an iconic herb. It can get confusing, as it shares a name with the relative of the banana, but alas! It is a humble, low-growing herb. The Plantago species have been used around the world for wounds, burns, ulcers and to stop bleeding, to absorb infection, and to generally treat the nasty sorts of things that can happen to a body. Norwegians and Swedes call this plant *groblad*, which can be translated as "healing leaves." Crushed fresh leaves and juice applied directly to wounds is mentioned as an effective cure in the ethnobotany of many countries and cultures from Russia to India.

Through its long history of use worldwide, as well as information gathered from the many studies done upon these plants, we know the crushed leaves have styptic, antioxidant, antimicrobial, antifungal, antibacterial, analgesic, anti-inflammatory, antiviral, and immunomodulation benefits, just to name a few. We can see from the pollen record that broadleaf plantain (*P. major*) entered the Nordic lands around 4,000 years ago and, from Europe, spread almost worldwide.

Romeo and Juliet (Act I, Scene 2):
> **Benvolio:** Take thou some new infection to thy eye,
> And the rank poison of the old will die.
> **Romeo:** Your plantain leaf is excellent for that.
> **Benvolio:** For what, I pray thee?
> **Romeo:** For your broken skin.[63]

The time of Shakespeare seems like a long time ago now, but plants in the *Plantago* genus have been used as medicine for a long, long time by people all over the world. The *Plantago* genus has 275 species worldwide, which, as we'll see, was used for everything.

Plantain has been used in a variety of magics, especially those of Midsummer. In French folklore, it is said to disorient the wits. If you pick nine flowers or the leaf of plantain and put it under the pillow, you will dream of your future spouse on Midsummer Eve. Magically, the seed stalks were used in love divinations. People throughout Western Europe would strip the stalks of flowers and if the next day some still persisted, it meant the prospect of a marriage was good. Much like mullein, the stalks were also bent or broken, and if they grew back or upright, it meant your true love returned your affections. When children in Cheshire, England, see the first plantain stalk they say this rhyme for good luck: "Chimney sweeper all in black, go to the brooke and wash your back, wash it clean or wash it none, Chimney sweeper have you done?"[64]

Everywhere Europeans went, it followed (sort of like a plant marker of European colonization). This is one of the reasons certain Indigenous peoples in North America came to call it the "White man's footprint," or more specifically, "Englishman's footprint."[65] Sometimes I think of this fact when I look upon *P. major*, but I can't blame this plant for the terrible things done by my ancestors. It more than makes up for this association with its ready availability, ease of harvest, and amazing medicine and food. I want things to be right and wrong, good and evil. It's simpler that way. But it is never that way. Things are almost always nuanced and complex.

Food and Medicine: Plantain is mentioned throughout the world in medical writings from Greece to medieval Islamic Spain: it was used as crushed whole leaves or mixed with honey for wounds. It was believed it could heal any organ in the human body when boiled in butter and eaten. I cannot argue against adding butter to everything to make it better. One of the herbs mentioned in the Nine Herbs Charm from the 10th century, it was gathered from Anglo-Saxon England and used to treat infection and poisoning. Plantain was known as weybroed or waybread. Culpeper said in his *Complete Herbal* (1649) that plantain is under the planet Venus.

More people in the herb world are finally having conversations today about the lack of visibility around the specific Indigenous medicines shared with colonists and especially the contributions of African and Caribbean people's knowledge and plant uses to herbalism in general. In the South I see this is especially present. If people weren't able to use their native plants, some of which they did still have access to, they were still pioneering and adapting their own healing knowledge base and using what was around them. It is always important to note that folk medicine is not a stuck or static practice, but rather it is constantly evolving and changing.

Plantain is sometimes known as snakeroot or snakeweed and was used by Appalachians and people of the Deep South of all races for snakebite. And it was an African slave named Caesar who discovered this use and how to best fix it. It was so effective he was remarkably rewarded for his discovery and was set free by the South Carolina General Assembly in 1750 and allotted £100 per year for the duration of his life. Something almost unheard of. And here is the healer Caesar's cure:

> Take the Roots of plantain and hoarhound fresh or dried 3 ounces boil them together in two quarts of water to one quart and strain it of this decoction let the patient take one third part three mornings fasting successively, from which if he finds any relief it must be continued till he is perfectly recovered; on the Contrary if he finds no Alteration after the first dose it is a sign that the patient has either not been poisoned at all, or that it is such a poison as Cesars antidotes will not Remedy (so may leave off the decoction).[66]

Plantain is clearly a medicine to celebrate. It's also a food to celebrate! Rich in vitamins C, K_1, and carotenoids, this plant has edible leaves, seed stalks, and seeds. In early spring, add some fresh young leaves to salads or sautés and enjoy. My favorite thing to do with tougher older leaves is to do a quick fry in coconut oil or lard and make plantain chips. Like kale chips with a slightly different texture. Crunchy and amazing. It is also interesting to note that the leaves are low in oxalic acid, which can be irritating to some people with kidney stones or certain autoimmune conditions.

Pine (*Pinus* spp.)

Remember that sometimes tree names include the word *pine*, but they are not actually in the *Pinus* genus. Norfolk Island pine (*Araucaria heterophylla*) and yew pine (*Podocarpus macrophyllus*) are some of the few toxic trees. This is a great reminder to always be doubly sure before harvesting any new plant or tree for consumption.

Habitat: Pine species grow all over the world! There are more than 125 species that can grow in wet, dry, maritime, and rocky conditions!

Identification: Most trees known as pines, spruces, and firs are somewhat edible and medicinal. However, the ponderosa (*Pinus ponderosa*), Monterey (*Pinus* *radiata*), and lodgepole pine (*Pinus contorta v. latifolia*) are reported to be toxic but mainly to livestock. Always be 100 percent sure of what pine species you are foraging and avoid them if pregnant or breastfeeding.

Pine trees (*Pinus* spp.) have needles that are bundled in clusters called fascicles of one to seven. Most species have two to five. The needles and branches grow in a spiral pattern.

Fir trees (*Abies* spp.) have short needles that are attached to their branch with what looks like a suction cup. The needles are soft and usually have two white lines on the underside. Fir needles sometimes point upwards, like their cones. I remember "frisky fir" and "saggy spruce" to help me remember who is who! Spruce's cones hang downwards.

Spruce trees (*Picea* spp.) have square, four-sided needles that leave behind a small woody peg when removed. Many spruces have stiff, pointy needles that grow all the way around their branches. They are painful to grab and quite sharp!

Parts Used: Resin, needles, cones.

Folklore and Magic: Pine trees of all species are some of the most abundant sources of magic and medicine one can forage. In some traditions they contain imprisoned spirits that moan as the trees sway in the wind. Pine cones have been used in ancient Rome to worship Venus; in Japan, the pine drives away demons. In Appalachia, they placed the tops of pine trees under the beds of sick people; simply being in the room with them was healing.

At winter solstice, we know the pine family as the emblematic Christmas tree, or to us, the solstice tree. It is difficult to tell exactly where this practice comes from, but it could be a melding of pagan and Christian beliefs: the old Roman custom of decorating houses with laurels and green trees at the Kalends of January, and the Christian belief that every Christmas Eve, apple and other trees blossomed and bore fruit. This Christian belief stems from the legend of St. Joseph of Arimathea. When the saint settled at Glastonbury in England he planted his staff in the earth, and it put forth leaves and blossomed every Christmas Eve.

We know from Libanius, Tertullian, and Chrysostom that Romans decorated with evergreens. Tertullian lets us know of his distaste for this pagan practice when he says the following:

"Let them," he says of the heathen, "kindle lamps, they who have no light; let them fix on the doorposts laurels which shall afterwards be burnt, they for whom fire is close at hand; meet for them are testimonies of darkness and auguries of punishment. But thou," he says to the Christian, "art a light of the world and a tree that is evergreen; if thou hast renounced temples, make not a temple of thy own house-door."[67]

It was also said the Druids decorated their huts with evergreens during winter as a winter home for the sylvan spirits. It is Germany, however, that is often credited for popularizing the practice of keeping a Christmas tree as we know it today. The Lutherans are specifically credited with decorating them and keeping them as we know now. They were the height of fashion by the 19th century and were vastly popular in North America, Austria, Switzerland, Poland, and the Netherlands.[68]

In Appalachia, it is said that the pine trees minister to a diseased mind. This spirit lifting accompanied by pine is further reason to bring some greenery inside. Further magic has been attributed to it, for in Bohemia it was thought that eating pine nuts could make one shot proof. In Germany, the pine is said to bear children, for from every hole a wood spirit may escape into the outer world, and sometimes, she may even become something like a human woman. In Christian mythology, Mary rested beneath a pine in her flight and took refuge in its sweet balsam fragrance. If you find a hairpin and hang it on a pine tree, you will have a letter by the next mail. Pine is also useful for driving away restless spirits.[69] If there are any envious neighbors about, you can also wipe some soft pine needles on a child's face to remove the evil eye.[70]

Due to the cleansing nature of pine, both spiritually and physically, I love to use resin from pine and spruce species that have been cut or knocked down in storms to make my own locally sourced, non-appropriative incense. It is a messy process, so be warned! I like to take a small pint mason jar with me and a butter knife coated in a little bit of olive oil (oil your hands and the knife first to prevent a mess). Use the oiled knife to scrape the dripping resin from a wounded tree. Make sure not to further damage the tree in your harvest and only take what is already on the outside of the bark—don't cut it deeply and make it bleed more. I also often find chunks of resin on the ground or coursing down the side of a tree—these are great bits to harvest as they are no longer directly covering the wound, like a scab. Allow them to dry and age for a few months before burning and use them just as you would copal or frankincense, on a coal.

Food and Medicine: All of these trees can be used to make tea, but some are more tasty than others. I focus on white pine, as it is abundant, easily identified, and delicious. Pine can be used as a medicine for a variety of ailments, but it is best known for its vitamin C content. First Nations people of many tribes harvested pine nuts, used needles of pine, fir, and spruce for teas, and chewed their resin and sap. Colonists also used their wisdom to avoid scurvy (a deadly condition from lack of vitamin C). Many conifers also contain vitamins B, A, iron, and a slew of minerals, antioxidants and flavonoids, antiinflammatory, cardiovascular-protecting, and triglyceride-reducing properties as well. Conifer needles are a great source of polyphenols that stimulate the immune system and have anti-stress, adaptogenic, and antiviral properties, making them great for colds and flu.

Make a pine sun tea by finding some conifers near you that are not sprayed and snipping a handful of needles. Finely chop them and place in a clean mason jar and fill with water. Set this jar in a sunny window and let the power of the sun infuse this vitamin C–rich beverage for you. This water can also be used in solar workings of magic and as a cleanser of spaces much like holy water. Aside from tea, you can also make infused vinegars, salts, salves, perfumes, syrups, sugars, and liquors from pine.

Violet (*Viola* spp.)

Wild violets are not the same as African violets (*Saintpaulias* spp.). African violet is neither edible nor a violet.

Habitat: They can be found in rich, shady, wooded areas. Most species are found in the temperate Northern Hemisphere. They do have a few divergent locales, however, namely Hawaii, Australasia, and the Andes.

Identification: Violet is one of 525 to 600 species in the Violaceae family, all of which are edible. My favorites are *Viola odorata* and *Viola sororia*. Violets grow low to the ground and never get very tall. They have a basal rosette of heart-shaped leaves with toothed edges and drooping flowers that do not produce seeds. I always remember violets because their teeth all point downwards towards the point of the leaf: "Violet gets to the point." Their flowers have five petals; four are upswept or fan-shaped with two per side, and there is one broad, lobed lower petal pointing downwards. This petal may be slightly or much shorter than the others, and in some species, has small stripes.[71]

Parts Used: Leaves and flowers. The roots are strongly purgative.

Folklore and Magic: Strangely enough, the happy purple, yellow, and white flowers are often associated with death in old plant lore, as well as constancy and innocence. This may have to do with the ancient Roman practice of strewing violets on the graves of the very young. This association with death continued in the use of the roots as a scrying incense to enter the spirit world.[72]

Hamlet displays this play between hope and loss when Ophelia tells Laertes that the violets themselves have died of grief: "I would give you some violets, but they withered all when my father died."

Violets remind us that even in death there is a promise of birth, even in destruction there is a promise of growth. Despite violets' association with mourning, to dream of them is thought in many countries to be a herald of good luck. When I see them in large clumps, as they tend to grow, I feel the robust abundance of their medicine, food, and magic, as if unseen eyes are watching me from some dark place and whispering, "We have all you need, take care, o take care."

From the infamous Madame Grieve we know violets were even mentioned by Homer and Virgil. They were used by the Athenians "to moderate anger," to procure sleep, and "to comfort and strengthen the heart."[73] Interestingly enough, in Macer's herbal (10th century), the violet is among the many herbs that were considered powerful against "wykked sperytis." (Wicked spirits, for those of us unfamiliar with 10th-century creative spelling.) In rural Germany, they decked the bridal bed and cradles of girl children with violets—this was done by Celts and Greeks as well. According to Culpeper, this plant is ruled by Venus and can also be employed in all magical workings of love and the heart, especially where the passions have cooled and a long-lasting love is growing.

Use the powdered leaf of violet in your charm bags against evil, from both the dead and the living. The root is strongly purgative and laxative due to its alkaloid content, so do not ingest it as most species cause nausea and vomiting. However, the somewhat robust roots can be used for alraun magic or fetishes for love work. The violet's association with death, especially of the young, make it a fine root to work with in necromantic or ghostly endeavors when dealing with the spirits of departed children.

Food and Medicine: This beautiful, common wildflower has edible leaves and flowers. With over 400 species, it's great to know that they are all edible. Famous old-school forager Euell Gibbons found per 100 grams, fresh leaves contain 210 milligrams of vitamin C, which is four-and-a-half times more than oranges, and 8,258 IU (international units) of provitamin A. More recent analysis shows that if collected in spring, this early research reported that violets contain twice as much vitamin C as the same weight of orange and more than twice the amount of vitamin A, gram for gram, when compared with spinach.[74] One recent study concluded that an aqueous *Viola* extract (i.e., tincture) inhibited the proliferation of activated lymphocytes as well as negatively affected other hyper-responsive immune functions. This indicates that violets may be useful in the therapy of disorders related to an overactive immune system.[75] Violet leaves contain a good bit of mucilage, or soluble fiber, and thus are helpful in lowering cholesterol levels. Soluble fiber is also helpful in restoring healthy populations of intestinal flora, as beneficial bacteria feed off of this type of fiber.

The leaves are high in rutin, which is a glycoside of the flavonoid quercetin. Rutin has been shown in animal and in in vitro studies to be antioxidant, anti-inflammatory, and blood thinning. Many foods that are high in rutin, such as buckwheat (*Fagopyrum esculentum*), are eaten traditionally as a remedy for hemorrhoids and varicose veins.

In the Middle Ages we can see the great association of violet with the heart through its folk name "heartease." The little heart-shaped leaves could be seen through the doctrine of signatures to bring joy and settle an unquiet heart. It was not just used to gladden, though—this gentle plant also has been used externally for serious ailments of the skin. Leaf plasters were also used on nasty wounds and boils historically. This cooling, moistening plant is perfect for such applications. I like to make a cup of violet leaf and flower tea to settle anxiety that yields a fast beating heart by steeping a heaping tablespoon of the chopped herb in one cup of freshly boiled water for 10 minutes.

Yarrow (*Achillea millifolium*)

Habitat: Native to Europe and Asia but now has circumboreal distribution, with 140 species. Yarrow thrives in poor soil and is often ground among pasture grasses and along roadsides.

Identification: Yarrow is a hardy perennial and can reach about three feet in height when in flower. It has very aromatic, alternate, feathery leaves that give the plant a fernlike appearance. The flowers are densely bunched, small, and white.

Parts Used: Leaves and flowers.

Folklore and Magic: Yarrow has long been a tool of warriors and of lovers. Yarrow is very special in Scottish folk magic. The *Carmina Gadelica*, a compendium of folklore, songs, charms, and much more gathered at the end of the 19th century in Scotland recorded a few charms for gathering yarrow. One was a woman's incantation spoken when picking yarrow and goes as follows:

I will pick the smooth yarrow that my figure may be sweeter, that my lips may be warmer, that my voice may be gladder. May my voice be like a sunbeam; may my lips be like the juice of the strawberry. May I be an island in the sea; may I be a star in the dark time, may I be a staff to the weak one. I shall wound every man, and no man shall hurt me.[76]

Yarrow has a long history of use from ancient Greece and Rome, where it earned its Latin name, Achillea, from the legends of Achilles. In Greek mythology, Thetis bathed Achilles in yarrow, which gave the hero, Achilles, its protective powers to make him invincible wherever the liquid had touched his skin, save for his heel, which was never submerged. Achilles also healed his wounded soldiers with yarrow, a great styptic herb, the warrior's herb. The fae also have strong associations with this plant. It is disputed as to whether it repels or draws faeries, so take what you will. Yarrow is associated with the element of air, as it is aromatic. It is also useful in divination. I like to combine it with mugwort and chamomile as a tea and dream of things to come.

Historically, it was used for divining one's future lover or determining whether one is truly loved. In Appalachia it was stuffed up the nose to divine if one's true love reciprocated the sentiment: "Green yarrow, green yarrow, you bears white blow, If my love loves me my nose will bleed now."[77]

It was used in love sachets, because it is believed to be capable of keeping a couple together for seven years. It was also used protectively, much like mugwort, in England and to bring good luck to those who wear it when going courting. It was strewn across the threshold to keep out evil and worn in charms to protect against hexes. It was also tied to a child's cradle to protect it from those who might try to steal its soul. The Saxons wore amulets made of this plant to protect against blindness, robbers, and dogs. Northern Italians wear it as a talisman against ghosts.[78]

Food and Medicine: Yarrow is most loved for its wound healing medicine, but I also love to eat the small, young leaves in spring in salads and as a cooked green in small amounts. The leaves can be chewed and used as a spit poultice on stings, cuts, and burns. Yarrow is a styptic, meaning it helps to stop the flow of blood. I've used the dried leaves and flowers, ground into a powder and stored in a clean spice container, as dust on cuts to staunch the bleeding with great success many times.

Yarrow flowers and leaves are great as a tea for colds and respiratory congestion, and also make a great herbal steam along with rosemary and thyme to clear the sinuses. Yarrow tea is excellent for circulatory issues and as a blood tonic. I love yarrow for its drying abilities and also use it as a wash for inflamed tissues, especially vaginal, or for itchy skin from psoriasis. Yarrow is an excellent herb for menstrual issues as well, especially delayed, heavy menses. One of the most miraculous things about yarrow is that while considered a cooling herb by many, it is also stimulating. The pungent, almost minty smell and bitter taste remind us of the plethora of magical constituents that lie within this beautiful plant. I take one cup of the tea up to three times a day for fevers, colds, and infections.

IV

REMEDIES, SPELLS, RITUALS, AND THE WHEEL OF THE YEAR

Now you can use everything I've taught you and put it all into practice! In this section, I'll provide you with rituals, spells, and herbal remedies for the sabbats, or holidays, on the Wheel of the Year. The Wheel of the Year is the calendar of cyclical holidays we observe in modern Traditional Witchcraft that fall on either astrological occurrences (like the solstices and equinoxes) or are based on pre-Christian Irish agricultural holidays like Imbolc, Beltane, Lammas, and Samhain. I hope these recipes inspire you to look more deeply into the ways of the Old Ones and learn more about herbalism, wild foods, and pre-Christian practices in the place you dwell.

Before we begin, I want to remind you to always pay heed to our foraging rules: be 100 percent certain of plant identification before consuming them, and always respect the First Nations land we are on when working with plants of the bioregion. Never forget that we are all always learning, and it is always okay to ask for help. I know I am. I also want to provide us with some basic medicine-making practices before we jump in. So, first things first, let's start with tea.

Basic Folk Medicine Making

Tea

Aside from eating a plant whole, tea was most likely the first way in which humans used plants for medicine. Tea is essentially an infusion of plant matter in hot water. Teas are also called infusions in herbal literature. You can make tea from both fresh and dry herbs depending on what season it is and what you have on hand. This is how I make a basic herbal tea.

You Will Need:

- A mason jar of your choosing
- Freshly boiled water
- Strainers of multiple sizes

When choosing what herbs to make a tea or infusion with, it's important to note which part of the plant you are using. Delicate plant parts like leaves and flowers are great for tea since they are simply being infused in hot water and not boiled. Boiling herbs can damage the volatile oils and constituents that we want to make use of. Harder, tougher plant parts like stems, roots, and seeds are excellent for the next method of medicine making: decoctions or boiling herbs to make a stronger extract.

Measure out the herbs desired for your recipe. Most herbs have a recipe or recommended ratio of how much herb to add to a specific amount of water. Boil water and pour over your herbs. Steep for the recommended amount of time and strain out the herbs. Compost or discard them and enjoy the tea.

Decoction

Decoctions are boiled teas made from tougher plant parts like roots, stems, and seeds. Gently simmering these parts for 10 to 30 minutes is a great way to break down tough, woody plant material and unlock the constituents inside.

Plant parts like dandelion root, cinnamon bark, and cherry twigs are all great candidates for decocting. Just bring a quart of water to a boil, add the amount desired (usually two tablespoons to a quarter cup of plant materials), and simmer for 10 to 30 minutes. Strain and slightly cool before serving.

Tincture

Tinctures are herbal extracts made using water and alcohol. There are two general ways to make tinctures: the folk method and the weight-to-volume ratio method. Each one is more appropriate at different times depending on your end goal. Some plants are not suitable for making alcohol tinctures depending on their predominant chemical constituents. Marshmallow root, for example, is best made into a cold water infusion due to the fact that its most important plant chemicals are soluble in water but not soluble in alcohol. There are many solubility charts to look up this information in books on basic medicine making. Alcohol can extract phytochemicals like alkaloids, sugars, enzymes, essential oils, minerals, and vitamins.

If you are using a nutritive herb like calendula, chickweed, or cleavers that do not have intense action on the body, the folk method is a great way to make medicine. If you are making a tincture with an herb with intense actions and toxicity at certain dosages, like poke root (*Phytolacca americana*), for example, or an expensive or rare herb, taking the time to make a weight-to-volume tincture is a better choice. Using the specific recipes provided by the weight-to-volume ratio method is a great way to determine exacting dosages and ensure you get the most out of precious medicines.

The Folk Method

1. Wash and chop your fresh herbs or crumble your dry herbs into small pieces. The smaller you make the pieces, the more surface area is exposed to the alcohol, allowing more phytochemicals to be extracted into the tincture. With dry herbs, it's best to remove the leaves and flowers from the stems, as stems often contain little volatile oil.

2. Place the herbs in a clean, dry jar with a wide mouth. You will see why the wide mouth is key when it comes time to cleaning it later! Pour high-proof alcohol like vodka or grain alcohol over the herbs and cover it.

3. Seal it with a clean lid and place in a dark, dry place for four to six weeks to allow the herbs to infuse. Shake the jar every once in a while to help the herbs fully release their chemicals into the alcohol. Make sure the alcohol level does not go down, and if so, top it off with a fresh pour to prevent spoilage.

4. After four to six weeks, strain the herbs out with a strainer or cheesecloth, and squeeze or press out the excess tincture, ensuring you do not waste valuable medicine.

5. Place in tincture bottles or new, small, clean jars and label with the date, name of the herb, and the type of alcohol with the percentage. Store out of direct sunlight in a cool, dark place.

Tinctures can last for over a year when correctly prepared and stored.

6. With folk tinctures, adult dosages are typically 30 to 60 drops in a little water, taken three times a day, as long as it is a gentle herb with a low toxicity report.

Weight-to-Volume Ratio Method

This method is excellent for many reasons, with the most important being that you can be sure what the dosage is, which is vital when using strong medicinal plants. You can also reproduce a particular recipe more easily. Just remember that plants are not machines and are highly variable in their medicinal compound content, so some variation will occur naturally. When making a tincture there are a few terms that are helpful to know:

- **Marc:** Solid matter in a tincture; the plants.
- **Menstruum:** The liquid in a tincture.

You Will Need:

- Measuring cups and ounce liquid measures
- An herb scale
- Jars
- Sharp knife or blender

Weight-to-volume tinctures take two parts of medicine-making information into account: the ratio between the weight of the marc and the volume of the menstruum and the amounts of alcohol and water in the menstruum. When written, this looks like a ratio and a percent. For example, when we have one part marc to two parts menstruum in 75% alcohol and 25% water, that reads as 1:2 75%. This lets others know your recipe easily and quickly. In the ratio, the parts are often measured in ounces. However, unfortunately, liquid and solid measurements are different in ounces and that must be taken into account when making medicine.

Alcohol is a useful menstruum for many reasons. It both preserves the plant chemicals and breaks down plant cell walls to release their contents. More important, there are many herbal constituents, e.g., volatile and fixed oils, resins, and alkaloids that are not very soluble in water but which will dissolve in alcohol.

To make a 1:2 tincture, use one ounce of marc measured out on a scale for every two ounces of menstruum in a measuring cup (this is where those different ounce measurements must be taken into account). If you have more than one ounce of marc, multiply the weight of the marc by the second number in the ratio. For example:

- With 5 ounces of an herb at a 1:2 tincture,
  use 10 ounces of menstruum:
  - 2 × 5 = 10.
- With 5 ounces of an herb at a 1:3 tincture,
  use 15 ounces of menstruum:
  - 3 × 5 = 15.

Deciding what ratio to use can be confusing at first. I like to go by which plant part I am trying to make medicine from. In general, delicate plant parts like leaves and flowers will do great at a 1:2 to 1:3 ratio, while woody, fibrous roots and other hard plant parts do best at a 1:3 or 1:4 ratio.[1]

Salve

Any salve begins by first infusing an oil with the herbs of our choice, then making it solid with beeswax or candelilla wax if you would like a vegan salve.

Here are oils and fats commonly used in salves, which can be used alone or combined:

You Will Need:

- Extra virgin olive oil
- Jojoba oil
- Coconut oil
- Shea butter
- Tallow (bovine or deer)

Gather your dried herbs to be infused. Gently heat the chopped herbs in a clean saucepan over low to medium heat until the scent of the plant has filled the air (or for about three hours). For a more passive method, you can set a jar filled with herbs and cover them with the oil of your choice to slowly infuse next to the woodstove for a few days as well. Once the oil is fragrant, strain out the plant matter with a strainer.

In a double boiler, add $1/4$ cup beeswax or soy wax per I cup infused oil. More wax makes a harder salve, and less makes an oilier consistency. Heat them gently together until the beeswax is melted, stirring constantly. Pour into clean, dry jars or tins and label. Store in a cool place out of direct light.

The Wheel of the Year: A Witch's Journey through the Seasons

Storytelling has been the tool of knowledge transfer for centuries. Today it is no different, even if it is a less popular medium of exchange. In modern witch-craft, we call the passing of the seasons the Wheel of the Year. For the seasons go around and around, just as a wheel turns. This cycle plays host to a meta-phorical tale of the Goddess and the God as they are born, fall in love, mate, grow old, and die, only to be reborn again as reflected in what is happening in the natural world. We begin on the winter solstice, at Yule as it is known, with the birth of the God, as the sun returns to its waxing power.

Winter Solstice (Yule)

The light returns and the light half of the year begins. This day is an astrologi-cal holiday and so falls on different days some years, namely December 20th, 21st, or the 22nd. In the lore of the Wheel of the Year, God is reborn as the Sun Child. Yule comes from the Old Norse, Icelandic, Faroese, and Norwe-gian Nynorsk word *jol*.[2] The Saxons celebrated the winter solstice with a festival called Mother Night on December 24. This was dedicated to the goddesses Holda and Freyja and marked their New Year. Some witches celebrate Samhain as the New Year, others choose to do so at the winter solstice.

Celtic peoples also celebrated the winter solstice. At Newgrange in Ireland there's a passage grave built so that on the winter solstice, a ray of sunshine penetrates the inner sanctum and illuminates three spirals carved on a stone slab. That may have signified the sun fertilizing the body of the Earth, and so wakening her after her winter sleep to the renewed cycle of life. It may also represent the birth and rebirth of the Sun Child in the womb of the Great Mother Goddess.

A similar event occurs at Maes Howe in Orkney and several other stone circles throughout the British Isles. Perhaps these places were seen as gateways to the otherworld where the dead could be contacted or the living could pass between the worlds. This night does revolve around the dead (like Samhain) and keeping an iron blade at the door was believed to keep out trolls and other frightening figures in Scandinavia on this darkest night.

Esoterically, the midwinter and solstice period of Yule and the Twelve Days is known as the "in-between time" or the "time between time." As the sun appears to stand still in the sky, the old year is dying, and the new year waits to be born. It is a strange and magical time, still seen in secular society's tales of Christmas magic and miracles. These are folk memories that survive in the modern subconscious of the magic of this between-time where magic could happen.

In winter around the world, many folk rituals were performed to ensure the sun's return, such as the lighting of fires. The Yule log, or candle, comes from this practice and is burned down a bit each of the 12 nights. These nights were seen as liminal times of mystery and magic. Stories are told and much merrymaking occurs to celebrate the returning light.

Despite this aura of joy, the dark aspect of winter has not entirely given up its hold on the land yet, and ghost stories were also told at this time, much like at All Hallows. Burn candles in each window to stave off the still-lingering darkness and make space for the coming light. Decorate your domicile with ivy, holly, and evergreens to bring forth thoughts of everlasting life.

This is the celebration of the winter solstice or midwinter, the time when the light returns to the earth and is often seen as the start of the light half of the year as days begin to become longer. Yule and Yuletide have become associated with Christmas, which happened due to the early Christian church adopting pagan festivals to celebrate their own holy days. The church leaders saw that their pagan converts were still attending the old pagan festivals and sought a way to equate the "new" religion with the old.[3]

Many folk rituals were performed at Yule to welcome back the sun or to encourage its return with sympathetic magic. These often involved the lighting of fires and one custom that has been adopted by modern witches: the Yule log.

Ritual: Yule Log Ritual

The Yule log was traditionally a log of ash or oak, trees that were representative of the God. The log would be fashioned from the woods on Christmas Eve and taken home. On the way home, any stranger passing it had to bow and raise their hat to the log, otherwise it was believed that bad luck would follow in the new year.

In Scotland, the Yule log was called the Christmas Old Wife; the log was collected by the head of the household and then carved to represent an old woman. When it was thrown on the fire, it represented the ritual burning of the Cailleach or winter hag goddess. In Cornwall, the log was chalked to represent a male figure and stood in effigy of the God.

In some urban areas the Yule log was replaced with a Yule candle—this was a large red or white candle decorated with holly. This was burned for a short period each day of the Twelve Days of Christmas. The Yule candle has been adopted by some Traditional Witches today where central heating has replaced open fires in homes. This candle wax could then be smeared onto a plough to bring plenty to the crops.

You Will Need:

- Either a log or a large candle
- A bell
- Incense of your choice, preferably pine, mugwort, and rosemary

Log: Outside or in a fireplace, create a fire and prepare the space. Burn incense of pine, resin, and mugwort to cleanse the space. Ring a bell three times. This marks the beginning. Say,

As this bell rings so I mark the beginning of this rite.
All spirits who would meddle in my workings depart,
and all who aid me draw near.
Like this log blazes and burns so too shall the Sun return.

Place your special log on the fire and contemplate it as it burns. Take time to consider that which will return soon that you have sorely missed from the warm times. Give thanks for the solace of winter and its lessons, but let your heart melt to the promises of spring. Burn the whole log that evening or burn a little of it for the next 12 nights.

Save the ashes of the log and sprinkle them in your garden to bless it with fertility in the coming year.

Candle: This is performed in the same way, but it can be done safely in your home at an altar. Burn the candle down a little each night or burn it all the way down in one evening. Use the wax to anoint containers for growing herbs.

Spell 1: Ritual Incense for Winter Solstice

Crafting our own incense is lovely. I like to make loose incense from things I forage and grow, and luckily they are very easy to make. Many store-bought incenses have toxic binders or chemical scents in them that can be harmful to our respiratory tracts, so there is plenty of reason to make your own. The process of crafting our own ritual tools helps call us into accountability on how and why we use different plants, stones, and trees in our practice. If we use many crystals, we must know they have been pulled from a mine somewhere, by human hands, and ask how did they get to us? These questions and more are so imperative to me to practice magic justly.

Loose incenses do not require the binding woods, many of which are harvested in tropical climates and travel thousands of miles to get to you. Just as we are learning more and more to eat locally, so too are we learning to listen to the land around us and see which medicines and magics dwell there.

Here's how I craft my winter solstice incense: first, prepare the ingredients in separate small bowls or on large dried leaves.

You Will Need:

- $1/2$ part dried rosemary, crushed in a mortar and pestle
- 1 part well-aged conifer resin, crushed
- $1/4$ part mugwort leaf and stick, crushed
- 1 part birch bark, shredded and well dried
- $1/4$ part dried apple, crumbled

Place into a strong wooden or ceramic bowl and using a mortar, or your hands, blend well. To enchant this for the purpose of winter worship, imagine the golden light of the sun welling up within your heart space. As you breathe in, like a fire being blown upon gently, the light grows brighter and stronger, and as you breathe out, the light softens and becomes gentle. Sit in this moment, holding the golden light of the sun within you until you are ready, and imagine it pouring forth from your hands into the bowl. If you wish, say or think intently the following:

> By the light of the golden Sun,
> who now returns,
> I bless these herbs.
> For to burn them is to honor the Cold Ones,
> and to aid us,
> in finding the Solace of Winter.
> This is my Will,
> So mote it Be.

Sprinkle these herbs on a hot coal in your winter rites.

Spell II: Wilted-Rose Love Spell

This is a spell to begin on Midsummer Eve, June 21 or thereabouts, to be used at the winter solstice. Prepare yourself by bathing or burning the cleansing smoke of pine, juniper, cedar, or mugwort about yourself. At exactly midnight, gather a rose without speaking a word and wrap it up in a clean piece of brown paper. Do not look at it, and leave it to dry until midwinter somewhere hidden. At the winter solstice, unwrap the dried rose carefully. Wear it on your bosom with a clean pin to all the gatherings you attend around the winter solstice, and whoever plucks it off shall be your true love.

Remedy I: Hawthorn Heart Tincture

In winter, I sink into the medicines of my bioregion even when the earth is covered in snow. I make medicine from late rose hips and another rose family member whose berries I have freshly processed by early winter: hawthorn. Hawthorn (*Crataegus monogyna*) is an incredible medicine. A rose family tree, hawthorn has long been associated with fairies, and it is bad luck to cut an old or solitary faerie thorn. The hawthorn also serves as the meeting place of witches.[4] Hawthorns bear small fruits, not unlike their cousins, the little crabapples. Hawthorns grow all over the US along stream banks and in sunny spots on pasture edges and are native to temperate areas of America, Asia, Europe, and North Africa. Their thorny branches make them easy to identify. But watch out, they bite.

Hawthorn has long been associated with heart medicine and used as a circulatory tonic perhaps due to their red fruits, vital as blood. In Russian and German folk medicine, angina was traditionally treated with an alcohol extract of the haws, or fruits.[5] I use the elixir of hawthorn haws for improving circulation to the heart, a use it is documented to aid in.[6] To make an elixir of hawthorn, simply gather the fruits after they reach red ripeness and fill a clean glass jar of any size. Cover with good brandy (I like to use apple brandy), making sure all the berries are submerged. Allow them to tincture for four weeks in a cool, dry, dark place. I then strain out the fruits and compost them. Serve over an ice cube, two tablespoons each day, as a heart tonic, or add to hot ginger tea. This elixir also gives aid when the heart is ailing and in grief. Take as needed.

Remedy II: Evergreen Chest Rub

Pines and other evergreens have long been used as aromatic medicine to clear the sinuses with their sharp, clean scents. Use this salve to rub on the chest to open the air passages, as a solid woodsy perfume, or to ease sore joints.

Any salve begins by first infusing an oil with the herbs of our choice, then making it solid with beeswax or candelilla wax if you would like a vegan salve.

Here are commonly used salve oils and fats, which can be used alone or combined:

- Extra virgin olive oil
- Jojoba oil
- Coconut oil
- Shea butter
- Tallow (deer, sheep, or cow)

Gather pine, fir, or spruce needles and resin. Gently heat the chopped needles and resin in a clean saucepan over low to medium heat until the resin is melted or the scent of the needles has filled the air. For a more passive method, you can set a jar filled with chopped needles and covered with the oil of your choice to slowly infuse next to the woodstove for a few days. Once the oil is fragrant, strain out the needles.

In a double boiler, add ¼ cup beeswax per 1 cup infused oil. More beeswax makes a harder salve, and less makes an oilier consistency. Heat them gently together until the beeswax is melted, stirring constantly. Pour into clean, dry jars or tins and label. Store in a cool place out of direct light and wash your pan right away in hot water to help keep the wax from hardening. This makes the most lovely winter solstice gift.

Remedy III: Winter Cordial

Cordials are essentially sweetened tinctures. They are delicious ways to take your medicine. I love blurring the lines between a beverage of healing and one of pleasure, for why can they not be one and the same? Winter chills bring colds and challenge the immune system, so working warming, immune-boosting herbs and fruits into our diet and self-care practice is important.

To make a delicious winter cordial begin with a clean quart mason jar and fill halfway with whatever proportion of the following pleases you, chopped:

- Fresh rosemary
- Fresh conifer needles (pine, spruce, or fir)
- Dried or fresh orange peel
- Dried rose hips
- 2 cinnamon sticks
- ⅛ tsp of nutmeg
- ⅛ tsp of clove
- 1 split whole vanilla bean

Cover this with good vodka or brandy and let it tincture for four weeks. Strain and pour into a new clear jar. I usually add one part sweetener to one part alcohol. So for a pint batch, you would add one pint of honey to your one pint of tincture. Stir it up, label, and store in a cool, dark place. Take a splash over ice, with seltzer, or in tea to drive the cold away.

Imbolc (Candlemas), February 1–2

Imbolc, or Candlemas, comes February 1–2 and is a festival of lights that some call the Quickening in Traditional Witchcraft; it's the time of the Bone or Snow Full Moon. Its Gaelic name, Imbolc, means "ewe's milk" and refers to the start of lambing season. It's a time for driving out the old winter and further welcoming the returning light through spring cleaning rituals. It is a sacred day of the Celtic goddess Brigid or Bride. She is the star of this time between winter and spring. The cross of Brigid is her sign, which is traditionally woven of straw. Springs and wells are dressed for her this day to ensure the purity of the waters and their continued plenty. In Scotland, the Cailleach, a hag winter goddess, drinks from the spring of youth and becomes Brigid, the fair maiden, living the eternal cycle of youth and age.[7]

Imbolc was Christianized to become the purification of the Virgin Mary in the temple after childbirth.[8] The name Candlemas derives from the old pagan custom of lighting torches in honor of the winter goddess. The Church adapted the torches to the lighting of candles for the Virgin Mary and had a special mass to bless the candles to be used in church over the coming year.

Ritual: Weather Prediction Ritual

The lore surrounding this day comes from a couple of key sources. The best known is probably the European tradition of the Candlemas Bear or Badger. These animals would stir (or in some cases, be coaxed) from their winter dormancy, and observers would make note of their reaction to the environment outside. Then a prediction of spring's eventual arrival could be made, and plans could be laid for things like tilling and planting crops.

The selection of the groundhog as the New World substitute is outlined by Gerald C. Milnes in his book *Signs, Cures, and Witchery*:

> The badger was . . . used as a weather predictor in Germany, but in the New World, Pennsylvania Germans substituted the groundhog for this role because skunks [whose fat or "grease," the author notes, was used as Old World healers used badger fat], unlike badgers, do not hibernate. . . . German Protestants brought the old weather-predicting tradition to Pennsylvania, where it is still actively observed in some German communities. Groundhogs were substituted for the badger (and bear) traditions of Europe. Now the hibernating groundhog has their supposed powers to predict the weather.

To perform your own weather divination on Imbolc, or Candlemas morning, you can try this Scottish charm:

> If Candlemas be fair and bright
> Winter will have another flight
> If Candlemas be cloud and rain
> Winter will be gone and not come again.[9]

Much like a shadow is cast on a sunny day to scare a groundhog, so too will a sunny day portend more cold to come.

Spell I: Make a Foraged Grass/Reed Bridget's Cross

The primary symbol of Brigid is the sun wheel (or fire wheel), and it is a version of the ancient symbol that represents the cosmic life force. Brigid's sun wheel flows left to right in the deosil movement of the sun. This sun wheel appears in the celebration of Imbolc and is traditionally made from interwoven rushes and hung above doors, windows, and cradles to ward off evil and protect against fire.[10] You can make Brigid's cross from anything stout enough to tolerate bending. I make them from various wild grasses I harvest from around our home.

Gather up some stout and somewhat clean and strong straw, grass, or reeds.

1. Fold a straw in half around the center of a vertical straw and where they overlap, hold tightly between thumb and forefinger and rotate it once to the left.
2. Add another straw with its ends facing to the right and rotate it to the left again.
3. Add another and rotate the cross to the left and continue this process. Every time you add a new straw, you put it over all the pieces sticking up. Rotate and repeat.
4. When you reach your desired size, tie the ends of each of the arms together and trim to the same length. Tie over your door or in your vehicle for protection.

Spell II: Iron Nail and Red Thread Protection Charm

If one needs to protect a space or a person from evil, try an iron nail charm. Make a charm of two iron nails bound with red thread to protect against evil and spirits of malcontent. Iron nails and objects of metal have long been used as talismans by many different cultures. Iron has been used in the British Isles to protect from malevolent witchcraft, fairies of ill-intent, and other nasty forces.

The taboo on iron dates from the beginning of the Iron Age when religious conservatism forbade the use of the strange new material in

place of the usual bronze. It has been suggested that the magic significance of iron arose from its susceptibility to magnetism which, as
the superstitious Romans often believed, it derived from witchcraft.[11]

In Scotland, a charm was made of rowan tree crosses with red thread to
keep away evil.

> Rowan-tree and red thread
> Make the witches tyne their speed.[12]

I have adapted a charm for protection by combining the magical protection of iron with that of red thread. A species of rowan, the mountain ash
(*Sorbus americana*), does grow near us but only in the highest elevations, so I use
the ever-handy nail instead. Rather than use the wood of the rowan to make a
cross, create a charm against evil by binding two large iron nails in an X shape
in the center with red thread. Red thread, the color of the vital force of blood,
was alone a powerful charm in Scottish folk magic against bad witchcraft and
evil spirits.[13]

Hang this charm somewhere high up in the home, or better yet, hidden
somewhere no one but you knows.

Remedy 1: Vital Wild Onion Nutritive Vinegar

Vinegar has been used since the dawn of humanity as a medicine and condiment. It is made through the process of yeasts fermenting natural food sugars
present in fruits and other vegetative matter into alcohol. Next, acetic acid bacteria (*Acetobacter*) convert the alcohol to acetic acid. The culture of acetic acid
bacteria grows on the surface of the liquid, and fermentation proceeds slowly
over the course of weeks or months—it's much like making kombucha. The
longer fermentation period allows for the accumulation of a nontoxic slime
composed of yeast and acetic acid bacteria, known as the "mother" of vinegar,
which we often see merrily floating about in vinegar bottles. We've been using
vinegar for a long time, especially since it's easy to make from another favorite
concoction of humans: wine. It's been used as medicine and as a preservative of
food for many, many years.

Acetic acid is the main chemical present in vinegar which gives it its remarkable actions. It has been shown to kill certain bacteria and prevent them from multiplying and reaching harmful levels. Vinegar is an acid that can help to support better stomach acid levels, which can assist in more efficient protein and mineral absorption. In studies, apple cider vinegar has shown great promise in improving insulin sensitivity and helping to lower blood sugar responses after meals.[14] As a disinfectant and natural preservative, it makes a great homemade cleaning product! Generally speaking, when using vinegar for medicine, seek out 5 percent acidity, for some fruit vinegars are weaker.

Dosing Vinegar Medicine

The dosage of a vinegar-based tincture will be higher than an alcohol-based tincture made from the same herbs since the vinegar is not as powerful of an extractor. You don't have to be as careful about doses with vinegars made from gentle food herbs such as nettles (*Urtica dioica*), chickweed (*Stellaria media*), dandelion (*Taraxacum officinale*), cleavers (*Galium aparine*), and violet (*Viola* spp.) because they do not contain many irritating compounds. These herbs are generally considered nutritive because they are more on the food side of the medicine spectrum. You can take one tablespoon one to three times a day. I like to make mine in water to help it go down easier.

I love to make an infused vinegar with wild onions, or onion grass (*Allium vineale*). These lily family members emit their powerful fragrance when the lawn is cut! That smell always takes me back to springtime as a child. If a plant looks like an onion and smells like an onion, you can eat it. If a plant looks like garlic and smells like garlic, you can eat it. If you do not smell a garlic or an onion odor, but it looks like an onion, be careful! You might have a similar-looking toxic plant in the lily family. Smell is a powerful plant ID factor.

Wild onions come up in cool weather: spring and fall. I look for the green-blue hollow-stemmed and fragrant, grass-like patches in the lawn around my home and other places I know are not sprayed. The little bulbs are so sweet! To make an infused vinegar you'll need the following:

- Clean mason jar
- Enough wild onion to loosely fill said jar
- Good apple cider vinegar, 5 percent acidity

Gather and clean enough wild onion grass to loosely fill a mason jar of your choosing. Cover with apple cider vinegar and close with a plastic or wax paper–protected metal lid. Let steep for two weeks and strain out. I like to blend up the leftover vinegar-soaked onions and add salt and pepper. Spoon this flavorful chopped onion mash on eggs or mushrooms at your spring equinox feast table.

The vinegar, which often turns a lovely spring green, makes a beautiful salad dressing rich in sulphur-containing compounds that have been shown to help to prevent certain types of cancers.[14] Onions are also high in various antioxidants and the addition of the vinegar makes this tasty treat a great helper in digestion. I like to use it as a marinade as well for beef and mushrooms.

Remedy II: Dandelion Tonic

A simple way to define "tonic" is a preventative medicinal substance taken to give a feeling of vigor or well-being. Most tonics were imbibed as beverages usually made by making a strong tea or decoction (boiling the herbs, roots, or barks rather than just steeping them) and sweetening to taste with sugar or honey. Spring greens, such as dandelions (*Taraxacum officinale*), dock (*Rumex* spp.), wild onion (*Allium* spp.), wild cherry bark (*Prunus* spp.), and stinging nettles (*Urtica dioica*) could also have a tonic/purifying effect. Even the juice of certain plants, like cleavers (*Galium aparine*), was seen as a blood purifier in American folk medicine. Water with slices of burdock root (Arctium lappa) soaked in it was also used as a tonic.

You can use tonics when digestion feels sluggish or you've been overdoing it with rich or sweet foods and drinks during the holidays. I like to make dandelion tonic like this:

In the evening, gather up enough dandelion roots and greens to fill, when roughly chopped, a quart mason jar halfway. Wash them well, separating the greens and rinsing them. Then soak the roots in a big bowl of cold water and scrub them with a brush. Chop them all up and place in your jar. Boil enough water to fill the jar and pour it in.

Allow to steep overnight. In the morning strain and add one teaspoon of blackstrap molasses for iron. Mix well and store in the fridge. I drink a cup three times a day, and it keeps one week refrigerated. It's great for post-bleeding time as well as for those of us who menstruate.

Remedy III: Late Winter Hand Salve

Our hands take a beating in the cold-weather months, and even if you live in a tropical place, frequent handwashing and working in the earth can rob your hands of moisture and create cracks. A good hand salve is indispensable. Go ahead and follow the salve instructions a few pages back and use the following ingredients.

For a skin-healing hand salve try:

- Plantain
- Comfrey root
- Rosemary essential oil

Fetch ³/₄ cup of dried plantain leaves, ¹/₂ cup of dried comfrey root, and 2 cups of oil. I like half olive oil/half tallow for this one, but do what works for you. It's best to use dried herbs for salves as the water content in fresh herbs can cause them to spoil. Gently heat the chopped herbs and oil in a clean sauce-pan over low to medium heat for three hours. You can do this in a Crock-Pot as well! For a more passive method, you can set a jar filled with the herbs and covered with the oil of your choice to slowly infuse next to the woodstove for a few days. Strain out the herbs.

In a double boiler, add ¹/₄ cup beeswax per 1 cup infused oil. Heat them gently together until the beeswax is melted, stirring constantly. When the salve has begun to cool slightly, add 10 drops of rosemary essential oil. This will help to prevent infections in small cuts on the hands and to extend the life of your salve. Pour into clean, dry jars or tins and label. Store in a cool place out of direct light and wash your pan right away in hot water to help keep the wax from hardening.

Apply to chapped and cracked hands liberally, especially after washing.

Spring Equinox (Ostara)

To everything there is a season, and a time to every purpose under the
heaven: a time to be born, and a time to die; a time to plant, and a time
to pluck up that which is planted.

–Ecclesiastes 3:1-2

Ritual: Planting by the Signs

All the signs but Libra are named for animals or beings, so the zodiac means
the "belt of animals."

The signs always appear in a specific order. First comes the Ram, Aries,
or the head, and it proceeds down to Pisces, the Fish, or Feet. Following Pisces, the Ram appears again, beginning a new sequence. Each of the signs has
specific attributes, such as being either masculine, feminine, airy, dry, barren,
fiery, earthy, moist, watery, fruitful, or very fruitful. The best time to conduct
any garden chore is when a day falls on both an ideal sign and a good phase
of the moon. For example, a day in Cancer in a waxing moon is a great day to
plant seeds. Cancer is the most fruitful sign, and the moon growing inspires
the seeds we plant in the ground to follow suit.

Over the course of a $29^1/_2$-day lunar cycle, the moon goes through four
basic phases: new, full, and two quarter phases. For half of its cycle, between
the new and full phases, the moon is waxing (growing in illumination). Then,
after the full moon, it begins to wane (decreasing in illumination).

Aboveground Crops

All aboveground crops should be planted when the moon is waxing. During the
new moon is the best time to sow or transplant leafy annuals such as lettuce,
spinach, cabbage, and celery, while the first quarter phase is good for annual
fruits and foods with external seeds, such as tomatoes, pumpkins, broccoli,
and beans.

Belowground (Root) Crops

Root crops do best when the moon is waning. When the moon is just past full, it's a good time to sow or plant root crops and fruit trees like apples, potatoes, beets, turnips, asparagus, and rhubarb. During the last quarter phase, it's best to avoid planting at all. Work instead on improving soil, weeding, mulching, composting, et cetera.

But knowing the phase of the moon isn't enough. Planting by the moon also requires knowledge of the moon's place in the zodiac, based on ancient lore that each sign confers certain growing conditions.

The History

Planting by the moon may have been the first "use" humans made of the lunar cycle. Evidence of its practice dates back thousands of years to the ancient peoples of the Nile and Euphrates River valleys. Farmers of these civilizations planted by the moon's phase and its sign in the zodiac.

German settlers began arriving in America in the early 1700s via Philadelphia, settling first in Pennsylvania. They eventually moved down to Maryland and Virginia. By the 1800s, German settlers and their kin had moved farther south into the Carolinas as well as westward into Kentucky, Tennessee, Ohio, and beyond. Unlike many of their English and Irish counterparts, the Germans clung to their Old World culture and traditions well into the 19th century. More than any other people, they were responsible for many Americans' acceptance and practice of planting by the moon and the signs of the zodiac.

In America, by 1750 there were over 50 separate almanacs in print. No genre of print had more circulation in 18th-century America than an almanac. These publications were rife with agricultural lore, weather predictions, and astrological information. It was also a sure way to spread occult information, especially lunar and astrological lore, as it was the most accepted of the occult sciences because it was so in line with natural, observable phenomena.[16]

The miscellaneous character of the wisdom espoused around planting by the signs is due to a combination of regionally specific, experiential astronomical observations and the ways in which the Enlightenment affected magic and occult thought in the 18th century. As class lines began to more clearly define those who believed in and practiced magic and those who did not, so too did the ways in which the diversifying populace change to what extent they interacted with the occult.[17] This allowed magic and this type of folkloric astrological knowledge to become a series of distinct recipe-like rules rather than parts of a unified science.

Over the years, a more specific set of rules has grown up around the zodiac that governs activities, such as planting and harvesting. These rules take into account both the sign governing the day and the phase of the moon on that particular day. At the beginning of the planting season, for example, the farmer consults their calendar, picks out one of the 14 favorable days that occur every month, and plants only on one of these 14 "fruitful" days. Should they miss and plant their crops on one of the unfruitful days, their crops will not produce at half their ability, say the believers.

SIGN	BODY PART	CELESTIAL BODY	ELEMENT
Aries	Head	Mars	Fire
Taurus	Neck/Throat	Venus	Earth
Gemini	Arms/Chest	Mercury	Air
Cancer	Breast/Stomach	Moon	Water
Leo	Heart/Back	Sun	Fire
Virgo	Bowels	Mercury	Earth
Libra	Kidneys	Venus	Air
Scorpio	Loins	Mars	Water
Sagittarius	Thighs	Jupiter	Fire
Capricorn	Knees	Saturn	Earth
Aquarius	Legs	Uranus	Air
Pisces	Feet	Neptune	Water

Plant all things that yield above the ground during the increase or growing of the moon, and all things that yield below the ground (root crops) when
the moon is decreasing or darkening. Never plant on the first day of the new
moon or on a day when the moon changes quarters. In the fourth quarter turn sod, pull weeds, and destroy. This is when the moon has the least
gravitational pull and the least moonlight—its resting period—and it's best for
harvesting, cultivating, transplanting, and pruning, but not good at all for
planting.[18]

When planting during the different phases of the moon, always plant on
days in the sign of **Cancer**, **Scorpio**, **Pisces**, **Taurus**, **Libra**, or **Capricorn**.
The first day of the sign is better than the second day. Do not plant in **Aries**,
Sagittarius, **Aquarius**, **Leo**, **Gemini**, or **Virgo**.

Planting/Harvesting

Planting is best done in the fruitful signs of Scorpio, Pisces, Taurus, or Cancer
(loins, feet, neck, breast). Always transplant in water or earth signs. There are
14 fruitful sign days every month.

Signs in order of effectiveness:

Cancer: *Breast.* A very fruitful water sign. Seeds germinate quickly. It
is favorable to growth and ensures an abundant yield. Most fruitful
sign. Crops planted in this sign will withstand drought.

Scorpio: *Loins.* A fruitful water sign. Ranks next to Cancer in fruitful-
ness.

Pisces: *Feet.* A fruitful water sign. Produces excellent results for fruits
and bulbs. Short growth; good roots. Don't plant potatoes in the feet,
or the potatoes will develop little nubs like toes. Best to plant them on
a dark night in March.

Taurus: *Neck.* Earthy and moist. A fixed earth sign. Productive sign,
especially for root crops. Crops planted in this sign will withstand
drought.

Libra: *Kidneys.* A strong movable air sign. Produces vigorous pulp growth and roots with a reasonable amount of grain. Produces many flowers (for beauty and fragrance especially), small leaves, few seeds. Best to plant flowers in Libra, as it is the sign of beauty. Plant flowers when the moon is in the first quarter.

Capricorn: *Knees.* A moist, earthy movable sign. Somewhat productive favoring root crops.

Barren Signs

Leo, Virgo, Gemini, and Aquarius are the most barren signs but great for weeding and cultivating. Aries and Sagittarius are movable fire signs, governed by the sun, and are best for cultivating but can be used for planting alliums.

Destroying Weeds

Destroy weeds, cut down trees, turn soil in the barren signs Gemini, Leo, or Virgo (especially if the moon is in the last quarter).

Leo: *Heart.* A dry, barren fire sign. It is favorable only for the destruction of weedy growth. Do not trim trees or vines when the moon is in Leo, for they will surely die. Never plant in this sign for it is one of the "death" signs.

Gemini: *Arms.* A dry, barren air sign. A good time to stir the soil and subdue all weeds. Cut the lawn to slow its growth; pinch buds to stop unwanted growth. Plant beans, pumpkins, and corn when the sign is in the arms, or Gemini.

Virgo: *Bowels.* A dry, barren earth sign. Cut weeds.

Aries. *Head.* Dry and barren. Plow, till, and cultivate. Never plant in this sign, for it is one of the "death" signs.

Harvesting

The best time for harvesting is in the dark of the moon (last quarter new moon) when the moon is "growing old." The best signs to use are Sagittarius, Aquarius, or Aries. Never gather fruit, grain, or vegetables in the water signs or during the new moon, as they will decay or sprout. Gather root crops in the knees and feet in the last quarter of the moon.

Fertilizing

Use fruitful signs like Cancer, Scorpio, or Pisces. Organic fertilizers should be applied during the decreasing moon between full and new.

Pruning

To discourage growth, prune in the signs of Aries and Sagittarius during the increase of the moon between new and full. To encourage growth, use signs Cancer or Scorpio during the decreasing moon.

Spell 1: Four Elements House Cleansing Spell

This is a simple spell for cleansing a new dwelling or a way to incorporate a spiritual cleansing practice into your cleaning routine after you have scrubbed away the physical dirt.

You will need the following on your altar or a table:

- A white or black candle
- A match
- Salt
- A bowl of water
- A smoke plant (try white cedar, mugwort, or pine)

Begin with the candle. Light it and chant the following, while walking every corner of your abode:

"I cleanse this space by Fire."

Place it back on the table and let it continue to burn.
Repeat with the bowl of water, sprinkling a little as you go:

"I cleanse this space by Water."

Repeat with the bowl of salt, sprinkling it as you go.

"I cleanse this space by Earth."

Repeat with the smoke plant:

"I cleanse this space by Air."

End the rite by blowing out the candle and sweeping up the salt.

Spell II: Green Oat and Egg Fertility Spell

Eggs are used in many traditions for charming, hexing, and curing. The Anglo-Saxons and Egyptians both placed eggs in their grave goods as well as on physical grave sites. There is no other symbol of new life so universal and apparent as the egg, lying in wait to birth whatever being or magical intention they hold. The tradition of egg dyeing that is quite popular in Easter customs today most likely comes from eastern Europe where the arts of Pysanky and Krashanka (two forms of decorated eggs) were born.

Pysanky are the blown, dyed, and decorated eggs that have long been used as protective amulets, as well as for fertility and prosperity. Wheat and images of flowers were drawn to create an amulet for an abundant harvest. These were then buried in the first and last furrow (or spadeful of dirt if you did not till or plough your earth) to ensure good crop growth. When dyed blue or green they were used to protect against fire.

The shells are dyed many colors to correspond to their uses and where they are from. Red-dyed eggs were thrown into rivers to alert those in the otherworlds that spring had come and the season of the sun had returned. These were also placed on the graves of loved ones and checked the following day for any disturbance. If any was detected, it was made known that their restless spirit was in need of a prayer, offerings, or other releasing rituals.

Eggs were also placed under beehives to keep bees from leaving and to ensure good honey crops. When rolled in green oats, the dyed eggs acted as fertility charms when buried in fields in Ukraine. You can also write upon an egg any spell or wish you have and bury it in some secret place. As it decays, so does your wish disseminate into the ether.[19]

To make a green oat charm for fertility (and remember fertility is of both mind and body if you are not trying to conceive) begin with the following:

- A raw brown egg
- Red cabbage
- Wheat flour
- Oats

Gently take a clean pin and poke a hole in both sides of the egg. Head outside where you won't make a mess and blow through one end and remove the yolk albumin. Rinse the egg gently and set on a paper towel to let dry. Make a glue with one teaspoon of flour and enough water in a small cup to make a thin paste. Dye your egg green with red cabbage. Chop one cup of red cabbage and cook down in one cup of water for 15 minutes and strain out the cabbage. Allow to cool and add one teaspoon of white vinegar to set it. Soak your egg in it until the desired green is reached.

Once your now green egg is dried, apply some flour paste. Place a small sprinkle of oats onto a plate and roll the egg in them until they stick. Add more paste if they are not sticking adequately. Allow the oats to dry.

Bury this charm in the earth where you shall garden to bless your fields with fertility or in a flower pot in your home to bring fertility into your life. Beware, fertility charms work!

Remedy 1: Dock Liver Detox Decoction

You are not dirty. Your body is not dirty. Our bodies detox constantly on their own when in good working order, but plant friends can help a lot in that process. The dock (*Rumex* spp.) species help greatly with this through their stimulation of the liver. I am not a huge proponent of extreme fasts or cleanses as I believe that many of them are hard on the body and unnecessary, but fasting is a very effective healing tool, and it is also good to be mindful about how one views the self and one's body. You do not need to be hungry to be healthy, and you do not need to constantly withhold food to support the body's wisdom in cleansing itself.

That being said, a dock root decoction can help stimulate bile production and aid in digestion. It helps us get the most out of our food. Try this decoction for one week in spring to get things moving.

You Will Need:

- ¹/₂ cup chopped fresh dock roots
  (curly or yellow dock is great)
- A medium sauce pan

Simmer on low one quart of water with ¹/₂ cup of chopped fresh dock roots for 15 to 30 minutes. Strain and take ¹/₂ cup six times a day between meals until gone.

Remedy II: Turkey Tail Fungus Decoction Tonic

Turkey tail (*Trametes versicolor*) is a glorious fungus that is easy to identify and abundant in many temperate locations year-round. Though it's not a plant, I find these when foraging for plants all the time. The Chinese call them *yun zhi* (cloud fungus) and the Japanese call them *kawaratake* (mushroom by the riverbank). These polypores grow on dead hardwoods in unique shelves and rosettes of striped, velvet-topped, thin fruiting bodies. There is much to know about mushrooms, but these are a great one to start with if you have never worked with mushrooms in the wild.

How to Identify Turkey Tail Fungus

- Does it have small pores or pinprick-sized holes on a white underside?
- Is it flexible and thin?
- When torn, does it have what appears to be cotton wool inside?

- Is the top almost furry, or velvety looking?
- Is the top striped with different colors of brown, ruddy, tan, white, and even indigo or bluish hues (much like a turkey's tail!)?

If the answer is yes to all of these, then, absolutely, you have a turkey tail!

There are look-alikes to turkey tail, so remember to never ingest a mushroom if you are unsure of the ID. You can always ask a mushroom club or local group to check IDs. Don't rely on apps either as they can be wrong!

These mushrooms have been used in medicine for centuries in China. They are used as an immune booster and cancer preventative, and they even help fight HPV.[20] They contain polysaccharides that help to prevent the recurrence of cancer and have been used in conjunction with chemotherapy as well. I like to drink the decoction of these mushrooms often, and while the flavor alone is not very notable, it is lovely to mix with other tonic herbs for a daily tonic to help keep our defenses up. They also dry and keep in jars very well.

To make a decoction, simmer the mushrooms, fresh or dried, in good water on low heat. It should be one tablespoon of chopped, dried mushroom to two cups of water. You can mix them with pine needles and honey for a special warming drink in the cold months.

Remedy III: Cherry Bark Oxymel Cough Syrup

Wild cherry trees have provided medicine for humans in North America for a long time. Though there are some 400 species in the *Prunus* genus in the temperate world, three of our Eastern native cherries interest me: *Prunus serotina* (black cherry), *P. virginiana* (chokecherry), and *P. pensylvanica* (pin cherry) in abundance.

Though there are differences between these three species, biochemically and energetically they work in similar ways medicinally and can be used for food (the berries) and medicine (the bark and twigs). Wild cherry bark infusions and syrups are a well-known cough and cold remedy in southern Appalachia and have a long history of use by different First Nations people and settlers of the area.

Black cherry (or rum cherry/mountain black cherry) is a pioneer species, meaning it is one of the first trees to enter a disturbed area. This makes it a sort of forest marker, letting us know the history of a forest by its mere presence. It is shade intolerant, preferring to grow in open sunlight, so it tells us of a past disturbance that opened up the forest of the overstory, allowing more sunlight to hit the forest floor. The wild cherry is often found growing in areas that were once open pasture or high up on ridges that are exposed to high winds. It has been found at elevations of 3,200 feet.

The dried inner tree bark was commonly used by eastern First Nations people. They made infusions for colds, fevers, diarrhea, labor pains, and as a general pain reliever due to its tranquilizing and sedative qualities. They passed its use on to early European colonizers who included wild cherry in many cough elixir recipes. The root was also used for things such as intestinal worms, burns, cold sores, and other skin ailments. The fruits were used to make cough syrups by tribes such as the Delaware. The Europeans copied this practice. Wild cherry bark is still used in herbal syrups and teas for coughs and colds. Young trees were harvested in fall, when the chemical constituents are most mobile in the tree, and the shiny, birchlike bark of young cherries peels well.

In Appalachia, cherry bark was used in cough medicines, tonics, and mild sedatives. The fruits were used in pies, preserves, and as a flavoring in rum. This gives them their lesser-known name of rum cherry. The bark works as an antispasmodic, essentially helping to quell the cough reflex and allowing the ill person some restful sleep. For this reason, it was also used for treating asthma.

Like our friend the black walnut, cherry moonlights as a poison plant. The leaves, twigs, and bark of black cherry contain a cyanogenic glycoside called prunasin. All cherry trees contain this chemical as well as amygdalin, which converts into hydrocyanic acid (or prussic acid) in water. However, in small doses this chemical can stimulate the respiratory system, improve digestion, and give an enhanced feeling of well-being. The dose makes the poison.

Cherry bark is my favorite thing to use for cough syrup, and I love to make a simple oxymel-style syrup from honey and vinegar that requires no heating. Oxymels are herbal extracts made in honey and vinegar that mostly originated from ancient Persia and Greece. Select some small cherry branches and prune back to where they meet the trunk with sharp pruners. Peel the bark off or cut up the very small branches with your pruners and fill a mason jar halfway with them.

Here is one way to make an oxymel:

The desired ratio of dried herb to vinegar and honey is 1:3 or 1:4, or one part dried herb to three or four parts honey and vinegar. You can easily measure by filling a pint jar less than a quarter of the way with herbs and then topping with equal parts honey and vinegar. Most of the oldest recipes call for more honey, and today you'll see more vinegar called for in medicinal preparations, but follow your taste. Oxymels are great options for herbs like mint, lemon balm, and fruits. Blackberry and raspberry oxymel are amazing when stirred up with seltzer water and ice!

Place your cherry bark fresh into a pint jar (a quarter to one-fifth of the way full), cover with apple cider vinegar and honey, stir it up very well with a clean spoon (preferably one of wood), and let your jar sit somewhere cool and dark, stirring a couple of times a week for two weeks. Strain out all the bark bits and pour into a clean, labeled glass jar for storage.

Take one teaspoon for coughs up to six times a day.

Beltane, May 1

Beltane means the "fire of Bel" in Gaelic. It is the time of year when the symbolic great rite of the plough and the soil now begins, and the earth celebrates the sacred marriage between the Goddess and the Horned One in neopagan lore. "Bale fires," or large bonfires, are lit upon hilltops to ward away evil and bring a reminder of the power of the mighty sun. It's a fire festival celebrating the beginning of the summer season to those whose agrarian lifeway was the center of existence.

In F. Marian McNeill's book *The Silver Bough*, she says, "At Beltane, flocks and herds went to their summer pastures; at Hallowmas (Samhain) they returned to their winter quarters." These two fire holidays, which stand opposite each other on the Wheel, were great markers of the year for those who danced it. Today, even if we do not grow all our own food, it's still a time of honoring fertility, renewal, and purification.

The ashes of those sacred fires, most often kindled of sacred woods like birch, are sprinkled over the fields as blessings. Branches of rowan are hung to keep away the faeries, or fae, who are traveling that night. It's the day after Walpurgis Night (April 30), an ancient time for witches' meetings.[21] One tradition for this May morning is to rise with the sun to greet it while washing your face with the morning dew to keep yourself looking young and fresh. Sacred wells are visited and decorated. Prayers and candles are left behind to adorn them.

Ritual: Maypole Dance Ritual

In English folklore, a May queen and king are often chosen and decorated with flowers. Today still, May Day events and festivals are popular among certain small towns in the British countryside. Offerings of food and drink are made now and remind us of the time in which sacrifice meant something very different than it does today. Sacrifice meant insurance against illness and misfortune. By imitating the sacred dance of nature, humans seek to find both their place in that performance and to more intimately know the other dancers. This is why we dance the Maypole, which has been popular since the 16th century so far as we know. The Maypole represents the generative forces of nature as pole and earth.

How to Dance the Maypole

Dig a fine pit with your friends and family to dance the dance! We use a posthole digger, but a shovel will do! Find a stout tree or wooden pole at least 15 feet long, and ask for its leaves to be cut.

Tie colored ribbons to the top affixed by a large timber nail or screw. Now, get everyone together, for it takes many hands to lift it into place. Put the pole in the ground, and tamp it well to make sure it doesn't move as you dance it.

Once the pole is secure, gather two groups of dancers of equal number, team A and team B. From Rod Stradling, a Maypole dance musician:

> Members of Team A should partner Members of Team B. Make sure that As and Bs are spaced alternately around the maypole with each Team A dancer facing one from Team B and then start the music. Each of Team A should pass right shoulder with their first Team B dancer and then left with the next (do not turn back on yourself), carrying on alternately until the ribbons are again exhausted. As dancers pass each other, they should raise and lower their right arm rhythmically to guide the ribbon over the other dancer. To unwind, remember to retrace your

steps accurately, passing your last dancer first and then alternate shoulders until the ribbons unwind. Make sure that everyone dances at a constant pace and that no one overtakes. You have now completed your second ribbon dance. You can vary the dance by having pairs (or more) of dancers, joined arm-in-arm, weave in each direction together.

In each case, look at the beautiful pattern that you have made on the maypole during the dance.[22]

This dance is definitely most easily learned by watching!

Spell I: Seeding Your Future Spell

The power of a sprouting seed can break through the toughest seed coats. Tapping into the generative forces of a seed are incredible for magical uses. I plant a lot of things around Beltane in our garden, right before the last frost has graced our holler. If at Beltane you find yourself looking to the year ahead, as one is wont to do when planting, imagining future harvests, ask yourself, what shall I plant?

Each year, I take a large seed, like a squash or a morning glory, and I plant it as a spell. To draw the power of the newborn seed into bringing your desires into fruition, try this spell.

You Will Need:

- A candle
- A pot
- A seed
- A desire
- Water
- Smoke plant (try rosemary or a blackberry witches' whisk)

Light a candle (green is best). Prepare the pot, cleansing it with smoke and water and ridding it of all other energies. Come to a quiet place inside of yourself. Sit and breathe until you feel centered and ready. Fill it with good soil. Hold your seed. Bring to mind that which you desire to achieve. Be sure it does not bend the will of any other beings. Be sure it is for your highest good. Whisper to it, enlivening it with your breath and life force, and tell it of your secret desires that you wish to harvest by Samhain or All Hallows Tide at the end of October. Envision that nothing stands in your way from meeting your desire. Envision a clear road forward. Envision help coming to your aid when you need it.

Plant the seed gently in the soil and cover appropriately if needed. Pass the smoke over the soil, sprinkle it with the water, and begin caring for this being. As the plant sprouts and grows so too shall your desire. Every time you care for the plant, ask, am I doing all I can to achieve my desire? Allow the plant to reflect how you care for meeting your goals and achieving your dream.

Spell II: Egg Wishing Spell

This spell can be performed much like the green oat fertility spell. Poke two holes in either end of an egg and blow the innards out. Crack the egg carefully in half as best you can. Write your wish on a small piece of paper and seal the egg shut with wheat paste or nontoxic glue. Bury the egg somewhere and forget about it. As it is buried in the earth, so does it imitate the potential force of birth, and your wish shall ride upon that energy. Soon your wish shall come to pass.

Remedy I: Forsythia Tea for Coughs and Flu

Forsythia is a beautiful and abundant spring-flowering shrub planted ornamentally all over the country. The happy yellow flowers used to bedeck our May Day celebrations in Upstate New York, where I lived for a time, because they always bloomed around Beltane. Here in the South, they bloom as early as February. There are many species planted, but luckily the flowers of all are edible and medicinal, and the small fruits produced after flowering are medicinal. Used in Chinese medicine, *Forsythia suspensa*, or *lian qiao*, is used to deal with chronic inflammation and viruses, among many other things. This plant is in the olive family, many members of which are excellent infection fighters.[23]

Make a tea of the flowers for a sore throat thusly:

Take one loose handful of fresh flowers and remove the little green calyx (the little green bit still clinging to the base of the flower). Crush them gently in your hand and place in your favorite teapot. Boil a fresh pot of water and pour over the fresh petals. Let steep for five minutes, strain, and enjoy with honey. The flowers also make a beautiful honey syrup or jelly!

Remedy II: Lemon Balm Tincture for Viruses

Lemon balm is such an easy-to-grow, abundant plant. While they can get a bit tenacious and take over, they are always there when you need them. Lemon balm is a great helper for those of us with cold sores and other herpes simplex viruses (HSV). The tea or tincture is a great way to help mitigate the painful and stressful experience of having an outbreak. Lemon balm, as we learned, is a nervine and helps soothe the nervous systems. It also has many complex chemicals that have been studied and are shown to help with healing time in HSV infections.[24]

Sometimes the tincture can sting too much for topical uses, but the tea can be soothing. For cold sores or herpes sores, steep two to four teaspoons of crushed dried leaf in one cup of boiling water for 10 to 15 minutes. Cool. Apply tea with cotton balls to the sores throughout the day and make sure to dispose of them afterwards and wash your hands.

I like to take the tincture at the first sign of prodrome, or the tingling sensation that warns of a cold sore to come. I take 60 drops three times a day until the feeling passes.

There is some concern that lemon balm may interact with certain HIV medications and thyroid medications, so be sure to check with a professional herbalist or naturopath before beginning any new herbal protocol.

To make a tincture of lemon balm:

You Will Need:

- 80-proof good vodka or organic grain alcohol
- A clean mason jar of your choice
- Fresh lemon balm, enough to fill the jar

Chop the lemon balm and stuff it in the jar. I like to mash it in with a sauerkraut masher or a large wooden spoon to release the oils. Cover with alcohol, put a lid on, and label the jar. Let sit for four to six weeks in a cool, dark place.

Remedy III: Blueberry Leaf Tea for UTI

Blueberries are a wonderful plant to grow or wild harvest. Their fruits are of course delicious and nutritious, but the leaves are also an excellent medicine. Like cranberries, blueberry leaves have chemicals called proanthocyanidins that prevent bacteria from sticking to the walls of the urinary tract.

You Will Need:

- One loose handful of fresh blueberry leaves
- One half-gallon mason jar

Pour freshly boiled water over the roughly chopped leaves and steep for 15 minutes. Strain and drink freely. Drink plenty of clear water as well.

Summer Solstice (Midsummer)

When the sun is at its zenith, it's the longest day of the year in the Western Hemisphere. Sacred fires were lit on hilltops and wild processions of torch-bearing people roved the fields to burn away disease and protect the crops. People often dressed as animals and "guised" much like at midwinter. In old Ireland, cattle and corn were both blessed by the balefires of Midsummer. This is one of the four spirit nights (All Hallows, Yuletide, and May Eve) where divination is performed and plants for magical workings are harvested. Herbs harvested on this auspicious day are at their full power.

The evening before is known as St. John's Eve to those who were Christianized. There is much folklore surrounding this time between. The fae are active this night and many protections and offerings are left to defend against them and please them in equal measure. The days begin growing shorter once more and the reaper's scythe casts a long shadow over the verdant fields.

Ritual: Banishing Disease from the Garden

This is a ritual we delight in each year on our community farm. By walking flames about our land and garden, we use the force of fire to burn away those spirits and ills that would do our crops and the wild plants we steward harm. Ancient peoples in the British Isles used various bonfires and fire practices to ensure their cattle and corn's health and freedom from malady.

You Will Need:

- Torches: we use the tiki torches one can find at a hardware store
- A bucket of water nearby in case of errant flame holders
- A drum
- Instruments or noisemakers (this can include your own mouth)

Take up a merry hoard of revelers. Make sure they are of sound enough body and mind to not get too wily carrying flaming torches about, and make sure everyone with long hair has it tied back safely. In some places, one person has been the torch bearer, and the hoard follows along happily. Light your torch and the holders cry,

"We Banish Disease!"

This shall be chanted as loud and strongly as possible. If available, a drummer is an excellent help for this chant as the hoard marches about the land and garden, scaring away all evil spirits that would nip your crops and cause them disease. In many folk magic traditions around the world, loud sounds like those of horns, drums, bells, and gongs frighten away evil spirits. If you have little ones about, arming them with pots, pans, and a wooden spoon for striking is an excellent way to involve them in protecting the garden.

Spell I: Charm to Ask the Elder Tree for Some Wood

Few plants are as dangerous to harvest from spiritually as the elder tree. Legendarily, the witch spirit that resides within each elder will cause you much misfortune if you should harvest from them without asking proper permission. This charm from Lower Saxony was repeated three times with bended knees and folded hands:

Lady Elder,
>Give me some of thy wood,
>Then will I give thee some of mine,
>When it grows in the Forest.[25]

I like to use this before harvesting. I have also adapted it to a rhyme to be sung to any tune of your choosing:

Elder tree, elder tree,
>Won't you give some wood to me?
>And when I'm a tree too,
>I will give some wood to you.

I sit before this special being and sing this at least three times before harvesting.

Spell II: Plantain Love Charm

Plantain heals so many of our wounds, but it also helps us answer questions of the heart. Plantain has been used for love divinations in England.

To see if a potential match is good, strip the stalks of their little flowers. Check them the next day, and if some still persist, it means the prospect of a marriage or relationship is good.

Much like mullein, bend the stalk one evening. The next day, check to see if it grew back straight upright, and that surely means your true love will return your affections.

If you pick nine flowers or the leaves of plantain and put them under your pillow, you will dream of your future spouse on Midsummer Eve.

Remedy I: Mugwort, Chamomile, and Yarrow Divination Tea

There aren't many more plants that you need when you have mugwort, chamomile, and yarrow. All three have powerful magical histories. To me, a very effective tea for washing divination tools and for imbibing before bed for prophetic dreams or before trance work, is this tea:

- 1 teaspoon each of mugwort[26], chamomile, and
  yarrow flowers

Blend them together in a ceramic bowl with your hands. Center yourself and take a few mind-clearing breaths. Blend the herbs together as you focus your will on receiving aid in divination.

Boil a fresh pot of water and take one teaspoon of the mixture of herbs and place them in a tea ball or small strainer. Pour one cup of boiled water over it and steep for 10 minutes, covered. I like to use my saucer over my teacup for this purpose. Sip this tea before divining or before bed. Cool and use as a wash for crystal balls, scrying mirrors, and other divination tools, especially if you have lent them to someone and must clean them of strange energies. Save the best of the herbs in a clean, labeled glass jar for future use.

Remedy II: *Nocino*: Sacred Italian Black Walnut Liquor

Make this legendary walnut liquor on Midsummer Eve and serve at midwinter.

You Will Need:

- A clean quart gallon jar
- Freshly harvested black walnuts
- Gloves
- A sharp knife
- Vodka
- 3 cinnamon sticks
- 1 tablespoon of whole cloves
- 1 orange
- 1 cup of good brown sugar

Chop the walnuts carefully, for they stain mightily! I use a chopping board that is already dark brown because the dye rendered from the walnuts is about the same color. I cut them into four pieces, which is traditional in some recipes. Drop these into the jar with the cinnamon, cloves, cut orange, and sugar. Stir vigorously. I like to leave this out on Midsummer Eve to bless it in the dew. Store this in a cool, dark place and strain; enjoy at midwinter over a large ice cube in a tumbler.

Remedy III: St. John's Wort Oil for Nerve Pain

St. John's wort is one of the stars of the show on Midsummer Eve. The sunny yellow flowers blaze with the glory of this zenith in the sun's power. If you live in a region where it blooms around Midsummer, plan to gather some on this auspicious day. St. John's wort is a great nerve pain remedy and, when extracted in oil, is wonderful when rubbed on for this purpose. Remember, it can cause photodermatitis for some people, so try not to get too much sun after applying.

You Will Need:

- A clean glass jar
- Enough olive oil to fill said jar
- Enough St. John's wort, crushed, to fill your jar

When I make oils, I almost always use dried herbs to help prevent spoilage. However, the exception to this rule is St. John's wort. I prefer *Hypericum perforatum* for this purpose. Harvest your St. John's wort from a field or garden, and allow it to wilt overnight. I place mine on some clean towels in an out-of-the-way place, out of direct light. This allows some of the moisture to escape but preserves the delicate oils we desire for medicine making. Chop roughly the flowering tops and unopened buds, marveling at the red stains it leaves behind on your fingers. Cover with oil and place in the sun for one day. If you make it on Midsummer Day, and it happens to be a sunny day, all the better. After that, place it somewhere warm and dark for four weeks, or until the oil turns red. Strain the plant matter out and compost it. Store the labeled oil out of direct light. Apply to nerve pain or as a general massage oil for stiffness and muscle pain.

Lammas/Lughnasadh/Michaelmas, August 1

In folk tradition, Lammas or Lughnasadh was the time each early autumn where a huge cart wheel was heated till it was red hot. It was then rolled down a hillside, and its journey downwards was an omen for the harvest: free from obstacles meant a good harvest to come. The fire wheels used at Midsummer symbolized the motion of the sun in the sky, while the fiery wheel of Lughnasadh can be seen as the sun descending from the height of the sky into the underworld.

The purpose of the Lammas rites are to prepare for the harvest and to perform rituals of sympathetic magic to promote healthful harvests and fine weather to gather it in. In Buckinghamshire, witches went out into the fields before the harvest was finished and rode about on horse-headed staves. The purpose of this was that the steps of the "ride" were traced upon the ground to drive away illness and decay and call in the crops' increase.[27] The word *Lammas* comes from an Old English phrase meaning "loaf mass." In the early Christian Church, the first loaves of the season were blessed by the church during mass, a practice harkening back to much older harvest celebrations. Lammas for us is a time to celebrate the first of the harvests, for this is the first of three harvest festivals we shall celebrate. This is the harvest of the shoots.

Ritual: Offering of the First Fruits

Every year, we harvest something on August 1 to be baked into an offering that we call the Offering of the First Fruits. Historically, the bread baked with the first grain harvested this day was sacred and blessed in churches. It was itself a magical charm and the bread could be broken up into a grain storage barn to prepare it and to bless the grain that would soon be stored there. Sacrifice can be important, not just for the act of going without or suffering as some sort of offering, but as the sharing of plenty and abundance. It is a living act of gratitude. By sharing the first harvest, we offer back that which sustains us, to that which yields our life-giving food. Any fruit, flower, or edible seed will do for this ritual. See what is in season near you.

WHEEL OF THE YEAR

CHAMOMILE

Matricaria chamomilla

BELLADONNA

Atropa belladonna

HENBANE

Hyoscyamus niger

DATURA

HORI HORI

FEVERFEW
Tanacetum parthenium

HELLEBORE

Helleborus

MANDRAKE

Mandragora officinarum

You Will Need:

- A favorite bread recipe (we like to use cornbread)
- A harvested edible fruit, flower, or seed (try goldenrod flowers or dock seeds)
- A Dutch oven or cast-iron pan
- White or golden candle

Prepare to make your favorite cornbread recipe. To use goldenrod flowers, remove one-quarter cup flour and add one-half cup finely chopped goldenrod flowers. Mix well and pour into a well-greased baking pan (I like to use a cast-iron pan heated hot with butter) and bake.

Prepare your altar. Decorate it as a feast table, perhaps making your altar at your dinner table this evening. Set your freshly baked bread on the table and light a candle. Cut into your bread and make sure to really get a large slice—there is no reason to skimp for the spirit world. Set a piece of the bread on a plate and say the following:

> This is the Offering of the First Fruits,
> We sit in awe of the miracle of life that sits before us.
> The Earth feeds us, and so too someday,
> shall we feed the Earth.
> The Wheel turns and we are grateful,
> The Wheel turns and we dance on,
> The Wheel turns and now it is the time to harvest.
> It is with this offering that we speak our thanks.
> Thanks be unto the Old Ones for protecting us,
> To our kin of leaf and bone that feed us,
> Please receive this humble offering.

Enjoy the rest of your Lammas feast, but set the offering outside for the Wild Ones to draw nourishment from.

Spell 1: Nine Herbs Charm for Wounds

The Nine Herbs Charm was a magical, herbal charm gathered from Anglo-Saxon England. It was one part spoken spell and one part herbal remedy that was used to treat infection and poisoning. The herbs referenced in this charm were plantain, mugwort, chamomile, nettle, crabapple, thyme, betony, lamb's cress, and fennel. That said, there is debate here and there about a few of the plant's identities. The poem is also amazing because it is one of two known references to Woden (or Odin), the old god of the Nords, in Old English poetry.

This charm is recorded in *The Lacnunga*, which is an ancient 11th-century Anglo-Saxon manuscript written around 1000 CE. Stephen Pollington's book *Leechcraft; Early English Charms, Plant Lore and Healing* is a popular translation, but it is only one of many translations of an ancient book filled with remedies and magic from that time period. This is a long charm and one to perform in its entirety.

These herbs were given to humankind by Odin, or Woden, to heal them. In a world where demons and evil spirits caused most diseases, we see why illness is called the "roving foe" who moves throughout the land in this charm:

> Remember, Mugwort, what you made known,
> what you arranged at Regenmeld.
> You were called Una, the oldest of herbs,
> you have power against three and against thirty,
> you have power against poison and against infection,
> you have power against the loathsome foe roving through
>   the land.
> And you, waybread, mother of herbs,
> open from the east, mighty inside.
> Over you chariots creaked, over you queens rode,
> over you brides cried out, over you bulls snorted.
> You withstood all of them, you dashed against them.
> May you likewise withstand poison and infection
> and the loathsome foe roving through the land.
> "Stune" is the name of this herb, it grew on a stone,

it stands up against poison, it dashes against poison,
it drives out the hostile one, it casts out poison.
This is the herb that fought against the snake,
it has power against poison, it has power against infection,
it has power against the loathsome foe roving through
    the land.
Now, atterlothe, put to flight now, Venom-loather, the
    greater poisons,
though you are the lesser,
you the mightier, conquer the lesser poisons, until he
    is cured of both.
Remember, maythe, what you made known,
what you accomplished at Alorford,
that never a man should lose his life from infection
after maythe was prepared for his food.
This is the herb that is called "Wergulu."
A seal sent it across the sea-right,
a vexation to poison, a help to others.
It stands against pain, it dashes against poison,
it has power against three and against thirty,
against the hand of a fiend and against mighty devices,
against the spell of mean creatures.
There the Apple accomplished it against poison
that she [the loathsome serpent] would never dwell
    in the house.
Chervil and Fennel, two very mighty one.
They were created by the wise Lord,
holy in heaven as He hung;
He set and sent them to the seven worlds,
to the wretched and the fortunate, as a help to all.

This section is sometimes referred to as the "Lay of the Nine Twigs of Woden":

These nine have power against nine poisons.
A worm came crawling, it killed nothing.

For Woden took nine glory-twigs,
he smote the adder that it flew apart into nine parts.
Now these nine herbs have power against nine evil spirits,
against nine poisons and against nine infections:
Against the red poison, against the foul poison.
against the yellow poison, against the green poison,
against the black poison, against the blue poison,
against the brown poison, against the crimson poison.
Against worm-blister, against water-blister,
against thorn-blister, against thistle-blister,
against ice-blister, against poison-blister.
Against harmfulness of the air, against harmfulness
    of the ground,
against harmfulness of the sea.
If any poison comes flying from the east,
or any from the north, [or any from the south,]
or any from the west among the people.
Woden stood over diseases of every kind.
I alone know a running stream,
and the nine adders beware of it.
May all the weeds spring up as herbs from their roots,
the seas slip apart, all salt water,
when I blow this poison from you.

The final part of the charm describes how to prepare the salve:

Mugwort, waybread open from the east, lamb's cress, atterlothe, maythe, nettle, crab-apple, chervil and fennel, old soap; pound the herbs to a powder, mix them with the soap and the juice of the apple. Then prepare a paste of water and of ashes, take fennel, boil it with the paste and wash it with a beaten egg when you apply the salve, both before and after.

Sing this charm three times on each of the herbs before you prepare them, and likewise on the apple. And sing the same charm into the mouth of the man and into both his ears, and on the wound, before you apply the salve.[28]

You can also prepare a salve in the way I have instructed in this book with the dried herbs of the Nine Herbs Charm for a historically inclined and safe salve for minor wounds and abrasions. You can leave the soap and egg out for certain.

Spell II: Love Divinations with Yarrow

Many things we wonder about in divinations revolve around health, wealth, and love. These same worries were reflected by the ancestors, for there are more love divinations that one can shake a yarrow twig at. Historically, yarrow was used for divining one's future lover or determining whether one is truly loved. In Appalachia it was stuffed up the nose to divine if one's true love reciprocated the sentiment: "Green yarrow, green yarrow, you bears white blow, If my love loves me my nose will bleed now." This may involve a bit of digging around, but what don't we do for love?

In Ireland, yarrow plucked from a young man's grave was deemed the best for a love divination.[29] Sleeping with a yarrow twig beneath one's pillow will surely bring dreams of your love to be, whether from a grave or not. Snip a flowering top before bed and tuck it beneath your pillow to try this charm yourself.

Remedy I: Goldenrod Tea for Allergies

Goldenrod lights up our fields around Lammas. The heavy flower heads bend towards the earth on occasion, beautiful and bright. I gather the flowers and dry them for tea. Goldenrod often has a bad rap as an allergen but is in fact a great medicine to help combat allergies to a look-alike: ragweed. Ragweed also has yellow flowers and blooms around the same time as goldenrod in most temperate locations, so it is an understandable mistake. To make a beautiful tea to help combat fall allergies, try this goldenrod tea blend.

You Will Need:

- 1 part goldenrod flowering tops
- 1 part elderflower

- $1/2$ part peppermint leaves
- 1 part nettle leaf

Mix these in the quantity you'd like to create in a ceramic or wooden bowl and spoon out one tablespoon. Boil a fresh pot of water and steep one tablespoon of this blend in two cups of water. Steep for 15 minutes, sweeten with honey if you desire, and enjoy three times a day during sneezing season.

Remedy II: Regional "Gruitbier"

Gruitbiers are the herbal beers of yesteryear. You can make your very own for medicine, pleasure, or both using what's growing around you. Here is my favorite recipe.

You Will Need:

- 1 very clean half-gallon jar
- Fresh dandelion blossoms
- Fresh herbs of your choice (I like ground ivy [*Glechoma hederacea*], yarrow, lemon balm, and mints)
- Raw honey
- Water

Wash your hands well. Clean your jar very thoroughly with hot water and soap. Gather at least one heaping cupful of fresh dandelion blossoms—these will provide the yeast you need to ferment this magical brew. Place the flowers in the jar and chop the other herbs roughly. I like to use ground ivy and mint. Chop $1/4$ to $1/2$ cup of fresh bitter or aromatic herbs and add them to the dandelions. Add two cups of honey and fill the jar the rest of the way with water. Stir very well with a very clean spoon. Cover with a loose-fitting lid to let the CO_2 that is produced by fermentation to escape. I place the jar in a baking dish in case some liquid bubbles up and out to avoid a mess. You can make a "real" beer using store-bought yeast, but I like this wild way.

Allow to ferment for five days, occasionally "burping" the jar and letting the gas out. Taste it on the fifth day. It should have a complex and exciting flavor and be slightly effervescent. At this point it is very low alcohol, so enjoy as a wild soda, or let it ferment longer! Strain out the plant bits and compost them and continue to monitor and taste. Place it in the fridge when it gets to the point you like in order to slow fermentation. You can make so many flavors and kinds of fermented beverages like this. Just watch for mold and make sure to add enough honey!

Remedy III: Blackberry Root Tea for the Bowels

Blackberry root is a powerful astringent. When the bowels are loose, and one is experiencing diarrhea, this humble yet fierce plant is here to help. The leaves are helpful but the root is really the powerhouse of its tannin content. Tannins are the magical compounds in blackberry that tighten tissues and help to tone the intestinal lining. Take one tablespoon of chopped dried blackberry root and gently simmer on the stovetop in three cups of water until it is reduced by a third. Sip this with clear water in between to keep hydrated until symptoms improve.

Autumn Equinox (Mabon)

Kings had such a great responsibility over their people, and that responsibility extended into the realms of ensuring good harvests, weather, and freedom from plagues and diseases. Magically and physically, he had to provide. He was, in fact, married to the goddess of the land, and if he displeased her, all would suffer. It was nothing less than a sacrifice of his own body that would quell her anger if he upset her.

Similar beliefs are known to have been held worldwide, where a shaman-like king was held as sacral, as the preordained sacrifice at the end of a specific term, or in a time of crisis. He was the mediator of the divine but not always the theocratic leader of his people. His very position was of a sacred, if not ephemeral, nature.

Sir James George Frazer introduced the idea of the sacred king in his book *The Golden Bough*, which in my opinion is a must read for any studious witch. He saw the king as a sort of living representation of the vegetal "dying and reviving god" similar to the stories of many gods' lives in our human history (Osiris, Dionysus, and Attis, to name a few). While people may agree or disagree with

Frazer's thoughts on anthropology and magic, his conjectures strike a chord with me as I watch the seasons turn and see the story of life, death, and rebirth play out over and over again.

Most lingering references to king sacrifice seem to come from a place where Germanic and Scandinavian mythology and history meet. Ken Dowden, in *European Paganism*, speaks about the metaphorical renewals of kingship that may have been a more realistic explanation for these king sacrifices than Frazer hypothesized. Rather than offer their bodies as sacrifice, they would commune with the gods themselves and reveal their new knowledge as refreshed and renewed kings, in turn renewing their people and ruling as a "new" king. While monarchy is a pretty giant bummer, this archetype of kingliness is available to all who seek to hold leadership and guidance roles rather than rulership over others.

These ideas of the king as god and vice versa are very interesting, and whether or not these were widespread historical practices or metaphorical myths demonstrating the death and rebirth tropes of the lord of the harvest, these ideas are central to this time of year. They also explain some strange bodies found in the bogs of Ireland.

This is all to say, we've derived much strange pleasure from reenacting this sacrifice as a play each year. A ritual theater piece. This is how we perform the ritual of the death of the king:

Ritual: Sacrifice of the King Ritual

Choose a King. Our friend John has unfortunately often drawn the short straw and has been "sacrificed" in our plays quite a few times. Ensure the role is shared equally. It is important to note this role is not gendered and any willing human is excellent for playing this character. Prepare for them a bed; we have used a massage table with a cloth over it or a stout folding table covered in a favorite altar cloth. Decorate around and under the table with fruits of the season. For us, pumpkins, large bouquets of ironweed, goldenrod, and apples adorn the altar.

Dress your King. We adorn them in brightly colored cloths of burgundy, gold, and black. We form a procession and follow our King to the table. You may do this within or without a magical circle, but remember, a drummer to keep time is an excellent addition. Once you reach the table, the King shall dramatically die, perhaps casting themselves gently onto the ground. The participants all wail and sigh, for their King is dead. Allow the participants to grieve the summer's end. The death of the King. For it is a sad occasion, but one of renewal to come.

One participant should cover the now-dead King with a black cloth. When the group is ready, start to change the mourning cries to ones of jubilation. Raise your arms to the heavens and watch the King rise up again. Just as John Barleycorn is mowed down, so does the grain sprout up again in spring. Now that the great sacrifice has been received, the King shall live again, renewed, blessing the land with fertility.

Guide the King, draped in black cloth, to the table and shout and sing. For the land holds the promise of spring!

Spell I: Dandelion Root Poppet Spell

Making human shapes from roots and working magic on them is a near-universal act of folk magic. Using a human-shaped object to enact magic is a practical form of sympathetic magic to achieve a goal. One can certainly get up to a lot of mischief with this type of magic, but I have found it to be a great way to do distance healing spells. Historically, *alruna*, or mandrake root dolls, were very popular in England and Germany, but mandrake is hard to come by for most people outside of the Mediterranean and other warm climates where they grow. I like to use dandelion roots for poppet magic, as they are both a potent medicine and also often branch and make unique shapes suitable for such magic.

To make a dandelion root poppet:

Dig up a whole dandelion on the new moon. Find a nice stout one. Leave the leaves on, but take a sharp knife and carve a small face on the root however you like to most make it resemble a person. Prepare a special pot to replant the root in rich potting soil. I like to smoke the pot out with mugwort first. If I am making the poppet to heal my friend John, I will whisper the name "John" into the newly carved mouth of the poppet. Replant "John" gently and water them in. Care for them for one month, being careful not to overwater. On the next full moon, dig them back up. Their little face should be healed over. Remove the leaves and wash the root well. Allow to air dry, turning occasionally to avoid mold. Once they are wizened and look like a little wrinkled person, they are ready. I make them a special box I keep them in, dressed in silk cloth. An example of a healing rite I might use them for would be a spell to aid in healing a friend of an addiction or self-destructive behavior:

Prepare your poppet. Make sure they are clean and swaddled in a nice piece of cloth. Cleanse them by the four elements. Pass smoke of mugwort over them and pass a lit candle over them, sprinkle them with a very little bit of water, and sprinkle them finally with a bit of salt. Hold a hand mirror up to the face of the poppet and now say,

> My friend, John, see how I care for you.
> You are precious,
> You are loved.
> I invoke the good spirits of this land
> To show you your worthiness
> And as you see your reflection in this mirror,
> So too will you see the strength and beauty you contain
> And face all foes, asking for help when you need it
> I am here, see how I care for you.
> Your body is healing all the time
> Your mind is healing all the time.
> It is my will that your health should be sound
> That your heart shall find gladness.
> This is my will.

Breathe a breath of life onto the poppet and swaddle them gently. Leave them in a cozy place with a small offering of favorite food and repeat the ritual as needed. It is best done at the increase of the moon.

Spell II: Herb Cloth Charm for Safe Travel

To make a charm for protecting those you love while traveling, try this small cloth square filled with protective herbs. Take a piece of black cloth (I like to thrift silk, cotton, or linen clothing and cut it up for these types of projects) and cut out a rectangle that when folded in half, roughly makes a perfect small square no bigger than your palm. Sew up two of the seams, leaving one end open. Turn it inside out.

Choose your filling. I like mugwort, a few blackberry thorns snipped off with pruners, wormwood, St. John's wort, and other herbs that have long histories of use as talismans. Stuff some dried herbs into the little square you are creating and sew the final seam shut. I like to embroider runes or other protective symbols on the squares after this step. Hide away on your person, in a wallet, a purse, or tucked into a pocket. If it rips or gets damaged, bury it and make a new one.

Remedy I: Tulsi Tea for Nerves

Tulsi (*Ocimum sanctum*) is a popular herb that comes to us from Southeast Asia. Also known as holy basil and sacred in Hindu tradition, tulsi is very easy to grow outside in zones 10 and 11 year-round, but as an annual almost everywhere, and in a container, anywhere! I love to grow a large amount of tulsi every year. Tulsi has a long history of use as a medicinal plant and makes a beautiful tea. There are a few varieties of tulsi, my favorite being Kapoor tulsi. Plant some in a pot with rich potting soil and keep evenly moist and in some good sun. I always harvest it all out of the garden in our zone 6-7 climate, in September or October, and dry it for winter tea.

I like to make tea from tulsi for anxiety. Tulsi is great for chronic stress due to its high flavonoid content.[30] To make this delicious, fragrant tea, do the following:

Chop one large handful of snipped tulsi tops (it's okay if they are in flower) and place in a clean quart jar. Pour four cups of boiled water over the tulsi and let it steep for 20 minutes. Strain and sweeten with honey. Drink up to six cups a day for mild anxiety and nerves.

Remedy II: Sweet Annie Tincture for All Ills

We've met wormwood and mugwort, but the other artemisia I love is sweet Annie (*Artemisia annua*). Sweet Annie has incredibly tiny seeds and does great as a self-seeding annual in most places. I grow this one in my garden, and aside from smelling like heaven and making beautiful wreaths, it is a potent medicinal. Sweet Annie has been used as an anti-malarial and antiparasitic and is native to northern China. It has been used to treat fevers in Chinese medicine for 2,000 years. Sweet Annie has even been studied for use against coronavirus and showed effective action against the 2005 SARS virus due to a chemical it contains called artemisinin.[31]

You Will Need:

- A clean jar in a size of your choosing
- Enough sweet Annie freshly chopped to loosely fill said jar
- 80-proof vodka to cover the plant material

Chop the sweet Annie and mash it into the jar. Cover with alcohol and let tincture for four to six weeks. Strain out the plant matter and compost. Take one-half tincture dropper a full four to six times a day in water for suspected viral fevers and use for no more than one week. Not to be taken by those pregnant or nursing.

Remedy III: Mullein Leaf Tea for Phlegm

Mullein has many magical uses, but the power this plant has to move stuck phlegm is one of its most useful in the fall. I like to gather a nice big handful of good-looking leaves and prepare them for colds and respiratory illnesses that feel like they are "stuck." Mullein contains saponins, which can be thought of as natural cleansers that make a cough more productive in their effort to expel phlegm from the lungs. It also has mucilage, one of the most interesting words in herbalism. Mucilage is a gelatinous substance that soothes irritated membranes, in this case, the lung and throat tissues.

I like to chop up two to three heaping tablespoons of mullein leaf and gently simmer it for five minutes on the stove top. I then strain and pour that tea over one tablespoon of mint leaves (fresh or dried). Steep the mint leaves for 10 minutes, strain, and sweeten with honey if desired.

Drink this tea freely when dealing with a phlegmy cough to help expectorate and bring up all that mucus.

Samhain

We're now in the dark time of the year. Though the days are still warm, the leaves are drying a crinkly brown and the hillsides are aflame with red, gold, and yellow leaves. The chickens are starting to slow their laying, huddling together to fluff warm and close on the ever-colder nights. The pumpkins are orange, the squash are all harvested, and the red peppers hang in heavy bunches from the eaves, drying to warm us this winter. The Bone Mother and Witch Father will soon run their icy fingers along the green stalks of goldenrod and joe-pye, rendering them lifeless and crisp, to rot away in the soil and feed next year's sproutlings.

This part of the year, when the veils separating the living and the dead are the thinnest, there are whispers in every wood and the smell of grandmother's perfume hangs in the air. These are the times we feel the exhilarating tingle of fear at strange shadows around the edge of the campfire, the first real cold that will envelop us for the next three months, and we celebrate all of the death around us, for we know it will be the soil of the New Year when the sun warms our faces once more.

This time around early November was when animals were slaughtered and put up for winter fare by Anglo-Saxon peoples. Writing in the eighth century, the Venerable Bede said that the pagan Saxons called November Blodmonath, or "blood month." Blót was also performed during this time, also giving the month its name, for it was a time to sacrifice animals to the gods to gain their aid and survive the sharp winter ahead.

Celtic, Saxon, and Norse peoples celebrated this time of the year as a time for the dead. The times between summer and winter give rise to wandering spirits and active shades. All Hallows, or Samhain, is one of the three "spirit nights" of the year when the veil between the worlds is thin and spirits and the fae are especially restless.[32] Beltane and Midsummer Eve are the other two nights, which we see in all the herbal protection lore that was born from these times of year. Protecting the home from errant ghosts, warming oneself by the comforting light of bonfires, and "souling," or going house to house to beg a treat in exchange for a prayer for the dead, were all practices that have persisted in some ways today despite the Church's efforts at erasing these traditions.

Ritual: The Dumb Supper

It's hard not to allow Samhain to nestle in my heart as my favorite sabbat, or festival celebration, on the Wheel of the Year. I have always been drawn to and loved spooky things and ghost stories. As a witch, I can't help but feel a little proud when I see the world around me light up with pumpkins, costumes, and revelry and giggle that many people do not know the long history of Samhain and its pagan roots. One of the most meaningful rituals I have come to observe over the years is the ritual of the Dumb Supper.

A Dumb Supper calls upon another meaning of the word *dumb*: silent. It is an older word that was often used to describe those who could not speak, and is not a kind word to use today to describe someone with that quality; however, in this context, it is evidence of the age of the ritual. It is essentially a supper eaten for the dead and with them, at Samhain. This meal is taken in total silence, hence the name, Dumb. The silence creates a space for the Old Ones to be with us. When we do something unusual, or against the grain, that opposition, such as being silent during a normally boisterous suppertime, is a potent magical space that can be utilized. In some cases the meal is enjoyed as a way to commune with loved ones passed on, yet in other cases the ritual is also a love divination.

A Dumb Supper as a love divination ritual involves setting the table backwards, as well, and leaving an empty seat. If a girl were to do this, during the course of the meal, the shade of her future husband would appear in the empty chair while they dined, a custom popular in England and some parts of Scotland that made its way into America.[33]

To perform this ritual, do the following:

Gather your friends or do it alone, whichever works for you. Prepare a meal. It can be whatever you like, but seasonally appropriate fare is always welcome. I like to make goldenrod cornbread and baked apples due to the fact they are folkloric foods of the mighty dead, a nice roast of venison my sweetheart hunted, or a good piece of beef from our neighbor's farm. I will make a salad of the last lettuces and wild greens from the garden with a homemade vinaigrette dressing using an oxymel like elderberry or birch bark mixed with olive oil, salt, and pepper. We have also hosted this ritual as a potluck-style meal, which does very nicely.

To begin, announce a welcome to the good spirits that reside around you.

Light some candles to decorate the table and hit a bell, drum, or other noise-maker three times:

> Hail and Welcome wandering shades,
> All who Hunger are welcome at our table,
> Find rest and peace in this sustenance,
> And we give good thanks for this bounty before us.
> Join us, ancestors and good friends,
> And then depart safely.
> Hail and Welcome.

Set the table backwards. Of course the table cloth must go first; I like to use a nice black linen one. As soon as the cloth is in place, begin the silence. Next place the cups, then the silverware, then the plates. As soon as the last plate is set, serve the food, being sure that there is a place set for the dead complete with a chair and nice silverware. Give them a little portion of every food and sauce. Let them have a taste of everything.

Sit down to your meal and enjoy it in silence. We also do it by candlelight. Notice in the shadows around you, do you see any movement? When you are done, blow out the candles and in the dark say,

> Hail and Depart,
> Spirits who have joined us/me here this All Hallows Eve.
> Go well back and away,
> Depart in love and take comfort in this nourishment
> Hail and farewell.

Ring the bell or hit the drum three times and turn on all the lights. We usually yell or jump for joy to further signify the end of the ritual and shoo out any lingering spirits.

Spell 1: Turnip Protection from Wandering Shades Spell

The pumpkin is one of the most easily recognizable icons of the All Hallows season. Jack-o'-lanterns were originally made from turnips, though, not the pumpkin, which only came into usage by Europeans after arriving in North America where it was a staple food of Indigenous peoples. Before pumpkins were carved into faces and lit with candles on doorsteps, turnips were the original jack-o'-lantern. This is an Irish tradition and the act of carving ghoulish faces onto root vegetables most likely came to America via Irish immigrants.[34] Hollowed out and lit up with a candle, these little root faces were set in windowsills to ward off evil spirits.[35]

Turnips are easy to grow in many climates with some cool weather, even Florida! I love turnips to eat, but this charm is also a beautiful way to use this affordable, easy-to-steward plant. To make a truly old fashioned jack-o'-lantern from a turnip, try this:

Get a large turnip, as the smaller it is, the more difficult to carve. Get a sharp knife and a cutting board. Slice the top off the turnip, saving it, as it will be the lid later on. Take the knife and cut around the interior of the turnip, leaving about a 1/2-inch away from the outside. Score this circle you've just carved with the knife and scoop out the turnip with a metal spoon. Once you've made a little cavity, you can carve a face onto the turnip just as you would a pumpkin. I find an X-Acto knife or a box cutter is very helpful.

Place a tealight inside and light. This charm works under an old belief that spirits can be scared, just as we can, by frightening faces. Place this on a fireproof plate or holder on your doorstep to protect your house on these nights when spirits roam so freely.

Spell II: Allan Apple Spell from Cornwall

The apple has long been considered a symbol of immortality, which is strange, because it's also legendary as a food for the dead. In Celtic myth, an apple branch bearing grown fruit, flowers, and unopened buds was a sort of magical key to the underworld. There are many love divinations to be done with the apple, a fruit as red as the heart's blood. Wait until midnight and cut an apple into nine pieces. Take the pieces into a dark room with a mirror (either hanging on the wall or a handheld one will do). At midnight, begin eating the pieces of apple while looking into the mirror. When you get to the ninth piece, throw it over your shoulder. The face of your lover should appear in the mirror.[36] You can also play a daring and slightly dangerous game called Allantide Apples if you wish. This game is a love divination in and of itself.

It involved suspended apples and became popular in the area of Penzance in England around the turn of the 19th century. Allantide is another name for Samhain, or All Hallows.

To play, do the following:

Two strips of wood, each between 18 to 20 inches long and about 1 inch to 1¹/₂-inch wide, must be nailed together to form a simple cross. Four candles should be placed on the top of each arm of the cross and then the cross should be suspended from the ceiling (this is usually in the kitchen of the home). Then, an Allan apple is hung by a short string from each arm of the cross.

In many households, as with bobbing apples, young ladies of a marriageable age would have placed their initial, or their "mark," on one of the apples before it was suspended from the cross. When it came time to play the daring game, the candles were lit, and the boys gathered beneath this Allantide "chandelier." Each boy took turns jumping up to try to catch an apple in his mouth. The most exciting bit of the game, and what really gives it some teeth, is the falling hot wax that could land on a person's face as they attempted to bite the apple.[37] Certainly play this one with care, and of course you don't need to gender this magical game either.

We play this game minus the jumping and so far no one has lost an eye. Some guests to this game have even worn safety goggles, which adds a delightful silliness to an already very fun and silly event.

Remedy 1: Wild Rose Hip Elixir for Colds and Flu

Roses are one of the most beloved flowers to humans; just look at the importance placed on giving them to loved ones, and even how many people have emblazoned their flesh with rose tattoos. One of my favorite cold-weather forageables is the wild rose hips that dot the hillsides in late fall and persist all through the winter where I live. When it seems there is nothing to sustain, there is always something, maybe hidden, awaiting. I gather these little fruits, so reminiscent of their larger apple family cousins, and dry them for tea. If you are blessed to live in a maritime climate you may have some of the large fruiting varieties around you like the rugosa or beach rose (*Rosa rugosa*). These are large enough to make jam!

I harvest the abundant and invasive multiflora rose. Originally native to eastern Asia—China, Japan, and Korea—this hated plant is very useful. The rose hips provide winter forage for birds, deer, and other wildlife, including us! The leaves and flowers are useful from this species (and all rose species) as a cooling remedy for skin issues and gut healing.

You Will Need:

- 2 cups of rose hips
- Brandy
- Honey
- Muslin cloth or nut milk bags
- Clean pint jar
- Clean quart jar

Gently heat the rose hips in a pot of water until just soft. Using a food processor, blend them carefully. (If you need to let them cool first, that is just fine!) Strain the rose hip solids out and save them in a clean pint jar. Rinse the pot out. Measure the liquid you strained and pour it back in the pot. Gently heat it and measure out the same amount of honey. Gently stir on low heat until the honey is mixed in well.

You can go ahead and use this water-based medicine as a syrup and take it by the tablespoon for colds and flus to get that vitamin C kick. To make the elixir, follow these steps:

Take the leftover rose hip solids and pour brandy over them in the pint jar to cover them by one inch. Add one-half cup honey. Tincture this for two to four weeks, stirring occasionally. When ready, warm this gently on the stove top in a pot to let the honey flow more freely. Strain, bottle, and you have an elixir to be enjoyed over ice with seltzer or taken by the spoonful for colds.

Remedy II: Sage for Sore Throats

Sage is a powerful antibacterial helper and a folk remedy for sore throats in Appalachian folk medicine. I love the tea for gargling when stuck with a painful sore throat. Take two heaping tablespoonfuls of dried sage and pour four cups of freshly boiled water over and steep 10 minutes. Sweeten with honey and sip to soothe the throat or chill and use as a gargle and spit it out.

An amazing way to preserve and use sage is to make an infused honey. Fill a clean quart jar one-quarter of the way full with dried sage, preferably from the garden, and cover all the way, filling the jar to the top with honey. Take this jar and place it somewhere warm but out of direct sunlight for one month. I like to infuse honey near, but not too near, the woodstove to get the gentle heat, or even over an air vent in an apartment. You can speed up the infusion process by heating the jar in a double boiler with water for three hours, then straining out the plant matter if you wish. Use this honey by the teaspoon dissolved in hot water for sore throats at any time. It also makes a beautiful addition to salad dressings and marinades. Let food be thy medicine!

Remedy III: Mugwort Wild Soda

This is a spectacular beverage for those who abstain from alcohol, though it has the slightest bite (similar to a kombucha, really, so just be sure to inform any friends who might imbibe). To make this magical concoction perfect before bed as a dreamwork enhancer or post-feast digestive, gather the following:

- Clean quart jar
- 2 cups chopped mugwort leaves and tops
- 2 cups honey
- 9 dandelion blossoms

Take your clear jar and pour in your chopped mugwort leaves. Cover them with the honey and add water to fill the rest of the jar. Drop the dandelion blossoms in and stir carefully. Lid loosely and place on a baking dish to catch any liquid—the fermentation goes a little faster than you think and escapes—to avoid a mess. Place it somewhere out of direct light and in a place with good airflow. Let it ferment for three to five days, occasionally "burping" the lid to allow the CO_2 to escape to avoid an explosion! Once you see bubbles, you know it's active! I taste it with a clean spoon each time, so as to not add more bacteria until I like it. Strain out the mugwort and compost, bottle in a pretty bottle, and store in the fridge for up to two months. Enjoy by the glassful or add seltzer to cut the sweetness. You should not drink if you are pregnant or nursing.

Conclusion

I envision a future very different from our current reality. I'm not sure what the governing bodies will look like, or how we'll power cars, or if they will even still exist. All I know is that I want all humans to feel at home in nature once more. I dream of the boundaries that keep us in and the wild out dissolving away. I dream that the wall of green most of us see outside becomes instead populated with unique, individual plants and trees we know by name and greet as allies. It is my hope that if you have never felt cared for by the incredible, complex, sacred, and special Earth you live on, that after learning more about stewarding some of their denizens, you feel like less of an outside observer, and more like a main character in the story of empowering yourself to heal and practice the magic you love.

Taking the time to get to know the history of where you live and what it has taken for us to have access to the spectacularly diverse plant knowledge we do in Western herbalism and American folk healing is one of the most worthwhile pursuits we can take on as plant people. Bridging the gap between the armchair herb crafter and a person grounded in the just recognition of the unique history of their dwelling place can seem daunting, but I believe we can all do it by tapping in to patience and humility and asking for help when we need it. My hope is that this book is one tool in your toolbox to meet those goals and once again feel at home outside of four walls, among the plants.

Acknowledgments

This is the first of what I hope will be many books. It feels monumental, scary, exhilarating, and precious. I would like to acknowledge the many people who supported me, both in this world and the other, on my journey. Thank you to my beloved partner, Corby, for your tireless support and love, giving me feedback, and troubleshooting wording with me. To my best friend, Saro, who supports me in all I do and gives me the strength to speak my truth when I feel too self-critical to do it alone. To my dear friend John who is my eternal editor and believes I am at least a foot taller than I really am. To my beloved friend Liam, who helped inspire in me a living practice of folklore. To my beloved friend Baylen, who has believed in me and given me a new life by teaching me to tattoo, and therefore the space and time to make this work. I love you all.

Thank you to my brothers, Kurt and Will, for both loving me even though I am definitely the strangest big sister you could have never asked for and to my father for instilling an endless effort to work within me. To all of my community of friends, allies, and comrades who inspire me and push me to ask hard questions and take on the work of always striving to reflect and improve myself as a practitioner and person. This book would also not have been possible without the ideas and spark blown into a fire by Natasha Yglesias, the one who sought me out and asked me to birth this work.

ACKNOWLEDGMENTS

Thank you to the many unseen people of this land I dwell in, the Indigenous, Black, and brown herb people whose knowledge I now benefit from as a white Western folk herbalist. Thank you to my ancestors for their herbal traditions, and thank you for allowing me to live this beautiful, painful, perfect, messy life I have been gifted. I promise you, I shall not waste your gift. Last but not least, thank you to the Wild Green World for allowing me congress with you and for healing my body, mind, and spirit as I seek closeness with you all, plant, shrub, and tree.

Notes

Part I: The Legacy
A History of Witchcraft

1. Petrovska, B., "Historical review of medicinal plants' usage," *Pharmacognosy Reviews* 6, no. 11 (2012): 1–5.

2. de Divitiis, Enrico, et al., "The 'schola medica salernitana': The forerunner of the modern university medical schools," *Neurosurgery* 55, no. 4 (2004): 722–44; discussion 744–5.

3. Howard, Michael, *Children of Cain: A Study of Modern Traditional Witches* (Richmond Vista, California: Three Hands Press, 2011), 17.

4. Inspired by the late Michael Howard's descriptions.

5. Bailey, Michael David, *Historical Dictionary of Witchcraft*, Historical Dictionaries of Religions, Philosophies and Movements (United Kingdom: Scarecrow Press, 2003).

6. Bailey, *Historical Dictionary of Witchcraft*, xxxii.

7. O'Connor, Bonnie B., and David J. Hufford, "Understanding folk medicine," in *Healing logics: culture and medicine in modern health belief systems* (2001), 13.

8. Duffy, John, *From Humors to Medical Science: A History of American Medicine* (Urbana: University of Illinois Press, 1993), x.

9. Cavender, Anthony P., *Folk Medicine in Southern Appalachia* (Chapel Hill: University of North Carolina Press, 2003).

10. Eijk, P.J. van der, *Hippocrates in Context: Papers Read at the XIth International Hippocrates Colloquium* (University of Newcastle upon Tyne, United Kingdom, 2002), 17.

11. Light, Phyllis D., "A History of Southern and Appalachian Folk Medicine," *Journal of the American Herbalists Guild* 8, no. 2 (Mar. 2008): 27.

12. Light, "A History of Southern and Appalachian Folk Medicine," 33.

13. Hand, Wayland, *Magical Medicine* (Berkeley: University of California Press, 1980), 44.

14. Hand, *Magical Medicine*, 46.

15. Araujo, Elcida, et al., "How Ethnobotany Can Aid Biodiversity Conservation: Reflections on Investigations in the Semi-Arid Region of NE Brazil," *Biodiversity and Conservation* 18, no. 1 (n.d.): 127–150.

16. Turner, Nancy Jean, and Patrick von Aderkas, "Sustained by First Nations: European Newcomers' Use of Indigenous Plant Foods in Temperate North America," *Acta Societatis Botanicorum Poloniae* 81, no. 4 (2012): 295.

17. Pongsiri, Montira J., et al., "Biodiversity Loss Affects Global Disease Ecology," *Bioscience* 59, no. 11 (Dec. 2009): 945.

18. Sale, Kirkpatrick, "Bioregionalism—a Sense of Place," *Nation* 241, no. 11 (Oct. 1985): 336.

19. "What Is Human Rewilding?," last modified March 19, 2021, https://rewildu.com/what-is-rewilding/.

20. Harvey, Graham, *Animism: Respecting the Living World* (Australia: Wakefield Press, 2005), xi.

21. Harvey, *Animism: Respecting the Living World*, xviii.

Part II: The Relationship
Gardening Your Own Magical and Healing Herbs

1. Magdoff, Fred, *Building Soils for Better Crops* (United States: Sustainable Agriculture Network, 2000), chapter 2.

2. Gatiboni, Luke, "1. Soils and Plant Nutrients," NC State Extension Publications, North Carolina Extension, Feb. 14, 2018, http://content.ces .ncsu.edu/extension-gardener handbook/1-soils-and-plant-nutrients.

3. Magdoff, *Building Soils for Better Crops*, 282.

4. "Essential Nutrients for Plants," last accessed Mar. 6. 2020, https:// bio.libretexts.org/@go/page/13781.

5. Zeder, Melinda A., "The origins of agriculture in the Near East," *Current Anthropology* 52, no. 4 (2011): 221–235.

6. Navazio, John, "A Short History of Agricultural Seed," *A Short History of Agricultural Seed*, Chelsea Green Publishing Mar. 3, 2021, http://www .chelseagreen.com/2021/a-short-history-of-agricultural-seed/.

7. "Seed Saving and Heirloom Gardening at the Wylie House," *Wylie House Museum*, Indiana University Bloomington, Feb. 3, 2015, http://libraries .indiana.edu/seed-saving-and-heirloom-gardening-wylie-house.

8. Burrows, Rhoda, "Saving Seed: Will the Seed Produce Plants Similar to the Plant It Was Collected from?," SDSU Extension, South Dakota University Extension, Aug. 30, 2019, http://extension.sdstate.edu /saving-seed-will-seed-produce-plants-similar-plant-it-was-collected.

9. Pleasant, Barbara, "How to Make Your Own Potting Soil," *Mother Earth News*, Ogden Publications, Dec. 2008, http://www.motherearthnews. com/organic-gardening/how-to-make-your-own-potting-soil-zmaz0 8djzgoe.

10. Ellis, Barbara W., *Starting Seeds: How to Grow Healthy, Productive Vegetables, Herbs, and Flowers from Seed* (North Adams, MA: Storey Publishing LLC, 2013), 80.

11. Raj, Abhay, et al., *Microorganisms for Sustainable Environment and Health* (Netherlands: Elsevier Science, 2020), 32.

12. Mazza, Charles P., Sally J. Cunningham, and Ellen Z. Harrison, "Using organic matter in the garden," 2014, http://www.michigan.gov/docu ments/deq/wrd-biosolids-using-organic-matter_556273_7.pdf.

13. Blankenspoor, Juliet, "Growing Herbs in Containers," *Chestnut School of Herbal Medicine*, Chestnut School of Herbal Medicine, Nov. 4, 2020, http://chestnutherbs.com/growing-medicinal-herbs-in-containers/.

14. Arrowsmith, Nancy, *Essential Herbal Wisdom* (Woodbury, CT: Llewellyn Publishers, 2009), 176.

15. Arrowsmith, *Essential Herbal Wisdom*, 179.

16. Thiselton-Dyer, Thomas Firminger, *The Folk-lore of Plants* (United Kingdom: D. Appleton, 1889), 264

17. Genders, Roy, *The Scented Wild Flowers of Britain* (United Kingdom: Collins, 1971).

18. Hyatt, Harry Middleton, *Folk-lore from Adams County, Illinois* (United States: Alma Egan Hyatt Foundation, 1965).

19. Schauenberg, P., and F. Paris, Guide to Medicinal Plants (London: Lutterworth Press, 1977).

20. Leyel, Hilda, *Herbal Delights* (New York: Houghton-Mifflin, 1938).

21. Trevelyan, Marie, *Folk Lore and Folk Stories of Wales* (Whitefish, MT: Literary Licensing, LLC, 2014).

22. Wiltshire, Kathleen, *Wiltshire Folklore* (United Kingdom: Compton Russell, 1975).

23. Watts, D.C., *Dictionary of Plant Lore* (Netherlands: Elsevier Science, 2007), 79.

24. Tongue, Ruth, *Forgotten Folk-tales of the English Counties* (London: Taylor & Francis, 2020).

25. Watts, *Dictionary of Plant Lore*, 79.

26. Vickery, Roy, *A Dictionary of Plant-lore* (Oxford: Oxford University Press, 1995).

27. Palaiseul, Jean, *Grandmother's Secrets: Her Green Guide to Health from Plants* (London: Penguin, 1976).

28. Grieve, Margaret, *A Modern Herbal, Vol. 1* (Mineola, NY: Dover Publications, 1971), 279.

29. Hatfield, Audrey Wynne, *A Herb for Every Ill* (United Kingdom: Dent, 1973), 76.

30. Cameron, Malcolm L., *Anglo-Saxon Medicine* (Cambridge: Cambridge University Press, 1993), 142.

31. Johnson, Thomas, and John Gerard, *The Herbal: Or, General History of Plants* (United Kingdom: Dover Publications, 1975).

32. Duke, J. A., *CRC Handbook of Medicinal Herbs* (New York: Routledge, 1985).

33. Alcock, Randal Hibbert, *Botanical Names for English Readers* (United Kingdom: J. Heywood, 1884), 172.

34. Pareek, A., M. Suthar, G. S. Rathore, and V. Bansal, "Feverfew (*Tanacetum parthenium L.*): A systematic review," *Pharmacognosy Reviews* 5, no. 9 (2001): 103–110, http://doi.org/10.4103/0973-7847.79105.

35. Arrowsmith, *Essential Herbal Wisdom*, 141.

36. Barber, E. J. W., *The Dancing Goddesses: Folklore, Archaeology, and the Origins of European Dance* (London: W. W. Norton, 2013), 79.

37. Rago, Linga Ours, *Mugworts in May* (West Virginia: Quarrier Press, 1995), 90.

38. Arrowsmith, *Essential Herbal Wisdom*, 448.

39. Arrowsmith, *Essential Herbal Wisdom*, 456.

40. Arrowsmith, *Essential Herbal Wisdom*, 461.

41. Opie, Iona Archibald, and Peter Opie, *The Lore and Language of Schoolchildren* (New York: New York Review Books, 2001), 362.

42. Higgins, Rodney, *Plants of Courtship and Marriage*, Plant Lore Studies, edited by Roy Vickery (London: Folklore Society, 1984).

43. Napier, James, *Folklore: Or, Superstitious Beliefs West of Scotland Within This Country* (Arden Library, 1980).

44. Watts, *Dictionary of Plant Lore*, 324.

45. Waring, Phillipa, *A Dictionary of Omens and Superstitions* (Souvenir Press, 1978).

46. Miles, Clement A., *Christmas in Ritual and Tradition* (Forgotten Books, 1912).

47. Grieve, Margaret, *A Modern Herbal: Volume 2* (Stone Basin Books, 1992), 682.

48. Fahrun, Mary Grace, *Italian Folk Magic* (Weiser Books, 2018), 97.

49. Whitney, Anne, and Caroline Canfield Bullock, *Folklore from Maryland*, American Folklore Society Memoirs Vol. 18 (1925), 19.

50. Arrowsmith, *Essential Herbal Wisdom*, 483.

51. Browning, Gareth H., *The Naming of Wild Flowers* (Williams and Norgate, 1952), 89.

52. Wilde, Lady, *Ancient Legends, Mystic Charms and Superstitions of Ireland* (Chatto & Windus, 1902).

53. Bachtold-Staublie, Hans, ed., *Handwörterbuch des deutschen Aberglaubens*, vol. 3 (Berlin: Walter de Gruyter & Co., 1987), 1490.

54. Arrowsmith, *Essential Herbal Wisdom*, 274.

55. Stokker, Kathleen, *Remedies and Rituals: Folk Medicine in Norway and the New Land* (St. Paul, MN: Minnesota Historical Society Press, 2009).

56. Pennacchio, Marcello, et al., *Uses and Abuses of Plant-Derived Smoke: Its Ethnobotany As Hallucinogen, Perfume, Incense, and Medicine* (Oxford: Oxford University Press, 2010).

57. Grieve, Margaret, *A Modern Herbal: Complete Volume* (Stone Basin Books, 1992).

58. Müller-Ebeling, Claudia, et al., *Witchcraft Medicine: Healing Arts, Shamanic Practices, and Forbidden Plants* (Inner Traditions, 2003).

59. Gutch, M., and M. Peacock, *Country Folklore, Lincolnshire* (Folklore Society, 1908).

60. Walsh, William S., *Curiosities of Popular Customs and of Rites, Ceremonies, Observances, and Miscellaneous Antiquities* (United Kingdom, Lippincott, 1925), 18.

61. Allen, David Elliston, and Gabrielle Hatfield, *Medicinal Plants in Folk Tradition: An Ethnobotany of Britain & Ireland* (Timber Press, 2012), 224.

62. Moss, Kay, *Southern Folk Medicine, 1750–1820* (University of South Carolina Press, 1999), 94.

63. Lee, Michele E., and J. Douglas Allen-Taylor, *Working the Roots: Over 400 Years of Traditional African American Healing* (Wadastick Publishers, 2014).

64. Painter, Gillian, and Elaine Power, *The Herb Garden Displayed* (Auckland, New Zealand: Hodder and Stoughton, 1978).

65. Arrowsmith, *Essential Herbal Wisdom*, 537.

66. Blunt, Wilfrid, and Sandra Raphael, *The Illustrated Herbal* (Frances Lincoln in assoc. with Weindenfeld & Nicolson, 1979).

67. Padosch, Stephan A., Dirk W. Lachenmeier, and Lars U. Kröner, "Absinthism: a fictitious 19th century syndrome with present impact," *Substance Abuse Treatment, Prevention, and Policy* 1 (2006): 14.

68. Schulke, Daniel A., *Veneficium: Magic, Witchcraft and the Poison Path* (United States: Three Hands Press, 2018). Publisher's description.

69. Hildegard, *Hildegard Von Bingen's Physica: The Complete English Translation of Her Classic Work on Health and Healing* (United States: Inner Traditions/Bear, 1998), 32.

70. Gerard, John, *The Herbal Or General History of Plants: The Complete 1633 Edition as Revised and Enlarged by Thomas Johnson* (United States: Dover Publications, 2015), 340.

71. Höfler, Max, *Volksmedizinische Botanik der Germanen* (Berlin: VWB, 1908), 90.

72. Rätsch, Christian, and John Robin Baker, *The Encyclopedia of Psychoactive Plants: Ethnopharmacology and Its Applications* (United States: Inner Traditions /Bear, 2005), 209.

73. Rätsch and Baker, *The Encyclopedia of Psychoactive Plants: Ethnopharmacology and Its Applications*, 272–273.

74. Ritter von Perger, K., *Deutsche Pflanzensagen* (Stuttgart and Oehringe: Schaber, 1864), 181.

75. Rätsch and Baker, *The Encyclopedia of Psychoactive Plants: Ethnopharmacology and Its Applications*, 280.

76. De Laurence, Lauron William, Heinrich Cornelius Agrippa von Nettesheim, and Henry Morley, *The Philosophy of Natural Magic* (United States: de Laurence, Scott & Company, 1913), 137.

77. Bevan-Jones, Robert, *Poisonous plants: a Cultural and Social History* (United Kingdom: Windgather Press, 2009), 78.

78. Watts, *Dictionary of Plant Lore*, 239.

79. Watts, *Dictionary of Plant Lore*, 239.

80. Raedisch, Linda, *Night of the Witches: Folklore, Traditions & Recipes for Celebrating Walpurgis Night* (United States: Llewellyn Worldwide, Limited, 2011), 45.

81. Hildegard, *Hildegard von Bingen's Physica: The Complete English Translation of Her Classic Work on Health and Healing*, 33.

82. Hildegard, *Hildegard von Bingen's Physica: The Complete English Translation of Her Classic Work on Health and Healing*, 33.

83. Richo Cech of Strictly Medicinal Seeds.

Part III: Foraging Your Own Magical and Healing Herbs: Foraging Basics for the Wild Witch

1. Poe, Melissa R., et al. "Urban Foraging and the Relational Ecologies of Belonging," *Social & Cultural Geography* 15, no. 8 (Dec. 2014).

2. Love, Thomas, and Eric T. Jones, "Why Is Non-Timber Forest Product Harvesting an 'Issue'? Excluding Local Knowledge and the Paradigm Crisis of Temperate Forestry," *Journal of Sustainable Forestry* 13, no. 3/4 (Nov. 2001): III.

3. Michail, Niamh, "Can Sustainable Foraging Go Mainstream?," *Food Navigator*, William Reed Business Media June 24, 2015, http://www.foodnavigator .com/Article/2015/06/25/Can-sustainable-foraging-go-mainstream.

4. Conversations with Alan Muskat of Wild Foraging Business, No Taste Like Home, Asheville, NC.

5. Kloos, Scott, *Pacific Northwest Medicinal Plants: Identify, Harvest, and Use 120 Wild Herbs for Health and Wellness* (United States: Timber Press, 2017), 48.

6. "Native, Invasive, and Other Plant-Related Definitions," Natural Resources Conservation Service Connecticut, USDA, www.nrcs.usda .gov/wps/portal/nrcs/detail/ct/technical/ecoscience/invasive/?cid=nrcs 142p2_011124.

7. Nunez, Martin A., et al., "Invasive Species: To Eat or Not to Eat, That Is the Question," *Conservation Letters* 5, no. 5 (2012): 334–341.

8. Berkes, Fikret, et al., "Rediscovery of Traditional Ecological Knowledge as Adaptive Management," *Ecological Applications*, no. 5 (2000): 1251.

9. Hatfield, Gabrielle, and David Allen, *Medicinal Plants in Folk Tradition: An Ethnobotany of Britain & Ireland* (United States: Timber Press, 2004).

10. Grieve, *A Modern Herbal: Complete Volume*.

11. Hatfield, Gabrielle, *Encyclopedia of Folk Medicine: Old World and New World Traditions* (United Kingdom: ABC-CLIO, 2004), 310.

12. MacCulloch, J.A., *The Misty Isles of Skye* (Edinburgh: Oliphant, Anderson and Ferrier, 1905).

13. Friend, Hilderic, *Flower Lore*, 540.

14. Cullum, Elizabeth, *A Cottage Herbal* (United Kingdom: David & Charles, 1975).

15. Vesey-FitzGerald, Brian Seymour, *Gypsies of Britain: An Introduction to Their History* (United Kingdom: Chapman & Hall Limited, 1944).

16. Folkard, Richard, *Plant Lore, Legends, and Lyrics Embracing the Myths, Traditions, Superstitions, and Folk-Lore of the Plant Kingdom* (1884), 258.

17. Briggs, *Plantlore* (1980)

18. "359—Twigs," Museum of Witchcraft and Magic, http://museumofwitch craftandmagic.co.uk/object/twigs/.

19. Thayer, Samuel, *Nature's Garden* (Forager's Harvest, WI, 2010), 136–138.

20. Jones, Ida B., "Popular Medical Knowledge in sixth century England," *Institute of the History of Medicine Bulletin* 5 (1937): 405–451.

21. Montesano, Marina, *Classical Culture and Witchcraft in Medieval and Renaissance Italy* (Germany: Springer International Publishing, 2018), 159.

22. Watts, *Dictionary of Plant Lore*, 410.

23. Hyatt, Harry Middleton, *Folk-lore from Adams County, Illinois* (United States: Alma Egan Hyatt Foundation, 1965), 313.

24. Grieve, *A Modern Herbal*, 844.

25. Müller-Ebeling, *Witchcraft Medicine: Healing Arts, Shamanic Practices, and Forbidden Plants*, 15.

26. Davey, F.H., *Flora of Cornwall* (Penryn: 1909), 261.

27. Randolph, Vance, *Ozark Magic and Folklore* (United States: Dover Publications, 2012), 291.

28. Weston, Brandon, *Ozark Folk Magic: Plants, Prayers and Healing* (United States: Llewellyn Publications, 2021).

29. Moss, Kay, *Southern Folk Medicine, 1750-1820* (University of South Carolina Press, 1999).

30. Patton, Darryl, *Mountain Medicine: The Herbal Remedies of Tommie Bass* (United States: Natural Reader Press, 2004).

31. Daniels, Cora Lynn, ed., *Encyclopædia of Superstitions, Folklore, and the Occult Sciences of the World: Volume 2* (United States: University Press of the Pacific, 2003), 776.

32. Porter, Enid, *Cambridgeshire Customs and Folklore* (United Kingdom: Taylor & Francis, 2020).

33. Barbour, John H., "Some Country Remedies and their Uses," in *Folklore, Vol. 8* (1897), 386–390.

34. Gunther, Erna, *Ethnobotany of Western Washington*, rev. ed. (Seattle: University of Washington Press, 1973), 46.

35. Vickery, Roy, "Cleavers," *Plantlore*, http://www.plant-lore.com/cleavers/.

36. Hopman, Ellen Evert, *Secret Medicines from Your Garden: Plants for Healing, Spirituality, and Magic* (United States: Inner Traditions/Bear, 2016), 101.

37. Thiselton-Dyer, *The Folk-lore of Plants*, 123.

38. Bergen, Fanny D., "Current Superstitions: Collected from the Oral Tradition of English Speaking Folk," in *American Folklore Society, Memoirs, Vol. 7* (1896).

39. Culpeper, Nicholas, *Culpeper's Color Herbal* (United States: Sterling Publishing Company, Incorporated, 2007), 56.

40. Evelyn, John, *Acetaria: A Discourse of Sallets* (United Kingdom: Prospect Books 1982). [[page TK]]

41. Milnes, Gerald, *Signs, Cures, & Witchery: German Appalachian Folklore* (Knoxville: U. of Tennessee, 2007).

42. See Mandrake.

43. Mars, Brigitte, *Dandelion Medicine: Remedies and Recipes to Detoxify, Nourish, and Stimulate* (Storey Publishing, LLC, 2016), 80.

44. Kvideland, Reimund, and Henning K. *Sehmsdorf, Scandinavian Folk Belief and Legend* (United States: University of Minnesota Press, 1988).

45. Bonser, Wilfrid, *The Medical Background of Anglo-Saxon England: A Study in History, Psychology, and Folklore* (Kiribati: Wellcome Historical Medical Library, 1963), 138.

46. Leland, Charles Godfrey, *Gypsy Sorcery and Fortune Telling: Illustrated by Numerous Incantations, Specimens of Medical Magic, Anecdotes and Tales* (United Kingdom: T. Fisher Unwin, 1891), 29–30.

47. Porter, Enid, "Some Folk Beliefs of the Fens," *Folklore* 69 (1958).

48. Müller-Ebeling, *Witchcraft Medicine: Healing Arts, Shamanic Practices, and Forbidden Plants*, 46.

49. Hoffman, David, *The Herbal Handbook: A User's Guide to Medical Herbalism* (Healing Arts Press, 1998).

50. Kavasch, E. Barrie, "Ethnobotany of Elderberry," in *The Herb Society of America's Essential Guide to Elderberry* (2013).

51. Bergner, Paul, "Sambucus: Elderberry," in *Medical Herbalism: Materia Medica and Pharmacy* (2001).

52. Thiselton-Dyer, *The Folk-lore of Plants*, 270.

53. Daniels, *Encyclopædia of Superstitions, Folklore, and the Occult Sciences of the World: Volume 2*, 802.

54. Müller-Ebeling, *Witchcraft Medicine: Healing Arts, Shamanic Practices, and Forbidden Plants*, 10.

55. Young, Merlin, *The Moon Over Matsushima—Insights Into Moxa and Mugwort* (United Kingdom: Godiva Books, 2012).

56. Nelson, Max, *The Barbarian's Beverage: A History of Beer in Ancient Europe* (United Kingdom: Taylor & Francis, 2005).

57. Hatfield, *Encyclopedia of Folk Medicine: Old World and New World Traditions*, 247.

58. Watts, *Dictionary of Plant Lore*, 260.

59. Cockayne, Thomas Oswald, *Leechdoms, Wortcunning, and Starcraft of Early England* (United Kingdom: Longman, Green, Longman, Roberts, and Green, 1864), 177.

60. Lehner, Ernst, and Johanna Lehner, *Folklore and Symbolism of Flowers, Plants and Trees* (Literary Tudor Publishing, 2011).

61. Mitich, Larry W., "Common Mullein: The Roadside Torch Parade," *Weed Technology* 3, no. 4 (1989): 704–705.

62. White, Newman Ivey, and Frank Clyde Brown, *The Frank C. Brown Collection of North Carolina Folklore; the Folklore of North Carolina* (Durham, N.C.: Duke University Press, 1952).

63. Shakespeare, William, *Romeo and Juliet*, Act 1, Scene 2, Lines 45–57a (1597).

64. Thiselton-Dyer, *The Folk-lore of Plants*, III.

65. Leyel, *Herbal Delights*.

66. Moss, Southern Folk Medicine, 1750-1820, 12.

67. Miles, Clement A., *Christmas in Ritual and Tradition* (United Kingdom: Terrace, 1912).

68. Grieve, Margaret, and Maud Grieve, *A Modern Herbal, Vol. 1* (United States: Dover Publications, 1971).

69. White, *The Frank C. Brown Collection of North Carolina Folklore; the Folklore of North Carolina.*

70. Elworthy, Frederick Thomas, *The Evil Eye* (United Kingdom: J. Murray, 1895), 98.

71. Ballard, Harvey E., Juliana de Paula-Souza, and Gregory A. Wahlert, "Violaceae," in *Flowering Plants, 11 Eudicots: Malpighiales*, ed. Klaus Kubitzki (Springer Science & Business Media, 2013), 303–322.

72. Arrowsmith, *Essential Herbal Wisdom*, 525.

73. Grieve, *A Modern Herbal: The Complete Volume*, 834.

74. Erichsen-Brown, Charlotte, *Medicinal and Other Uses of North American Plants; a Historical Survey with Special Reference to the Eastern Indian Tribes* (New York: Dover Publications, 1979), 330.

75. Hellinger, R., et al., "Immunosuppressive activity of an aqueous Viola tricolor herbal extract," *J. Ethnopharmacol* (January 10, 2014): 299–306.

76. Carmichael, Alexander, *Carmina Gadelica* (United Kingdom: Scottish Acad. Press, 1900), 95.

77. Britten, James, *Folk-Lore Record*, (1. Folklore Enterprises, Ltd., Taylor & Francis, 1878), 32, 156–157.

78. Arrowsmith, *Essential Herbal Wisdom*, 295.

Part IV:
Remedies, Spells, Rituals,
and the Wheel of the Year

1. Carr, Julliette Abigail, "Making Weight-to-Volume Tinctures," Basic Recipes for Kitchen Witches, Old Ways Herbal, Nov. 18, 2019, http://www.oldwaysherbal.com/2013/12/15/making-weight-to-volume-tinctures/. From numerous lectures and classes with 7song, the owner of the Northeastern School of Botanic Medicine.

2. Vladimir Orel, *A Handbook of Germanic Etymology* (Leiden: Brill Publishers, 2003), 205.

3. Hollander, M. Lee, trans., *Heimskringla: History of the Kings of Norway* (University of Texas Press, 2007).

4. Evans, Emyr Estyn, *Irish Heritage: The Landscape, the People and Their Work* (Ireland: W. Tempest, 1949).

5. Kurennov, Pavel Matveevich, *Russian Folk Medicine* (United Kingdom: W. H. Allen, 1970).

6. Hoffman, *Medical Herbalism*.

7. Hutton, Ronald, *Stations of the Sun: A History of the Ritual Year in Britain* (United Kingdom: OUP Oxford, 2001), 134.

8. Ferguson, Diana, *The Magickal Year* (United Kingdom: Batsford, 1996), 78.

9. Walsh, *Curiosities of Popular Customs and of Rites, Ceremonies, Observances, and Miscellaneous Antiquities*, 171.

10. Berger, Pamela, *The Goddess Obscured: Transformation of the Grain Protectress from Goddess to Saint* (Boston: Beacon Press, 1985), 42.

11. Burriss, E.E., *Taboo, Magic, Spirits* (New York: Macmillan Company, 1931).

12. Davidson, Thomas Davidson, *Rowan Tree and Red Thread* (Edinburgh, 1949), 76–77.

13. Stewart, William Grant, *The Popular Superstitions and Festive Amusements of the Highlanders of Scotland* (1823), 114.

14. Kausar, Sofia, Muhammad Arshad Abbas, Hajra Ahmad, Nazia Yousef, Zaheer Ahmed, Naheed Humayun, Hira Ashfaq, and Ayesha Humayun, "Effect of apple cider vinegar in type 2 diabetic patients with poor glycemic control: A randomized placebo controlled design," *International Journal of Medical Research & Health Sciences* 8, no. 2 (2019): 149–159.

15. Fujiwara, Y., et al., "Onionin A, a sulfur-containing compound isolated from onions, impairs tumor development and lung metastasis by inhibiting the protumoral and immunosuppressive functions of myeloid cells," *Mol Nutr Food* Res. 60, no. 11 (2016): 2467–2480.

16. Butler, Jon, "Magic, Astrology, and the Early American Religious Heritage, 1600–1760," *The American Historical Review* 84, no. 2 (1979): 317.

17. Eisenstadt, Peter, "Almanacs and the Disenchantment of Early America," *Pennsylvania History: A Journal of Mid-Atlantic Studies* 65, no. 2 (1998): 143.

18. Llewellyn, George, *Powerful Planets Astrologically Considered* (Kissinger Publishing, 1931).

19. Campanelli, Pauline, and Dan Campanelli, *Ancient Ways: Reclaiming the Pagan Tradition* (United States: Llewellyn Worldwide, Limited, 2015).

20. Donatini, Bruno, "Control of Oral Human Papillomavirus (HPV) by Medicinal Mushrooms, Trametes Versicolor and Ganoderma Lucidum: A Preliminary Clinical Trial," *International Journal of Medicinal Mushrooms* 16, no. 5 (2014): 497–498.

21. Thiselton-Dyer, *The Folk-lore of Plants*, 62.

22. Stradling, Rod, "May Pole Dance Steps," All About Maypole Dancing, 2020, http://www.maypoledance.com/maypoledance.html.

23. Muluye, R.A., Y. Bian, and P.N. Alemu, "Anti-inflammatory and Antimicrobial Effects of Heat-Clearing Chinese Herbs: A Current Review," *Journal of Traditional and Complementary Medicine* 2 (April 2014): 93–98.

24. Blumenthal, M., A. Goldberg, and J. Brinckmann, "Herbal Medicine: Expanded Commission E Monographs," (Newton, MA: Integrative Medicine Communications, 2000), 230–232.

25. Friend, Hilderic, *Flowers and Flower Lore*, 39.

26. Do not use mugwort if you are pregnant or breastfeeding.

27. Howard, *Children of Cain: A Study of Modern Traditional Witches*.

28. Storms, Godfrid, *Anglo-Saxon Magic* (Germany: Springer Netherlands, 2013), 187.

29. Mac Coitir, Niall, *Ireland's Wild Plants—Myths, Legends & Folklore* (Ireland: Collins Press, 2010).

30. Tierra, Michael, and Karta Purkh Singh Khalsa, *The Way of Ayurvedic Herbs* (Lotus Press, 2008).

31. Nair, Manoj S., Yaoxing Huang, David A. Fidock, Stephen J. Polyak, Jessica Wagoner, M. J. Towler, and P. J. Weathers, "*Artemisia annua L.* extracts inhibit the in vitro replication of SARS-CoV-2 and two of its variants," *Journal of Ethnopharmacology* 274 (2021): 114016.

32. Howard, Michael, *Liber Nox: A Traditional Witch's Gramarye* (United Kingdom: Skylight Press, 2014).

33. Hand, Wayland D., "Anglo-American Folk Belief and Custom: The Old World's Legacy to the New," *Journal of the Folklore Institute* 7, no. 2/3 (1970): 136–155.

34. Smith, Andrew F., *The Oxford Companion to American Food and Drink* (Oxford University Press, 2007), 269.

35. Palmer, Kingsley, *Oral folk-tales of Wessex* (David & Charles, 1973), 87–88.

36. Rogers, Nicholas, *Halloween: From Pagan Ritual to Party Night* (Oxford University Press, 2002).

37. Kane, Kathryn, "Halloween in Cornwall: Allantide and Allan Apples," The Regency Redingote, The Regency Redingote, Nov. 1, 2015, regency redingote.wordpress.com/2015/10/30/halloween-in-cornwall-allantide -and-allan-apples/.

Index

About the Author

Rebecca Beyer is an Appalachian folk herbalist, Traditional Witch, huntress, and wild food forager dedicated to living simply on the Earth. She has taught and presented at universities, conferences, and gatherings over the last nine years with the hope of showing people that living a seasonal life grounded in connection with the Old Ways is possible. Through growing, foraging, hunting, fishing, and preserving her own food, she strives to create a life as close to her ancestors as possible while paying homage to the diverse peoples who created her beloved Appalachia.

She makes her living tattooing, making medicines, and selling wild foods, writing, and running her school, called Blood and Spicebush School of Old Craft. Rebecca currently spends her days living in community and dedicating herself to Appalachian folk arts, primitive skills, folk music, and learning the names of all the beings she shares her bioregion with.

Image Credits

Vintage Card Design with Bird and Hand Drawn Poisonous Plants
by Yevheniia Lytvynovych/Shutterstock

Insect Illustration and Medicine Bottle Illustration
by Bodor Tivadar/Shutterstock

Retro Floral Frame by song_mi/Shutterstock

Black Pepper Set in Vintage Style by Arthus Balitskii/Shutterstock

Vector Illustration of Strawberry by Dn Br/Shutterstock

Hand Drawn Mushrooms by Spicy Truffel/Shutterstock

Five of Cups by Vera Petruk/Shutterstock

Funeral Service Set by Alex Rockheart/Shutterstock

Tattoo Roses with Leaves by bioraven/Shutterstock